Divided Sun

*MITI and the Breakdown of Japanese High-Tech
Industrial Policy, 1975–1993*

D1193389

Divided Sun

MITI and the Breakdown of Japanese High-Tech Industrial Policy, 1975–1993

Scott Callon

STANFORD UNIVERSITY PRESS

Stanford, California

Sponsored by the Northeast Asia–United States Forum on
International Policy of the International Strategic Institute at Stanford

Stanford University Press
Stanford, California
© 1995 by the Board of Trustees of the
Leland Stanford Junior University
Printed in the United States of America

CIP data appear at the end of the book

TO JANEL, WYNNE, SAM, AND TED

Acknowledgments

In writing this book, I have been blessed with the advice and the support of a large number of individuals. The book would not have been possible without them. First and foremost, I have benefited immensely from the opportunity to interact with colleagues at Stanford University. I most especially thank Daniel Okimoto, who has been unstinting in his patience and generous encouragement of this effort. I am also much in debt to Yoshio Nishi, who on numerous occasions shared many hours with me in discussions that ranged from his experiences within the Ministry of Trade and Industry (MITI) VLSI consortium to the technical details of advanced semiconductor manufacturing. Henry Rowen and Stephen Krasner were particularly helpful in their suggestions for improvements; I am lucky to have been able to tap into their deep experience and intelligence.

I thank the participants, including a group of MITI officials, at seminars in Stanford's departments of Political Science and Economics and schools of Business and Engineering; at the Export-Import Bank of Japan; at the Kansai colloquium of the Abe Foundation and the Center for Global Partnership of the Japan Foundation; and at the Research Institute of Capital Formation of the Japan Development Bank for their useful criticisms, rebuttals, and other feedback. In addition, a number of other individuals generously read all or substantial portions of the manuscript and offered valuable suggestions and criticisms, among them Michael Anderberg, Mike Caldwell, Jack Callon, Sun-ki Chai, Sandy Faber, Ryū Fukui, Bob Johnstone, Wen-Jeng Kuo, Susumu Kurokawa, Satoshi Nishimura, Toshiro Sasaki, Frank Schellenberg, Edward Steinmueller, Tarō Tanimitsu, Brian Woodall, Akiko Yamazaki, and several interviewees who will have to remain anonymous. I am lucky to be able to count among my long-term friends two exceptionally talented computer scientists, Dave Hitz and J. P. Singh, whom I called upon when I wanted to discuss some of the technical aspects of this book's argument.

I was (mostly) resident at Stanford University's Asia/Pacific Research Center for the several years during which I worked on this book. In addition to those already named, I wish to thank all of those at the center for their help, most especially Jim Raphael, Jean Lee, Carol Tao, Mariko Jitsukawa, Nori Shirouzu, and the exceptional group of visiting mid-career fellows from Asia from whom I learned much, particularly Katsusada Hirose, Yasukazu Irino, Yoshihiro Tamura, and Kōichirō Urabe, four outstanding MITI officials who epitomize MITI's deep intellectual resources and a commitment to public policy for the public good. I remain deeply grateful to Kent Calder of Princeton University, an exceptional scholar of the Japanese political economy, who was my first teacher in Japanese politics many years ago and who first inspired me to pursue the path of scholarship.

In Japan, I offer thanks to the talented group with whom I had the honor to meet and work at the Japan Development Bank, especially Fumiyuki Kashima, Motoo Kishi, Hiroyasu Sugihara, and Noritada Terasawa; to Yasunori Sone of Keio University for his generous and ongoing assistance; to Makoto and Yasuko Inagawa and Masafumi Handa, who sent me needed material from Japan during the times that I could not be there; to Mary-Lea Cox, Toshiyuki Minami, Norio Furushima, and Takeshi Matsuda for setting up an excellent colloquium in Kansai to discuss this book's themes; and to Shunji, Ako, and Nene Ito and Maruo Moriya, who extended their warm hospitality to me during my several extended visits to Tokyo. After a day dashing all over the Kantō region conducting interviews, it was a pleasure to return to the friendship and lively after-dinner conversation of the Itos rather than the solitude of a hotel room.

I might add that research in Japan was facilitated by the outstanding quality and quantity of information available in the Japanese business press. Japanese mass media have a reputation for being toothless in pursuit of stories that are controversial or challenge powerful entrenched interests. I found, however, that in the case of the Japanese electronics and computer industries, the reporting was excellent and abundant. It was also frank, hard-nosed, gritty. I literally felt physically uncomfortable at times reading articles where interviewers from, for example, *Nikkei Electronics* (Japanese-language) or *Nikkei Intelligent Systems* (Japanese-language) grilled highly respected figures in the Japanese computer industry, challenging their statements, their policies, and at times their failures. This was "in-your-face" journalism driven by a Ben Bradlee-esque pursuit of the inside story and shorn of the deference typically accorded major figures in Japan. It was exciting and refreshing to read, but more important, it offered dependable information and analysis in immense quantities, a godsend to any researcher.

My sincere thanks go as well to all the anonymous informants—nearly one hundred of them—who took time from their busy schedules to grant me interviews, sharing their private insights into their hopes and frustrations, their day-to-day doings, and their long-term plans. They were to a person exceptional, some already in high positions, others clearly destined for such, and they took me inside Japanese high-tech industrial policy as no other group could have. Many of them introduced me to colleagues and other contacts and helped me gather additional information. This book could not have taken the shape that it did without their help.

I would gratefully like to acknowledge the financial support of the Alfred P. Sloan Foundation and Stanford University Computer Industry Project and the Asia/Pacific Research Center, Stanford University, as well as the leadership of Hirsh Cohen at Sloan and of William Miller in making the Computer Industry Project possible. In addition, I thank the Research Institute of Capital Formation at the Japan Development Bank for providing me with an office during a critical working period, and Muriel Bell, Peter Dreyer, and John Feneron at Stanford University Press for expert guidance of and support for this book.

Finally, I would like to thank my family, my wife, and my children, who stood by me (and in the case of the kids also crawled and toddled by me) during this effort. This book has been a long journey, both intellectually and geographically. It was a journey we made together as a family. I thank you for your patience and your support.

It is clear that what I have written here will not satisfy some of those who cooperated with me in this study, persons who had expectations of more positive findings about the role of MITI and cooperative high-tech consortia in stimulating high-tech innovation and industrial growth. I regret this fact, all the more because I remain truly grateful for their generous assistance. I have depicted recent Japanese high-tech industrial policy as I have felt it, read it, heard it, and seen it, and I take personal responsibility for the judgments here.

S.C.

Contents

Tables

Figures

Nothing in progression can rest on its original plan. We might as well think of rocking a grown man in the cradle of an infant.

Edmund Burke, *Letter to the Sheriffs of Bristol*

ONE

Divided Sun

The Rationale

Japan's is a system of bureaucratic rule. . . . Japan's postwar economic triumph . . . is the best example of a state-guided market system currently available; and Japan has itself become a model, in whole or in part, for many other developing or advanced industrial systems. . . . Collaboration between the state and big business has long been acknowledged as the defining characteristic of the Japanese economic system.
            Chalmers Johnson, *MITI and the Japanese Miracle*

The invisible hand is at work in Japan, but it is not Adam Smith's invisible hand—it is the invisible hand of the government working with Japanese industry. . . . It can no longer be doubted that foreign intervention in the high-technology industries exists and that it works to the competitive disadvantage of American producers.
            Laura D'Andrea Tyson, *Who's Bashing Whom?*

The Ministry of International Trade and Industry (MITI) has moulded, joined, and in other ways shaped industrial sectors to make them collectively fit for optimum performance on the foreign and domestic markets.
            Karel van Wolferen, *The Enigma of Japanese Power*

This book argues that the basis for Japan's postwar industrial policy has disintegrated since the 1970's. It is titled *Divided Sun* because the central argument stresses the coming apart of consensus and coherence in Japanese industrial policy. It therefore stands in sharp contrast to *cooperative-functional* theories of Japanese industrial policy, a broad body of work that includes among its sharpest advocates "revisionists" like Chalmers Johnson, Laura D'Andrea Tyson, and Karel van Wolferen,[1] and that argues that the policies of Japan's vaunted Ministry of International Trade and Industry, most recently embodied in MITI-led high-tech consortia, effectively enhance government and business cooperation to Japan's international competitive advantage.[2] In short, these theorists argue that MITI *plus* the market has outperformed the market alone.[3]

Whatever the past validity of this notion of a *cooperative* and *functional* Japanese industrial policy, it is now seriously out of date. There has been a major change in the policy environment facing MITI's industrial policy makers: specifically, the emergence of Japan as an economic and technological giant has seriously complicated the process of formulating industrial policy, making it much more difficult to achieve both cooperation and functionality.

In analyzing the new realities of Japanese industrial policy, this book focuses on what might be called the heart of Japanese industrial policy: the promotion of leading-edge or high-tech sectors, specifically through MITI's use of high-tech consortia. Three aspects of Japan's new situation have eroded the basis for these policies since the 1970's. First, as Japan moved to the leading edge of many technology sectors in the 1980's, it could no longer follow proven technology paths blazed by the world's leading high-tech economy, the United States. In this context, Japan's traditional industrial targeting strategies began to go astray. Simply put, it was no longer clear what to target. Second, the major Japanese companies that were dependent on MITI for protection against U.S. competition in the 1970's became increasingly confident of their own competitive strength by the 1980's and began to resent and resist MITI's industrial policy intrusions.[4] Finally, as the U.S. trade deficit with Japan soared in the early 1980's, U.S. government pressure on MITI became intense. The United States demanded that MITI abandon its aggressive promotion of Japanese industries.

This new policy environment has had crippling effects. Today, Japanese industrial policy in high technology is neither particularly cooperative nor successful. The domestic industrial policy-making process is torn by conflict and competition: between MITI and other government bureaucracies, between MITI and Japanese companies, and between the companies themselves. As a result, the elaborate structures to promote cooperation that appear in Japanese high-tech consortia are often nothing but a public show: seemingly cooperative institutions mask an underlying reality of fierce competition and conflict.[5]

The technologies emerging from the latest Japanese high-tech consortia have been little better. Recent Japanese efforts have frequently been the industrial-policy equivalent of flogging a dead horse. MITI has in recent years had a tendency to target technologies that are soon made obsolete in the rapidly changing high-tech marketplace, notwithstanding which it continues to adhere rigidly to the outdated plan.

What has made MITI's task more difficult is that, despite a huge pool of elite bureaucratic talent and deep experience and ties with Japanese industry, it finds itself hampered in putting these strengths to use, as other Japanese ministries have often played a negative, blocking role relative to new MITI policy initiatives. Thus, MITI's own interests increasingly (and some would say ironically) align with the forces advocating deregulation and decreasing the power of Japan's bureaucracies. Having been largely stripped of its own major regulatory powers by the early 1980's, MITI, too, requires a level playing field—the knocking down of bureaucratic regulations and barriers that prevent it from entering new policy areas.

In the shadow of these new realities, MITI finds itself at a turning point. It will have to redefine itself and carve out a new role in the Japanese political economy and among Japanese government ministries. Its primary focus cannot be industrial policy as traditionally defined, where MITI sought primarily to promote the international competitiveness of Japanese companies. Since industrial policy has historically been its raison d'être, a failure by MITI to seek out a major new role will result in its slow, but inevitable, decline.

It is important, however, to separate the success of Japanese industrial policy (or the lack thereof) and overall Japanese economic success. This is no doom-and-gloom "the end is near" assessment of the Japanese economy, the kind that seems to surge in popularity in the West (and interestingly enough in Japan) every time there is a decline in the Japanese business cycle. In fact, it is precisely the point of this book that the two—MITI industrial policy and Japanese economic success or failure—now have very little connection with each other.

The center of gravity in the Japanese economy has long since shifted away from the industrial-policy bureaucrats at MITI to the managers and workers at Japan's firms. It is *companies*, not government bureaucracies, that have been at the heart of Japan's stunning postwar ascent to international competitiveness and its overseas export and investment surge. MITI's industrial policy may have waxed and now wanes, but the companies remain world-class competitors who have to be taken very seriously.

It bears emphasizing that this is an analysis of MITI industrial policy *from the mid 1970's through 1993.* The time dimension is important. In asserting that MITI efforts launched in the *1980's* have met with serious problems, I am not making any claims about earlier MITI policies. Indeed, one of the cases studied here, the VLSI consortium that targeted advanced semiconductor technology in the late 1970's, is clearly an example of policy success, although not for the reasons usually put forth. Moreover, there is no question in my mind that despite certain negative costs, MITI policies from the 1950's through the 1970's in the main played a positive, if *limited*, role in promoting Japanese economic development and growth.[6] The point here is that times have changed. That role is no longer so available to MITI, and it must change too.

Underlying Rationale

This book focuses on MITI's industrial policy efforts in high technology, specifically joint high-tech consortia, in the period since 1975. By industrial policy, I mean simply government policies to improve the relative competitiveness of specific domestic industries or industrial sectors. It is this sectoral focus that distinguishes industrial policy from national economic policies, such as policies to promote domestic saving, with a broad impact across all sectors of the economy. In order to focus this analysis, industrial policy is surveyed here in five contexts: (1) Japan; (2) MITI; (3) high technology; (4) high-tech consortia; and (5) the post-1975 period. Let us explore the rationale behind each of these choices:

1. Japan's economy is the second largest in the world, racking up huge trade and foreign investment surpluses year after year. Moreover, in terms of state/society relationships, the role of the bureaucracy, and industrial organization, all issues that impinge on industrial policy, Japan offers an interesting contrast to advanced industrialized countries in the West, particularly the United States. Accordingly, this book seeks to consider Japan on its own terms and on its own merits—Japan as Japan, not just Japan as a model case.

2. MITI's role in the Japanese postwar economic "miracle" helped resurrect the idea of the "effective and efficient" state in economic policy. It can even be said that MITI as a phenomenon *created* industrial policy as a major subject of analytic and academic investigation. Much of recent scholarship on industrial policy was born out of the need to understand and explain MITI. Previously, there had been no significant debate about "an appropriate government role": it was well understood that the major job of government was to get out of the way and let dynamic free-market forces do their competitive and efficient work. But MITI's successes rocked these neoclassical economic tenets to their foundations. Focusing on MITI thus tests the merits of indus-

trial policy at its best. Since Japanese industrial policy, as formulated by MITI, is widely considered to be the most successful example of industrial policy in the world, the deterioration of recent MITI industrial policy, the central finding of this book, is significant in terms of its potential lessons about the limits to industrial policy. Problems with MITI industrial policy clearly have implications for policy makers elsewhere.

(3.) If one is going to cast doubt on the effectiveness of industrial policy, for credibility's sake, one has to choose a strong and successful example of industrial policy making, rather than a weak straw man. MITI's high-tech industrial policy is precisely such a "tough test." Not only is MITI considered to be highly successful in general, but high-tech ("sunrise") industries are considered to be its most successful area of endeavor.[7] In particular, since the 1970's, MITI has made a major commitment to high technology—to promoting high-value-added, knowledge- and information-intensive industries, including computers and microelectronics. MITI has clearly indicated this priority in publications such as its 1980's "vision" targeting microelectronics. Thus, by focusing on these high-technology areas, particularly microelectronics, I attempt to address MITI policies where they are strongest, where MITI has concentrated its intellectual and financial resources, and where the policies thus have the greatest likelihood of success.

(4.) High-tech *consortia* are the fourth choice defining this study. By consortia, I mean institutionally independent organizations that bring together competing companies for joint research and development (R&D) or for work on common technology issues. I focus on consortia for two reasons.

First, by the mid 1970's, MITI-sponsored high-tech consortia had become MITI's primary tool of industrial policy in high technology and its primary method of influencing Japanese corporate behavior. This rising importance of joint consortia was really the flip side of MITI's loss of its more direct and substantial regulatory powers. With respect to microelectronics, in 1975–76, MITI relinquished its ability to impose quotas on imports and restrict foreign investment, powers with which it had protected domestic electronics and computer firms and fought off foreign producers since the early 1950's. The abdication of most of MITI's regulatory powers over trade and capital flows was completed with the revision of foreign exchange–control laws in 1980. In the absence of these more direct methods of control, MITI put an increasing emphasis on one of the few remaining tools available:

MITI-led consortia. Since MITI's structural transition, consortia have claimed center stage in MITI's high-tech policies, so a study of consortia gets to the heart of MITI industrial policy for high technology.

Second, a focus on high-tech consortia also has the advantage of providing a degree of consistency and ease of comparison in assessing why certain policies worked and others did not. We can compare 1975 apples to 1985 apples to 1990 apples, rather than having to sort out the more difficult issues of cause and effect when a study chooses to compare different policy instruments over different time periods—for example, if we were to compare the VLSI consortium of the late 1970's to the import controls in the 1960's.

5. Finally, with respect to the choice of time frame, this book focuses on MITI industrial policy since 1975. There are two reasons for this. *First*, the late 1970's to the mid 1980's were a critical transition period for Japan. With massive trade surpluses making Japan the largest creditor nation in the world in the mid 1980's, and all of its major trading partners clamoring for relief from a deluge of Japanese products, this was the period in which Japan clearly established itself as a world economic power. It was also the period of Japan's transformation from a technology "follower" that reproduced and tried to improve upon more advanced products from the United States to a world leader in the production of high-technology products, products that were on par with those of the United States and came to surpass them in a number of areas.

In 1975, however, Japan was reeling from the inflationary body blows of the first oil shock and technologically appeared to lag several years behind the United States in all key sectors. Few saw any chance of it rivaling the United States anytime soon. Thus, by beginning the analysis in 1975 and continuing into the 1990's, we have an opportunity to look at Japan in the period immediately before and after this key transition in its techno-economic position in the world economy. This transition is also important because one causal argument at the heart of this book is that the transition in the decade following 1975 seriously complicated the task of MITI industrial policy and directly resulted in a deterioration of MITI's policy effectiveness.

Second, many of the prevailing impressions of Japanese industrial policy date from the pre-1975 period. For example, Chalmers Johnson's seminal work *MITI and the Japanese Miracle: The Growth of Industrial Policy, 1925–1975*, which helped define MITI's international reputation as an industrial policy maker par excellence, ends its analysis in the very year this analysis begins. Johnson's more recent work continues to make claims about MITI's power and effectiveness, claims that are now highly dated.[8] Similarly, the major work on MITI's postwar computer industrial policies, Marie Anchordoguy's *Computers Inc.: Japan's Challenge to IBM*, takes as its primary analytic focus the period up through the early 1970's, giving scant attention to later MITI efforts. If a structural transition in Japan's political economy has occurred that has dramatically transformed the policy context and content of Japanese industrial policy, as this book suggests, then these earlier analyses of MITI policies appear less relevant. A closer look at "late" MITI industrial policy, as opposed to the early "classic" MITI industrial policy, is necessary for a true understanding of the merits and demerits of Japanese industrial policy.

In sum, by examining the high-tech consortia where MITI has directed much of its energies in the past few decades, this book hopes to provide a richer sense of the context for MITI policy making and the tensions between various actors, bureaucratic and corporate. It presents a much less harmonious and much more critical view of MITI industrial policy than the one that dominates not just the literature on industrial policy but also popular discourse. This is a view of Japan that is very different from the notion of Confucian order and harmony that seems to grip the Western (and, indeed, the Japanese) imagination. It is a Japan of fissures and factions, where great efforts are made to paper over irreconcilable conflicts in order to transmit a surface impression of cooperative harmony.

Basic Structure and Approach

The core of the book consists of controlled case studies of the four major Japanese high-tech consortia in computers and electronics since the mid 1970's: (1) *VLSI*, an attempt to catch up with the United States in advanced semiconductor technology for computers, the single example of success among the four consortia studied (1975–79)[9]; (2) *Supercomputer*, which pushed the technology envelope in supercomputers (1981–89); (3) *Fifth Generation*, an effort to develop the basic building blocks for "thinking machines," computers able to reason, understand human speech, and so on (1982–93); and (4) *TRON, The Realtime Operating System Nucleus*, an ambitious bid to revolutionize Japanese (and ultimately world) computing based upon new computing standards and architectures (1984–ongoing).

These cases are the major efforts in microelectronics (indeed, in all

TABLE I

Research Focus: Major Japanese Computer Consortia, 1975 to Present

Category	VLSI		Super-computer	Fifth Generation	TRON
	MITI	NTT			
Time period	1976–79	1975–81	1981–89	1982–92[a]	1984–present
Years	4	6	9	11[a]	10+
Billions of yen	74	40[b]	18	54	70–100?
Corporate participants	5 (NEC, Fujitsu, Hitachi, Toshiba, Mitsubishi)	3 + NTT (NEC, Fujitsu, Hitachi)	6 (5 MITI VLSI firms + Oki)	Main firms: 8 + NTT (Super-computer firms + Matsushita + Sharp)	Main firms: 7 + NTT (Fifth Generation firms less Sharp) TRON Assoc. Affiliates: 75–150
Financing	40% MITI, 60% companies	100% NTT	100% MITI	100% MITI	100% companies
Did a central, joint lab exist?	Yes, but only 15–20% of total funding	Yes—NTT effort's main research site	No	Yes— approx. 20% of total funding	No
Technology focus: future or current technology?	Joint Lab— mostly future; Company labs—current	Mix of future and current	Mix of future and current	Future	Current

NOTE: The dates listed under "Time period" list the relevant Japanese fiscal years, rather than calendar years. The Japanese government fiscal year runs from April 1 to March 31. Budget totals are actual funds spent, rather than funds budgeted to the consortium at launch. These two figures can differ substantially—the Supercomputer consortium was originally funded at ¥23 billion, but it ultimately only received less than 80% of that, approximately ¥18 billion. By "technology focus," I mean whether the consortium focuses on more current, status quo technologies or more futuristic, basic research and development (R&D).

[a] JIPDEC, the Japan Information Processing Development Center, a public/private body sponsored by MITI, continued funding efforts to propagate Fifth Generation technologies through FY 1994. If one were to include these additional two years, the total Fifth Generation consortium length reaches 13 years.

[b] The NTT effort consisted of two three-year plans. The first three years were funded at ¥20 billion. This budget estimate assumes that the second three-year plan continued the funding levels of the first three years.

high-tech sectors) in the period under study. They also present a good variety of both organizational structures and outcomes, with sufficient variation in these variables to draw conclusions about effective organization for technological innovation. Table 1 gives a brief summary of all four high-tech consortia along several key dimensions, including time length, budget, number of participants, financing, the existence or nonexistence of a common, joint research lab, and the consortium's technology focus. A fuller introduction to each consortium is provided in Chapter 2.

The first three consortia, VLSI, Supercomputer, and Fifth Generation, were all MITI-run high-tech consortia. MITI organized them, funded them, and ran them. The final consortium, TRON, on the other hand, is privately funded and organized, so MITI clearly did not exercise the kind of direct, highly involved leadership and control that it had in VLSI, Supercomputer, and Fifth Generation. This being the case, a natural question arises: since this is a book on MITI industrial policy, why analyze TRON? There are two reasons:

1.   In the BTRON (*Business TRON*) effort to create a TRON personal computer, the central technology focus of the TRON consortium in the mid 1980's, MITI *did* in fact play a highly significant role, albeit one that was more indirect and behind-the-scenes. Although MITI had no official position in the TRON consortium, it shared control with the Ministry of Education of a government/industry consortium called CEC, the Center for Educational Computing, that sought to determine the specifications of a national Japanese school personal computer standard. It was largely through its activities in connection with this body that MITI exercised substantial influence over the future of the BTRON personal computer. Thus, this book's assessment of the rise and fall of BTRON offers an opportunity to study one aspect of MITI's 1980's policy behavior in the crucial technology area of personal computing.

2.   The very lack of an overt role for MITI in the TRON consortium gives insight into the changing nature of Japanese industrial policy, a core concern of this book. Launched in 1984, TRON is the last historically of the four consortia studied here. It was a natural candidate for a MITI technology initiative—it brought together Japanese firms to bootstrap up Japan's capabilities and competitiveness in a broad array of computing technologies, both hardware and software. MITI was highly interested in this effort, and it ultimately sponsored the TRON Association's application to become a semi-public foundation (*shadan hōjin*), along with assigning some of its personnel to informally monitor the effort.

Nevertheless, MITI did not formally push for control of the TRON consortium, probably because by the time the TRON consortium was officially convened in 1984, trade tensions with the United States made such overt MITI action impossible. TRON was deliberately aimed at creating something new, something Japanese, that would erode Microsoft's and Intel's lock on the world personal computer market. As an official government effort, it would have likely been perceived as yet another example of unfair Japanese business/government alliance fostering competitive advantage and would have inflamed trade tensions with the United States, so it could absolutely not take the shape of the other three, official MITI consortia.[10]

Sources and Evidence

This book draws extensively on Japanese-language materials, including contemporary reports in newspapers and mass-market and trade magazines as well as Japanese government documents. In addition, it makes use of data from previously published English-language analyses of Japanese high-tech industrial policy. While the basic assumptions and ultimately the conclusions of these analyses often differ quite strikingly from those of this study, I have tried to build upon these past efforts as best I can.

I have also made much use of interviews to supplement and cross-check information in these written sources. In 1992–93, I conducted nearly 100 interviews (98, to be exact), which typically ran from one to two hours and were recorded either on tape or in detailed written notes. Most of the interview sources were Japanese researchers, bureaucrats, and academics who had been active in the planning, management, or research activities of one of the consortia analyzed.[11] With some exceptions, the interviews were in Japanese; I have translated the remarks quoted in the text.

Almost all of the interviews were off the record; the few exceptions were with persons such as Ken Sakamura (TRON) and Kazuhiro Fuchi (Fifth Generation) who, as pivotal figures in their respective consortia, granted me the privilege of on-the-record discussions. For the rest of those interviewed, however, the promise of confidentiality was essential to a frank airing of opinions.[12]

In piecing together the story of Japan's high-tech consortia from these written sources and interviews, I have maintained a certain (but, I hope, not overly suspicious or unfriendly) skepticism. I am well aware that certain kinds of information can be unreliable. Although this reliability problem is often thought of with respect to interview sources, it also applies to written sources, even published ones. Human error and frailty in the form of faded memories play a role here, as do various institutional and personal agendas, which can feed the desire to exaggerate or criticize, play up or play down. Consequently, I have put a great deal of effort into confirming and cross-checking information, so that no finding in this book, no interpretation of events, springs from a single source.

What Comes Next: Chapter Organization and Content

Seven chapters follow. Chapter 2 introduces the four high-tech consortia that have been a major focus of Japanese industrial policy over the past two decades. This chapter is intended to give the reader a foothold, a factual point of reference, before proceeding to more detailed analysis. In each case, I address issues such as: Who were the main players? Why was the consortium launched? What were the goals?

Chapters 3, 4, and 5 address the role of cooperation, competition, and conflict in the formation and implementation of MITI policies. The basic thrust is that conflict and competition between (1) MITI and other bureaucracies, (2) between MITI and Japanese companies, and (3) between the companies themselves frequently undercuts Japanese industrial policy's cooperative goals. For the sake of clarity, I have analyzed each of these three levels in a separate chapter.

Chapter 3 tackles *interbureaucratic* competition and conflict, the turf wars and struggles for power between MITI and other bureaucracies that are an artifact of Japanese bureaucratic life. It describes, for example, the media war that took place between MITI and NTT, Japan's then-public telephone monopoly, as they fought for control over the VLSI consortium, and the discreet face off between MITI and the Ministry of Education when the two tried jointly to set up a new personal computer standard for Japanese schools based on TRON.

Chapter 4 proceeds to the divergence in goals and interests *between MITI and the companies*. In the 1980's, MITI increasingly pushed companies to participate in consortia against the companies' explicit wishes. The chapter details, for example, MITI's overriding of company resistance to the Fifth Generation plan and the companies' retaliation by withholding funds and personnel, and how NEC was cornered by MITI and forced to join the TRON personal computer effort, even though NEC was violently against this threat to its near-monopoly in the Japanese personal computer market.

Finally, Chapter 5 details *intercompany* competition and conflict, finding no evidence of any spirit of cooperation between corporate competitors. Companies do not like to be forced to cooperate on MITI's terms, and largely do not. As a matter of basic principle, they are against joint research with one another, and fight to constrain or eliminate MITI's hoped-for joint R&D labs.

The low point of intercompany cooperation described in the book is the large supercomputer that was supposed to be jointly built by Hitachi, Fujitsu, and NEC in the Supercomputer consortium. Hitachi and NEC engineers at a Fujitsu factory to integrate the components of the supercomputer in the final year of its development were treated more like the enemy than as allies. For fear that they might overhear Fujitsu secrets over ramen and rice, they were forbidden to eat in the cafeteria, and food was brought to them in special isolated rooms. Forbidden for the same reason to ride the Fujitsu commuter bus, they took taxis an hour a day for six months from the nearest train station. Forbidden even to *see* the main computer that they were working on, they had to ask Fujitsu employees to test their subcomponents and come back and tell them what had happened. It was an engineer's and manager's nightmare.

Chapter 6 moves on to an evaluation of the success or failure of the four high-tech consortia. It suggests that the VLSI consortium is the single example of success; the three 1980's consortia have not been able to match MITI's earlier achievements.

In pointing to the success of VLSI, it is important to understand that the primary influence of the VLSI consortium was financial, not technological. Although the Japanese VLSI effort has been proclaimed by Western and Japanese analysts to be a triumph of Japanese joint R&D over splintered U.S. efforts, the reality is that an estimated 85 percent of VLSI research and development was done separately by the Japanese firms *in their own labs*. And much of the remaining 15 percent of the funds that *was* devoted to joint R&D went to a particular technology bet (equipment that used electron beams to draw microscopic integrated circuits), which did not pay off.

In fact, the real key to the VLSI consortium was MITI's money. MITI VLSI subsidies, amounting to 40 percent of consortium funding, were critical to the companies' decision to invest in advanced semiconductor technology. In 1975, when the decision to launch the Japanese VLSI effort was being made, all of the Japanese firms were in financial crisis. Being highly dependent on foreign oil imports, Japan had been clobbered by the OPEC oil shock; its inflation rate soared to 18 percent, the highest in the industrialized world, and the Japanese economy shrank for the first time since World War II.

In the midst of this oil-shock recession, not only were the big Japanese companies losing money in semiconductors, they were also having their trade protection stripped away. MITI had agreed in 1973, before the oil shock, to throw open the Japanese market to U.S. semiconductor imports in 1975–76. It was in this context of financial turmoil and market risk that MITI subsidies stimulated corporate investment and played a role in the ultimate Japanese conquest of the world market in computer memory chips. In contrast to VLSI, the three 1980's consortia proved to be ineffective instruments of both subsidy and technological innovation.

Chapter 7 explains the decreased effectiveness of MITI policy in terms of the changing policy environment that envelopes MITI. The chapter's main goal is to illustrate the linkages between Japan's transformation into a leading high-tech economy and the erosion of MITI's ability to execute its industrial-policy agenda.

As Japan entered the 1980's, its growing economic and technological power represented a structural transition in its position in the global economy. Japan had moved from being a follower, both technologically and economically, to being a world-class competitor in a broad array of high technologies. This combined with a robust economy of continuing high growth rates and massive trade surpluses to establish Japan as an economic powerhouse.

This new techno-economic situation seriously eroded MITI's ability to run an effective industrial policy. First, increasingly confident Japanese firms cast off their dependence on MITI and refused to contribute funds to MITI consortia. MITI's technology budgets shrank drastically in size in comparison to the surging technology investments of Japan's electronics firms. Second, MITI discovered that pushing out on the technology frontier was substantially more difficult than pursuit of "catch-up" policies that targeted existing technologies perfected by the United States. Third, trade pressures, exacerbated by Japan's huge trade surpluses and its inroads into high-value-added, high-tech markets overseas, increasingly constrained MITI's policy options.

The result was that MITI's two major technology efforts in the 1980's, Supercomputer and Fifth Generation, were hamstrung by small budgets, company resistance, and a focus on highly speculative, futuristic technologies in an attempt to create original Japanese technologies and avoid the trade frictions caused by MITI's previous focus on targeting current technology areas dominated by the United States.

MITI was also hamstrung in its policies toward the third major consortium in the 1980's, TRON. Trade tensions kept it from playing a more active role, and it was forced to depend upon the Ministry of Education in setting standards for the TRON personal computer, which had promised to be the first truly original Japanese personal computer. Unfortunately for MITI, it and the Ministry of Education had totally different interests, and the TRON PC standard for schools was killed off in 1989. Today, much to the TRON backers' dismay, the Japanese personal computer industry continues to be dominated by American hardware and American software.

In conclusion, Chapter 8 briefly (1) summarizes the main arguments; (2) offers a critique of "revisionist" views of the Japanese political economy; and (3) assesses the competitive and policy implications of my findings for government and business decision makers. The most important conclusion is that Japan's experience gives us reason to be extremely cautious about government industrial policy in high-tech sectors. Despite bringing substantial advantages over other national bureaucracies to the making of industrial policy, MITI found itself outmatched in high technology in the 1980's. Unable to predict technology trajectories accurately, it constantly struck out when it tried to swing for technological home runs.

TWO

First Impressions

Basic Details of Four Major Japanese High-Tech Consortia, 1975–1993

> The Japanese are a homogeneous race, and the ability to achieve consensus easily makes joint government-industry research possible.   Fujitsu executive

> Japan has a culture which promotes cooperation between government, industry and labor to achieve national goals once a consensus is reached.
> U.S. Department of Commerce report, 1989

This chapter briefly describes the four major high-tech consortia whose stories form the core evidence of this book: VLSI, Supercomputer, Fifth Generation, and TRON. The aim is to provide the reader with a basic level of detail and understanding of where these consortia arranged themselves in time, what their goals were, and how they were organized. More details are, of course, provided in the chapters that follow.

Chasing America: The VLSI Consortium, 1975–1979

It was the VLSI consortium that really propelled MITI's cooperative ventures onto the world stage. The earliest of the consortia analyzed here, VLSI was a catch-up project that targeted advanced semiconductor technologies for use in computers. These were so-called VLSI (Very Large-Scale Integration) integrated-circuit technologies, highly miniaturized semiconductor technologies that have allowed for the placement of computer functions on ever-smaller computer chips. Today, because of advances such as the transistor, the integrated circuit, and VLSI, computers that used to weigh several tons and occupy whole rooms, or even several rooms, have shrunk to small pieces of silicon that weigh only grams and are about the size of a fingertip.

The VLSI effort brought together NEC, Toshiba, Fujitsu, Hitachi, and Mitsubishi and coincided with Japan's rapid advances and ultimate conquest of the world market for DRAMs (Dynamic Random Access

Memory), the memory chips used in almost all computers today. The apparent success of joint R&D in VLSI, along with Japan's new Fifth Generation, spawned a host of imitators worldwide, including the U.S. Department of Defense's VHSIC semiconductor initiative, the Microelectronics and Computer Consortium (MCC), and Sematech in the United States, and the Alvey and Esprit programs in Europe. To avoid U.S. companies falling behind, U.S. anti-trust law was even amended to allow companies to work together on R&D "like the Japanese do."

However, the most important thing to know about the VLSI consortium was that it was at heart *not* a joint research effort. As already noted, in actuality, an estimated 85 percent of the research was done separately by companies in their own independent facilities.[1] Thus, the VLSI consortium was more an example of high-tech subsidies than of high-tech joint R&D. This flew in the face of MITI's original intent, which was to make it a 100 percent joint operation, a story that is told in Chapter 4.

The process leading up to the launch of the VLSI consortium is described in detail in Chapter 3. The immediate precipitant was the acquisition of secret documents belonging to the International Business Machines Corporation (IBM) that described work on a new IBM computer, code-named "F/S," or the "Future System." The most shocking revelation in these documents was that the Future System intended to employ highly miniaturized VLSI DRAMs. The Future System's DRAM specification was for placing 1 megabit (1 million "bits," or units of information) on a single chip, far beyond Japanese capabilities. Thus, the VLSI consortium that took shape as a response to the IBM Future System made improving Japanese DRAM capabilities its major focus, although it also funded work on "logic" devices, the computing engines or "brains" of computers.

VLSI is the most complicated organizationally of the four consortia analyzed here. The five participating companies, Fujitsu, Hitachi, Mitsubishi, NEC, and Toshiba, were the major computer manufacturers in Japan. Another company, Oki Electric, was also a candidate for participation, but as punishment for Oki having dropped out of the computer business in early 1975, MITI did not let it into its VLSI effort. It is somewhat ironic that VLSI, a semiconductor R&D effort, did not include any semiconductor equipment manufacturers as members, but MITI positioned the consortium as a *computer* development effort. The semiconductor technologies developed were to be applied to the manufacture of high-end Japanese computers. This computer "spin" on the consortium appears to have been both a response to IBM's Future System computer and to MITI's needs in wresting control of the VLSI effort away from NTT, Japan's domestic telephone monopoly, which was at the time a public corporation. Since MITI regulated the computer industry and NTT did not, if the VLSI consortium targeted computers, MITI would run it.

The clash of interests between MITI and NTT (described in Chapter 3) is the reason VLSI consortium details are listed in two separate columns—MITI and NTT—in Table 1. Despite being publicly portrayed as a single, unified Japanese effort that brought together MITI and NTT under MITI's control, the reality was that the VLSI consortium housed two different efforts, one controlled by MITI and one by NTT. Since the NTT and MITI efforts were not only distinct, but also different in form, it makes sense to list the key details of each separately.

While this analysis does look at some aspects of NTT's VLSI effort, it focuses primarily on the VLSI consortium efforts more fully under MITI's control: the MITI joint lab and the so-called company "group labs" affiliated with the VLSI consortium. The NTT program is addressed primarily to describe the competition between NTT and MITI.

There are three reasons for the focus on MITI. First, the MITI program was the larger and more significant of the two. Second, I am most interested in Japanese industrial policy as articulated and implemented by MITI, the primary postwar actor in Japanese industrial policy, so I have tried to achieve a greater level of detail on the MITI program. Third, information on the NTT program is not readily available, so given its lower analytical priority, I have devoted more attention to MITI.[2]

Turning to the organization of MITI's VLSI consortium, Figure 1 shows the R&D lab structure that emerged. A joint R&D lab was created to bring together all of the companies and ETL, the Electrotechnical Laboratory, MITI's central research lab. Within the joint lab, there were six sublabs, each headed respectively by one of the five companies or ETL. The sublabs did basic research in microfabrication (three labs), semiconductor devices, semiconductor manufacturing processes, and silicon crystals and wafers.

There were also the "group labs" run by two joint venture companies that did the actual application of VLSI technologies to competitive products. One group was CDL, the Cooperative Development Laboratories, consisting of Fujitsu, Hitachi, and Mitsubishi. The other group was NTIS, NEC-Toshiba Information Systems. Finally, there

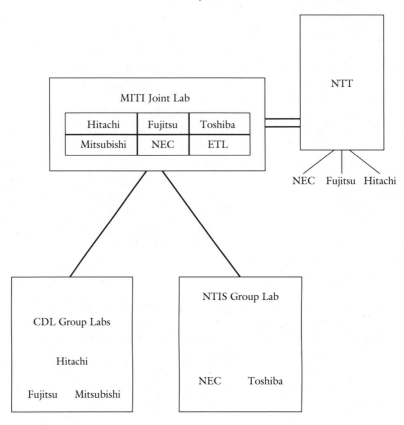

1. VLSI Consortium Lab Structure

was also the NTT effort, in which NTT allowed only Hitachi, Fujitsu, and NEC to participate, and that nominally cooperated with the MITI joint lab.

We Will Build the World's Fastest Computer: The Supercomputer Consortium, 1981–1989

Supercomputers are sexy. They are also phenomenally expensive, costing on the order of several millions to several tens of millions of dollars apiece. But if you want the biggest, the best, and the fastest, if you have problems to solve of mammoth complexity and mammoth size, supercomputers are the only solution. In the late 1970's, there was one dominant supercomputer manufacturer in the world, and it was based not in Japan but in the upper reaches of the great plains, in Minnesota. This was Cray Research, headed by the iconoclastic supercomputer visionary Seymour Cray, who formed the company in 1976.

There were those in the Japanese scientific community who felt it was important for Japan, too, to be a player in this highest end of computing—that leading-edge science would increasingly be done on such machines, and that if Japanese researchers did not have access to their own supercomputers, in the words of one leading Japanese computer scientist, "Twenty-first-century science could not advance."[3]

After all, speed is essential for certain applications. In modeling the earth's atmosphere for tomorrow's weather forecast, for example, it might be cheaper to try it on a smaller machine, but when it takes a day to churn through the immense weather datasets that are used, "tomorrow's" weather prediction arrives *after* tomorrow's weather.

In areas such as the aerodynamics of new aircraft designs, moreover, where the number of different design iterations can be in the thousands, not being able to do it fast can mean not being able to do it at all. When NASA's Langley Research Center did a computational model of the space shuttle's solid rocket booster, the component that failed on the *Challenger* in 1986, for each iteration, the model took fourteen hours on a mid-range computer. When computed on a top-of-the-line Cray Y-MP supercomputer, it took just five seconds, a speedup of over 10,000 times.[4] A five-second analysis can be done hundreds of times a day; a fourteen-hour analysis obviously cannot.

It was this kind of performance gain that Japanese scientists and MITI bureaucrats dreamed of when they pushed for a consortium for supercomputers made in Japan. The MITI Supercomputer consortium that emerged was the first MITI computer consortium to follow on the heels of VLSI. It was a relatively small effort, funded only at about 20–25 percent the level of VLSI, and began at the beginning of 1982 (the end of FY 1981). Six companies participated: the five firms in VLSI—Fujitsu, Hitachi, Mitsubishi, NEC, and Toshiba—plus Oki, which seems to have won its way back into MITI's good graces after pouring tremendous investments into its independent VLSI efforts. The aim of the consortium was quite clear: in the words of a senior academic involved in consortium planning, it was "to build a better Cray-1"—the computer Seymour Cray was selling worldwide.[5]

In pursuit of this end, the Supercomputer consortium split its funds equally between R&D on (1) computer systems and architectures and (2) new high-speed computer "devices," or components (see Table 2). On the systems side, there were three projects. The primary effort,

TABLE 2

Supercomputer Consortium: Research Program and Division of Labor

Systems/Computer architecture				Non-silicon devices		
Vector supercomputer	Graphics supercomputer	Data-flow supercomputer	HEMT		Gallium arsenide	Josephson junction
Fujitsu	Mitsubishi	ETL	Fujitsu		ETL	ETL
Hitachi	Oki		Oki		Hitachi	Fujitsu
NEC	Toshiba				Mitsubishi	Hitachi
					NEC	NEC
					Toshiba	

which got the bulk of the systems funds, brought together Fujitsu, Hitachi, and NEC, Japan's three largest computer makers, to build a huge vector supercomputer that would be able to drive sixteen different CPUs (Central Processing Units, the "brains" of computers) simultaneously.

Vector supercomputers were the kind Cray built: they arrange data in large vector matrices, which can be solved simultaneously by a CPU. This is a kind of limited parallel computation, because a single CPU operation can solve parts of multiple equations. Vector supercomputers can also increase the amount of parallelism by having multiple CPUs work on the same problem simultaneously. More processors attacking the same problem means that solutions come faster, and getting things done faster is what supercomputers are all about.

In 1982, Cray was working on stringing together up to four CPUs to do parallel computation, so the Japanese consortium's 16-processor goal suggested a major increase in complexity and speed. The consortium aimed to achieve a computation speed of 10 gigaflops (10 billion floating-point operations per second; "giga" in the computer world means a billion, and "mega" means a million), up to a thousand times faster than existing supercomputers. This vector supercomputer was to be the showpiece of the entire Supercomputer consortium, both because of its projected computational power and because it would incorporate the exotic high-speed device technologies that were being developed simultaneously.

In contrast to this large-scale effort to extend and improve upon existing vector supercomputer designs, the Supercomputer consortium launched two other smaller systems projects aimed at exploring new approaches to supercomputing. Mitsubishi, Toshiba, and Oki, led by Mitsubishi, were to tackle a specialized graphics supercomputer for image-processing applications. It would crunch imaging data beamed down from satellites and would employ newer, more aggressive techniques of parallel processing to increase speed, including so-called "massively parallel processing."

Parallel processing is the next great leap forward in computational power. Parallel processing can come in various flavors, ranging from limited parallelism or multi-processing, which starts at two parallel processors, to massive parallelism, where the number of parallel CPUs can be in the tens of thousands. Massively parallel machines tend to differ from vector machines on two dimensions: (1) the number of CPUs, and (2) the complexity and power of each CPU. Vector supercomputers in their limited parallel forms employ a few (typically 2–8) extremely fast CPUs. Each CPU is composed of a group of specialized computer chips that when put together on a computer board comprise a single computational unit. In contrast, the basic concept in massively parallel supercomputers is to string together many slow CPUs. This means putting lots and lots of microprocessors—CPUs that have been shrunk down to a single chip—into a single computer. Microprocessors are ubiquitous in the computing world: for example, they drive all personal computers today. While single-chip microprocessors are extremely slow when compared to the complex, multi-chip CPUs of vector supercomputers, they are also extremely cheap, because they are made by the millions for use in personal computers and workstations by semiconductor manufacturers such as Intel and Motorola.

The massively parallel processing idea is that if you can get enough of these microprocessors to work on the same problems in parallel, they will be orders of magnitude faster than the few CPUs in vector machines. The underlying logic is that vector supercomputer makers have pushed the limits of speed of the few processors that they employ and have hit a wall of diminishing marginal returns, so that the search must turn away from the vector machines' focus on increasing the speed of each and every CPU, and toward figuring out ways to get lots of CPUs to work together—an army of ants overcoming a few giant elephants.

The third systems project in the Supercomputer consortium also attempted to apply new parallel processing techniques aggressively. It was a "data-flow" machine, which tries to ease programming burdens and create a form of "natural" parallelism through an innovative system architecture. Since the data-flow approach was fairly speculative—there were really only two efforts going on in the world, at the Massachusetts Institute of Technology (MIT) and at MITI's ETL—ETL was left by the companies to do the data-flow supercomputer on its own.

In tandem with these three systems projects, the other half of the

Supercomputer consortium's funds were to be used to develop new computer "device" technologies, new components that aimed at huge improvements in speed and decreased power consumption over existing devices. In 1982, all mass-market semiconductor devices for computers were made out of silicon. Silicon is abundant and cheap; it is, after all, the basic element in sand. Moreover, the processing technologies for turning this element of sand into sophisticated computer components are well known. Based upon these strengths, silicon continues to be king in the computer industry today. There are no general-purpose computers that use anything but silicon components. But in 1982, MITI, along with many others active in the computer industry worldwide, saw a number of alternatives to silicon that seemed to offer substantial performance improvements. MITI proceeded to fund research in these areas.

Three device technologies were chosen as particularly promising. Josephson junctions, components that have a totally different physics from existing semiconductor devices, were the first. They are based on the discoveries of Brian Josephson, who as a graduate student at Cambridge University in 1962 observed what came to be called the Josephson effect, research that eventually won him a Nobel Prize in physics in 1973. Josephson found that certain materials when cooled to near zero Kelvin—this is *absolute* zero, $-273.15°C$ $(-459.67°F)$—become superconductors that can form the basis for extremely fast computers. IBM had had a large effort going on in Josephson junctions since the mid 1960's, and as a catch-up effort in the Supercomputer consortium, MITI's ETL and the Big Three, Fujitsu, Hitachi, and NEC, undertook Josephson junction R&D.

The other two device technologies, gallium arsenide and HEMT (*High Electron Mobility Transistor*) were not quite as radical as Josephson junctions, although HEMT promised to achieve speeds in the range of Josephson junctions. Like existing computer components, these two approaches were based on semiconductors; however, they used different materials. Instead of silicon, they employed types of gallium arsenide, a compound of two elements, gallium and arsenic, which had good semiconductor properties and was expected to offer improvements in speed and lower power consumption over silicon devices. MITI's ETL, Hitachi, Mitsubishi, NEC, and Toshiba took on research on conventional gallium arsenide compounds. These had no possibility of offering the speed improvements or low power consumption of Josephson junctions, but could be used at room temperatures and offered a more certain technology payoff.

Fujitsu and Oki were to investigate a specialized type of gallium arsenide called HEMT, which had layers of both gallium arsenide and gallium arsenide aluminum compounds. HEMT devices when cooled to the temperature of liquid nitrogen ($-196°C$) experienced dramatic speedups to the level of Josephson junctions. They were primarily a Fujitsu innovation, and Fujitsu expected them to be easier to build and cheaper than Josephson junctions, since they could be cooled with liquid nitrogen, rather than the more expensive and difficult liquid helium required for Josephson junctions.

This was the Supercomputer research plan that the companies ultimately acceded to. Unfortunately for MITI, the companies may have agreed to it, but they were far from enthusiastic. In fact, to say that they were dragged by MITI kicking and screaming into the consortium is probably a better way of putting it, as we shall see in Chapter 4. The lack of corporate enthusiasm had a major effect on the organizational shape of the consortium. MITI had expected that it would repeat the experience of VLSI: Supercomputer was to have a joint lab and the companies were to kick in half of the consortium funding. However, MITI could not win acceptance of a joint lab or corporate funding contributions. The Supercomputer consortium companies would target these technologies on MITI's money and in separate labs.[6]

Machines That "Think": The Fifth Generation Consortium, 1982–1992

MITI's Fifth Generation project was designed to forever break the hold of IBM on the Japanese computer industry. It aimed to push out along a computer technology frontier where no man and no nation had gone before. At the same time, it was to demonstrate that Japanese computer scientists had become world-class *creators* and *inventors*; that Japan was no longer a mere copier of U.S. computer designs.

The Fifth Generation consortium started up only months after Supercomputer in 1982, and had a budget several times larger. It was also more ambitious technologically, and a lot more organizations were involved. For one, the firms represented on the board of directors of the consortium increased from Supercomputer's six to nine. Matsushita, Sharp, and NTT were the new arrivals. (At Fifth Generation's startup, NTT was still the public telephone monopoly—it would lose its long-distance monopoly and be privatized in the middle of Fifth Generation's research effort in 1985.) In addition to these core firms, a number of firms and research institutions participated in the consortium in a more reduced way. In 1991, for example, researchers from seventeen different organizations were at the ICOT joint lab.

ICOT is the acronym of the independent foundation that MITI set up to run the Fifth Generation consortium: the *I*nstitute for New Generation *CO*mputer *T*echnology. ICOT housed the joint research lab in the Mita International Building, near Tokyo Tower and the Mita campus of Keio University, one of Japan's elite private universities.

Fifth Generation got its name from its technology goal: to build "Fifth Generation" computers that were one step closer to human beings in their ability to reason and infer from large knowledge databases. The first generation of computers had been based upon vacuum tubes. Generation two was built with transistors, followed by integrated circuits (third generation), and then VLSI-based integrated circuits (fourth generation).

The fifth computer generation was going to break away from the design philosophy that had governed all these previous generations. Previous generations had all processed information serially—they were so-called von Neumann machines, named after the mathematician John von Neumann, who has been widely regarded as the first person to articulate the concept of a modern digital computer in the 1940's. Recent historical work has now come to question von Neumann's right to this claim to fame, but, be that as it may, computers with a single CPU that processes information one portion at a time are frequently referred to as von Neumann machines.[7]

The Fifth Generation consortium aimed to put an end to this von Neumann approach to computing. Fifth Generation computers would not have a single CPU slowly grinding its way through data; instead, they would have lots of processors that would be able to solve problems by computing simultaneously. The multiple-processor vector supercomputer and massively parallel computers described above as part of the Supercomputer consortium's research agenda could thus also be considered a part of this fifth computer generation.

However, the Fifth Generation consortium had a specific computational goal that was in stark contrast to the Supercomputer program. While supercomputers and almost all conventional computers process numbers, the Fifth Generation consortium's computers were going to process *knowledge* and compute *concepts*. In short, the computers of the Fifth Generation consortium were meant to take a major step closer to the holy grail of artificial intelligence (AI) research: thinking machines, machines that reason and even understand. Thus, the performance measurements that the consortium adopted were not conventional ones such as millions of instructions per second (MIPS) or millions of floating-point operations per second (MFLOPS). These are performance measures that come from the world of numerical computing. Rather, Fifth Generation machines were going to be measured in terms of a *higher-order* computational activity, logical inferences per second (LIPS).

The Fifth Generation consortium also embarked upon a focused technical strategy to achieve its goals. It proposed the use of techniques of "logic programming," a particular subfield of computer programming that was deemed particularly suited to programming for parallel inference. The basis for this approach was to be a computer language called Prolog, created at the University of Marseilles in the early 1970's. After LISP, invented by John McCarthy at MIT in the late 1950's and heavily used in the United States, the dominant center of world AI research, Prolog was a prominent programming language for AI and was particularly popular in Europe. In Japan in the late 1970's, however, Prolog was an obscure programming language known only to a few and used by even fewer.

Creating the Fifth Generation was a grand concept, and called for highly futuristic basic research that was a striking departure from that of past MITI high-tech consortia. Even the Supercomputer consortium was status quo in comparison, given that a good chunk of its effort was going into better-known, and therefore more readily applied, technologies such as vector supercomputing and gallium arsenide. In part owing to its expansive goals, as with supercomputers, MITI had trouble getting the major Japanese companies to buy into the Fifth Generation dream, a face-off described in Chapter 4. In the end, financing for the effort was provided 100 percent by MITI. MITI did manage to get the companies to agree to a joint lab, although like the VLSI joint lab, it was small—only about 20 percent of the consortium's funds was spent there. The rest went to contract work at companies.

Japanese Visions of Japanese Computers: The TRON Consortium, 1984-Ongoing

TRON (The Realtime Operating system Nucleus) has its roots in the late 1970's. It is a computer and semiconductor R&D effort that brings together an extremely diverse set of activities under a single umbrella. To understand TRON, one must understand the man who created it and drove it: the University of Tokyo professor Ken Sakamura. TRON is Sakamura's brainchild, and his imprint can be felt everywhere on it.

Ironically, the roots of TRON are tangled up with those of Fifth Generation. In 1979, Sakamura, a newly minted Ph.D. in computer science from Keio University, won a position as a lecturer at the University of Tokyo, Japan's premiere academic institution. (To give an indication of its status, it is as though Stanford, Princeton, Yale, Harvard, and MIT were a single place, with all the assembled intellectual talent, prestige, and tradition, and vast alumni networks that these institutions could bring to bear.) While at the University of Tokyo, Sakamura joined the deliberations committee for the Fifth Generation project. Hideo Aiso of Keio University had been Sakamura's advisor at Keio, and Sakamura joined Aiso's subcommittee investigating computer-architecture issues related to the Fifth Generation. Chapter 4 describes how the proposals for the Fifth Generation consortium of the architecture group, which largely represented the interests of the major Japanese computer manufacturers, were shunted aside in favor of the more radical logic-programming approaches that became the Fifth Generation consortium's agenda.

Sakamura disagreed with this Fifth Generation approach. Having noted the rapid progress that microprocessor-based personal computers were making in the United States even prior to the introduction of the IBM PC in 1981, he argued very forcefully that Fifth Generation should focus on microprocessors and personal computers, rather than large-scale AI machines. His argument was rejected, and he ultimately resigned from the Fifth Generation task force based upon these disagreements. Sakamura recalls, "[Kazuhiro] Fuchi and the others thought PCs were toys. They told me: 'You want to build a toy, build it yourself. Go find yourself a garage like they do in America.' "[8]

Garages were scarce in Japan, but Sakamura did find support for his concept in JEIDA, the Japan Electronic Industries Development Association, a public/private industry association aligned with MITI. JEIDA gave Sakamura some funding and clerical support to pursue his TRON concepts. The first creation of Sakamura's lab, developed with the help of five or six graduate students, was ITRON: software to control a variety of electronic equipment, such as robots and numerically controlled machine tools. Its key characteristics were that it was (1) multi-tasking, meaning that it could switch between a variety of computational tasks at the same time; and (2) real-time, meaning that it had a prioritization scheme built into it to complete high-priority tasks within a specified time limit.[9]

Sakamura's charisma is his genius. He is engaging in conversation, humorous, driven, confident and confidence-inspiring (some would say arrogant), and highly persuasive in argument. It is these qualities that allowed Sakamura to build TRON from these small beginnings into a large-scale R&D consortium that brought together all of the major Japanese electronics companies. What is particularly startling about Sakamura's achievement is his relative youth at the time. Japan is a hierarchical society, where seniority weighs very heavily. Major projects of TRON's nature are usually headed by men at the peak of their power, having accumulated seniority and prestige over decades of proven accomplishments as scientists or academics. In contrast, Sakamura was still suspiciously young (in his early thirties when he started up TRON at JEIDA) and not even tenured as a professor.

Sakamura made an end run around the traditional power structures of Japanese academia and industry. He sold TRON hard through the mass media, writing over ten books on the subject in the 1980's and even hosting a week-long TV documentary series featuring TRON on the national public television network, NHK, in 1988.[10] (Unlike public television in the United States, NHK is Japan's number-one TV network.) Through the 1980's, TRON continued to gather momentum. In 1984, a special group was formed under the auspices of JEIDA to promote TRON, and a number of Japanese companies participated. In 1986, the TRON effort was attracting sufficient corporate interest and corporate funds to be able to break away from JEIDA and become a free-standing consortium, regulated by MITI, called the TRON Association.

The TRON Association's board of directors had all of Japan's microelectronics heavyweights on board: Fujitsu, Hitachi, Matsushita, Mitsubishi, NEC, NTT, Oki, and Toshiba. Moreover, outside of these main firms, TRON attracted an increasing number of companies who participated in TRON activities as members. The number of these member firms hit a peak of nearly 150 at the end of the 1980's. In contrast to VLSI, Fifth Generation, and Supercomputer, which all operated under MITI auspices and received MITI funds, the TRON consortium is a purely privately financed effort, drawing upon membership fees. Moreover, it is ongoing, with no scheduled end to its activities.

TRON's two main thrusts can be typified as *openness* and *pervasiveness*.[11] Openness means that TRON is committed to being nonproprietary and allowing equal access to all interested parties to its proceedings and outputs. This commitment to openness has a central position in the "Fundamental Concepts Governing the TRON Project" published by the TRON Association:

1.   The computer architecture TRON originated by Dr. Ken Sakamura is an open computer architecture. The TRON Specifications are made publicly available to anyone in the world.

2. Copyrights to the TRON Specifications belong to the TRON Association. Anyone is entitled to utilize the TRON Specifications in developing and merchandising products conforming to the TRON Specifications.

3. The TRON Association has been established as the core organization for the purpose of preparing the TRON Specifications, conducting conformance testing, and otherwise promoting the TRON Project. Membership in the TRON Association is open to anyone in the world who shares in the objectives of the TRON Project and agrees to observe the TRON Association's rules.[12]

The emphasis on openness is a direct response to what Sakamura and the major TRON members felt were the monopolistic activities of Motorola and Intel, who had cut off licensing of their new advanced 32-bit microprocessor designs to Japanese manufacturers in 1983 and 1985 respectively (32-bit microprocessors process data in 32-bit chunks, as opposed to earlier microprocessors, which could only handle up to 16 units of information simultaneously; handling more data simultaneously means faster computation). Sakamura and the Japanese companies also felt outraged by Microsoft's entrenched position. Microsoft's DOS was required for IBM-compatible personal computers, allowing Microsoft to dominate the market for IBM-compatible PC operating-system software. DOS (the *Disk Operating System*) was a humble operating system, which Microsoft had originally purchased for under $50,000, and it was ultimately worth billions of dollars in sales to the company. For Microsoft, it was a brilliant and lucrative deal, but the Japanese wanted out.

The second key dimension of TRON is pervasiveness. Sakamura wanted to smash the conventional way of thinking about computers, which held that "computers" were small boxes on desks or big boxes in rooms, specialized boxes holding information that was usually accessed by keyboards. Sakamura believed that computers could and should be everywhere, that TRON could bring computer intelligence to all sorts of everyday objects. Air conditioners could house microprocessors and be smart. So could washing machines, toaster ovens, garage door openers, cars, houses. All these things could be "computers." TRON's goal was to make this computerized society a reality.

TRON has had six key project areas.[13] BTRON is *Business* TRON; it aims to establish a new desktop standard for computers, a TRON personal computer. CTRON is Communication and Central TRON; it aims to create standard software interfaces for communications switching equipment and networks. ITRON or *Industrial* TRON has been described above. It specifies operating-system software to control industrial equipment of all types—from robots to refrigerators. MTRON or *Macro* TRON has yet to come to fruition—it aims to create a network-system architecture able to integrate all of the other TRON components. The TRON chip project proposes a new VLSI chip design to compete with existing microprocessors from the likes of Intel and Motorola.

In addition to these projects focusing on more conventional computing contexts, TRON has proposed a number of what might be called environmental or application projects, which attempt to introduce TRON concepts into atypical situations and applications. These number four: TRON House, TRON Building, TRON City, and TRON Car. Only TRON House has come to fruition. A house near the trendy Roppongi area of Tokyo was opened to the public from late 1989 to early 1990. This TRON House showcased the use of computers in everyday life. Computers controlled the air conditioning and heating, the stereo system, lighting, and even the toilets.

I shall not try to analyze and evaluate the full spectrum of these diverse TRON projects here. Rather, the focus is on the fate of the desktop computer standard, BTRON. BTRON is particularly interesting, first of all, because it was at the heart of Sakamura's initial vision for TRON. With millions of personal computers being sold annually, a new computer standard through BTRON would have the most direct impact on people's daily computing lives. BTRON would bring TRON functionality to the individual user: Sakamura wanted to create a new kind of computer with integrated Japanese-language capabilities and a Macintosh-like user environment for ease of use. In addition, Sakamura proposed other BTRON innovations, such as a split keyboard to reduce typing stress on hands and wrists.[14]

The second reason to focus on BTRON is that BTRON is the single area of the TRON consortium where MITI made its presence strongly felt. In the mid 1980's, the Japanese government decided to specify a standard personal computer for Japanese elementary, junior high, and high schools. A joint deliberation council, the Center for Educational Computing (CEC), was set up by MITI and the Ministry of Education (MOE) to decide what that computer should be. Chapters 3–5 describe how this school computer standardization process spun out of control and the conflict of interests that emerged between MITI, the Ministry of Education, and NEC, the dominant player in the Japanese personal computer market.

Finally, a word on TRON's budget: frankly, it is difficult to know.

There is the TRON Association's budget, of course, but the association is primarily a decision-making and promotional body. Actual R&D is done by individual members within their own research labs; these company budget numbers are proprietary and not released to the public. Be forewarned, then, that the estimate provided in Table 1 is no more than an educated guess, which is why it is preceded by question marks and encompasses such a broad range. It is based on some existing published estimates of the total costs of TRON activities and on a sense derived from interviews with corporate managers of the scale of internal development activities.

THREE

Turf Wars

MITI Against Other Japanese Bureaucracies

> The politicians didn't know that it was *tatemae* [a public
> fiction]. . . . we drew a picture that showed the MITI
> project. And, look, here is NTT cooperating with MITI.
> But it was just a picture.
> > NTT semiconductor research manager,
> > about the VLSI consortium

Japanese government agencies tend to be jealously territorial, and when
jurisdictions collide or overlap, the most common result is a bare-
knuckle brawl for control. In the case of the electronics industry, MITI
has been involved in two areas of bureaucratic conflict. The first is
MITI's traditional competition and conflict with Nippon Telephone
and Telegraph (NTT) and the Ministry of Post and Telecommunications (MPT). NTT, Japan's equivalent of AT&T, was until 1985 Japan's
government-owned monopoly on domestic telecommunications, and
the Ministry of Post and Telecommunications is the ministry that regu-
lates NTT. MITI, NTT, and MPT have long quarreled over policies
toward computer-related industries.

The second, newer pole area of conflict pits MITI against the Ministry of Education, Science, and Culture (hereafter the Ministry of Education, or MOE) and the Science and Technology Agency (STA) respectively in a struggle for control of Japanese government research and
development policies. Its increasing involvement in basic R&D, more
traditionally an area of funding for MOE and STA, has caused MITI to
clash more directly with these agencies in recent years.

This chapter first explores these two areas of interbureaucratic conflict, laying out in more general and historical terms the background to
the specific frictions that arise when MITI launches high-tech consortia. I then proceed to flesh out these frictions and conflicts with concrete
examples from VLSI, Supercomputer, Fifth Generation, and TRON.

MITI, NTT, and the Ministry of Post and Telecommunications

In the area of electronics research, there has been a long-standing rivalry between NTT's Electrical Communications Laboratory (ECL), the main R&D arm of NTT, and MITI's own central research lab, the Electrotechnical Laboratory, or ETL. In the postwar era, NTT's ECL has been blessed with much larger budgets and higher salaries because it is not part of the ministerial salary system. Moreover, owing to its huge annual procurement of electronics and communications equipment, it was in a much easier position to demand cooperation and loyalty from the so-called "DenDen Family," the family of electronics firms, chief among them NEC, Fujitsu, Hitachi, and Oki, that served NTT and built equipment for it.

NTT's Electrical Communications Laboratory and MITI's Electrotechnical Laboratory have thus competed, not just on the basis of promoting the goals of their separate political bureaucracies, but also in recruiting top-flight researchers and in vying for the reputation as the premiere government research organization in Japan. Thus, when called upon to cooperate on major projects by the Ministry of Finance or politicians, simmering rivalries frequently interfered. "In practice cooperation is at best superficial for they not only duplicate research topics and equipment but withhold information from each other, plot and fight over budgets, academic advisers, new recruits, company researchers, and access to politicians."[1]

This conflict between NTT and MITI will be seen below to have played an important role in the launching of the VLSI project, but the skirmishing between NTT and MITI over the shape of Japan's VLSI effort represents just one battle in a grand tradition of bureaucratic antipathy.

To draw upon an example from high-tech consortia, MITI and NTT also collided over R&D in optoelectronics, a technology area that integrates principles of light (optics) and electronics. MITI had tried to launch a large-scale project in optoelectronics in 1977, but NTT persuaded the Ministry of Finance, which vetted the budgets of all the ministries, that additional government funding would just waste taxpayers' money. This was, after all, an area where NTT was already doing major work—in its fiber-optic cable for telephone transmissions, for example. MITI's plan was withdrawn, and NTT thus preserved exclusive rights to do optoelectronics R&D. In the fall of that very same year, NTT threw a party at a restaurant in Hibiya Park in Tokyo at which it showed off its latest laser devices, examples of its technological prowess in optoelectronics. MITI officials were invited. At the party an NTT executive announced to his conversation partner, in a voice loud enough to be *clearly* overheard, "MITI's so-called research, compared to NTT's, is like a child's toy." [2]

Interpreting the party as a celebration of NTT's blocking of their own optoelectronics work, MITI personnel were furious and redoubled their efforts to launch MITI's own optoelectronics project. This time it was helped along by the leadership of an ETL scientist from a family with long-standing ties to the Japanese telecommunications industry, who succeeded in persuading NTT not to block the new MITI project.[3] The MITI consortium was launched in 1979, several years later than originally planned.

Similarly, in the 1980's, in the so-called "telecom war," the increasing overlap of the technologies of the computer industry and the telecommunications industry, brought the Ministry of Post and Telecommunications, NTT's oversight agency, and MITI into conflict. MPT regulated telecommunications; MITI regulated computers. But computers were becoming increasingly linked through networks and thus had a telecommunications component; similarly, telecommunications equipment was becoming increasingly digitalized and computerized, so the previous division of labor between MPT, which had the analog world of telecommunications, and MITI, the digital world of computers, came to be dysfunctional. This created tremendous tensions, inasmuch as both ministries tried to claim these new areas of overlap and in the mid 1980's battled, for example, over jurisdiction to regulate "value-added networks"—telecommunications networks that allow access to databases, computer "bulletin boards," and the like using a computer and a phone.

MITI, the Ministry of Education, and the Science and Technology Agency

The NTT/MITI conflict has faded recently, because NTT's 1985 privatization has lowered its profile in technology policy. At the same time, in the 1980's, frictions between MITI, MOE, and STA intensified. This is particularly the case with tensions between MITI and MOE, whose ministerial status makes them more powerful and aggressive than STA.

The increasing conflict from the 1980's onward largely flows from new MITI policies in response to a changing international policy environment. With the increased sense in Japan that it must do more basic research to meet its international obligations, and with MITI facing criticism for its promotion of Japanese companies, MITI has turned away from applied research projects to basic research. However, this new emphasis on basic research brings MITI squarely into what the Ministry of Education has always considered its domain. MOE has traditionally funded basic research in Japanese universities. Thus, when MITI has tried to recruit university participation in its basic R&D projects (including, for example, Fifth Generation), it has been blocked by MOE, which refuses to sanction university participation in projects under MITI control. It is even rumored that MOE has a standing policy that any university that receives MITI funding will have its MOE funding cut by an equivalent amount. In private, MITI officials insist that this rumor is true and complain about MOE obstructionism.[4] MOE officials, in turn, deny that there is any tension between MITI and MOE.[5]

The root of the friction lies in the way the R&D authority of MITI, MOE, and STA has been stipulated. In various ways, all three organizations have jurisdiction over the promotion of Japanese science and technology, although theoretically there is a division of labor, with MOE sponsoring basic research, MITI doing commercially relevant research, and STA coordinating overall policy. But the reality is that all three agencies are fiercely competitive with one another, constantly jockeying for bigger shares of the Japanese government's science and technology pie and making occasional raids into one another's spheres of influence (universities for MOE and industry for MITI).

As for STA's "coordinating power," it discovered very soon after its creation in 1956 that MITI and MOE had no interest in STA's "coordination," and brooked no transgressions onto their R&D turf. STA has learned that coordinating power without actual management control is like being a general without troops. STA is handicapped in the R&D tug-of-war because it is only an agency, not a full ministry, lacking the institutional power that ministerial rank and privilege brings with it.

The Translation War

One of the more bizarre ways in which the STA-MITI-MOE rivalry expresses itself is the "translation war." The names of Japanese government bureaucracies are determined by Japanese law, but each bureaucracy is free to *translate* its name as it wishes. While the Science and Technology Agency (Kagaku gijitsu chō) faithfully translates its Japanese name, both MOE and MITI have taken considerable license with

English translations in an attempt to express broader jurisdiction over science and technology issues.

The Japanese name of MITI's technology arm, the Agency for Industrial Science and Technology (AIST), does not include the word "Science," which MITI has inserted in the English to claim some authority over basic research, the domain of "science," and the prime area of STA and MOE activity. Similarly, AIST's Japanese title is more appropriately rendered as "Institute," not "Agency," in English. Since in Japanese governmental naming conventions, "agencies" have higher institutional status than "institutes," MITI has in effect given AIST a promotion, putting it on institutional par with STA.

Likewise, although MOE claims as its official English name "Ministry of Education, Science, and Culture," the word "Science" does not appear in the Japanese original (Mombushō); it has been added in English to express MOE's claim to manage science policy in the Japanese government. In sum, this war of words typifies the continuing free-for-all between MITI, MOE, and STA in Japanese technology policy.

Having laid out the general dimensions of interbureaucratic competition and conflict, let us now turn to specific instances in the VLSI, Supercomputer, and Fifth Generation consortia.

The VLSI Consortium

The VLSI consortium was the setting for a protracted power struggle between MITI and NTT for control over government-led efforts in VLSI technology. The truth of the matter is that NTT acted much more swiftly and aggressively to launch its project than MITI did. Indeed, MITI did not really become active in planning a MITI-led technology consortium until NTT's project was well under way. At that point, MITI decided that tolerating NTT's independent efforts in this area threatened MITI's authority over the computer industry and moved to seize control. Although MITI eventually won this struggle, and NTT was forced publicly to declare itself a cooperating branch of the MITI consortium, the private reality was that NTT remained a competitor to MITI during the entire length of the two organizations' efforts.

In the early 1970's, it was increasingly obvious that semiconductor technology was rapidly progressing in its performance and degree of integration, and that so-called VLSI technology was going to be a critical technological building block for the computer and electronics industries. In the case of NTT, this was made clear internally in January 1974, when NTT's President Shigeru Yonezawa met with his top officials to plot future R&D directions and it was decided that one focus should be VLSI. In 1973–74, MITI similarly sponsored a study by the Japan Electronics Industry Development Association (JEIDA), a MITI-sponsored public/private agency, that investigated future technology priorities and put a major emphasis on VLSI.

Codename "Future System": Secret IBM Plans Arrive in Japan

It was in this context that a shock from IBM launched a frenzy of discussion and activity in Japan over how best to bootstrap upward Japanese VLSI technology. Sometime in late 1973 or perhaps early 1974 (the exact timing is in dispute), a Fujitsu managing director, the late Toshio Ikeda (then *jōmu*, later *senmu*, or senior managing director), managed to get hold of highly detailed, secret IBM documents describing an ongoing IBM effort to build a revolutionary new computer that would leap far beyond existing technology. Code-named "F/S," or "Future System," this computer was to be introduced by 1980.

One of the most ambitious technological advances Future System promised was 1-megabit DRAMs, computer memory chips capable of storing 1 million "bits" or units of information. (In the computer world, "kilo" signifies thousand, "mega" million, and "giga" billion.) At the time Japan was just barely moving into volume production of the 4-kilobit (4,000-bit) generation of DRAMs, so the IBM Future System promised a 250-fold improvement in storage capacity over Japanese best efforts within a period of around seven years, far beyond what the Japanese semiconductor industry thought itself capable of.

With all of the Japanese semiconductor companies losing money in 1974 and under sustained competitive attack from U.S. semiconductor giants such as Texas Instruments, the Japanese industry was in a state of crisis. And IBM's fantastic Future System seemed to spell doom for the same Japanese companies who competed with IBM in their role as Japan's leading computer makers. What was particularly frightening was that, bowing to American pressure, MITI had agreed to liberalize the computer and semiconductor industries in 1975–76. Table 3 gives the liberalization timetable. No longer could the Japanese firms count on MITI trade and investment barriers to escape competition from the United States. The protectionist walls were coming down, and the Future System was coming along. For the frightened companies, the answer was clear: go to the Japanese government and plead for money.

Ironically, the Future System turned out to be a case of threat inflation, the kind of worst-case scenario and hyping of overseas threats sometimes seen in the U.S. defense establishment during the Cold War.

TABLE 3
Dates of Liberalization of Japanese Domestic Computer and Semiconductor Markets

Item	Capital liberalization		Import liberalization	Liberalization of foreign technology licensing
	50% liberalization	100% liberalization		
Electronic accounting machines & high-end calculators	8/4/74	12/1/75	4/19/73	7/1/74
Computers				
Main unit	8/4/74	12/1/75	12/24/75	7/1/74
Peripherals:				
Memory devices & terminals	8/4/74	12/1/75	12/24/75	7/1/74
Peripherals: Other	8/4/74	12/1/75	2/1/72	7/1/74
Computer parts	8/4/74	12/1/75	12/24/75	7/1/74
Software	12/1/74	4/1/76	—	7/1/74
Integrated circuits[a] (IC)				
IC: Fewer than 100 elements	8/4/71	12/1/74	9/1/70	6/1/68
IC: Fewer than 200 elements	8/4/71	12/1/74	4/19/73	6/1/68
IC: 200 or more elements	8/4/71	12/1/74	12/25/74	6/1/68

SOURCE: Japanese Fair Trade Commission 1985: 54

[a] Capital liberalization for "computer integrated circuits" took place at the slower computer capital liberalization schedule: 50% capital liberalization on 8/4/74, 100% capital liberalization on 12/1/75.

For not only were the Future System's technology targets unattainable for the Japanese, they were unattainable for IBM. As Charles Ferguson and Charles Morris describe it:

The scope of the F/S effort and the time schedule were utterly unrealistic. . . .
. . . F/S was absurdly ambitious; much of the effort was focused on technologies that are advanced even today [1993]. . . . [By the time it ended,] F/S flailed away expensively and hopelessly on multiple fronts, with surprisingly little to show for it.[6]

As a result, the secret project was canceled, also in secrecy, in 1976. Ironies abound, for 1976 was the very same year in which the MITI VLSI consortium, meant to be the Japanese response to the Future System, was launched. The F/S project ended up being "IBM's own quiet Vietnam," draining resources away from its 1970's mainframe computer development and giving its Japanese competitors "five years of breathing space" in which to catch up to IBM's mainframe technology.[7] IBM never reached the technology target of 1-megabit integration by 1980; indeed, in 1979, it was not even producing enough 64-kilobit

DRAM chips to be able to meet its internal needs and had to buy huge quantities of 16-kilobit DRAMs, which packed less than 4 percent of the information of the targeted F/S device, from the same Japanese suppliers who had thought they were doomed by the Future System.

But all of this was unknown in the frightening spring and summer of 1974, when IBM's Future System cast a shadow over the Japanese semiconductor and computer industries. Somebody had to act fast, it seemed, and that somebody turned out to be NTT. In the spring of 1974, Fujitsu managing director Ikeda lobbied NTT and MITI, arguing that the Japanese computer industry would not be able to survive in the face of the Future System, and that massive government subsidies of the Japanese computer industry were necessary, along the lines of the huge subsidies of the early 1970's to help the Japanese industry catch up with IBM's 370 mainframe.

In response, it does not appear that MITI reacted much. It did not mobilize for a Japanese response to IBM; indeed, according to a senior member of the JEIDA committee mentioned above, for a long time, MITI did not even seem to have heard the news of the IBM Future System.[8] The JEIDA committee did turn to investigating VLSI R&D issues, and it issued a report in December 1974 that called for a MITI VLSI program. "MITI did not seem to consider it important," however, and the report languished for several months.[9] Then, in early spring 1975, several months after NTT had launched its own VLSI program, one of the JEIDA committee chairman's former students, who had read the report, came racing into the chairman's office to push for the VLSI program to be put into action within MITI.[10] Ironically, this former student was not even a MITI employee: he was on loan to MITI from a different government agency.

NTT Moves Forward

In contrast, NTT's semiconductor research group acted swiftly. The head of the semiconductor group in the Electrical Communications Laboratory drew up a tentative research plan after meeting with Ikeda in April and verifying the reported nature of IBM's efforts. The proposed NTT research plan, completed in June, aimed to create an NTT technology initiative to target VLSI technology in cooperation with Fujitsu, Hitachi, and NEC. However, like its JEIDA/MITI counterpart, this plan, too, seems to have languished for a number of months. Approval of the proposal to launch a major spending program for VLSI technology did not occur in the summer of 1974, and the issue remained unresolved until that fall. Perhaps this was because as a telephone company, NTT's main barometer of technological prowess was not IBM, but AT&T, so IBM's activities did not strike fear into the hearts of top executives at NTT. Or perhaps it was that paper reports of IBM VLSI activities were not concrete enough to warrant major investments by NTT.

Whatever the reason, the semiconductor research lab's proposed VLSI program was not approved until after NTT's President Yonezawa visited Bell Labs in New Jersey in fall 1974, where AT&T showed him some of its most advanced projects, including electron-beam (e-beam) machines that were writing masks for VLSI-level integrated circuits.

Yonezawa was shocked. It was clear to him that Japan was at least three years behind in a technology area where time-to-market advantages of as little as a few months can be decisive. When he returned to Japan, he gave quick approval to the NTT VLSI program and urged publicly that Japanese firms and the government come together to launch a targeted, concerted effort in VLSI technology.

That NTT's VLSI program was precipitated by a visit to Bell Labs is in some sense an ironic, historical quirk, because public and private discussions of appropriate Japanese efforts in VLSI at that time continued to be dominated by the long shadow of IBM, the globe-straddling giant that dominated every computer market in the world and controlled half of Japan's. IBM could make or break Japan's computer manufacturers. In contrast, AT&T had virtually no presence in Japan.

So for the Japanese firms, as for MITI, the burning issue was how best to respond to IBM. This was the way the issue was also treated in the national press, which took to describing VLSI as the "basic technology that would decide future competitiveness in computers and electronics," and the proposed VLSI efforts as the "anti–IBM Future System VLSI project."

After the Bell Labs visit, in September 1974, NTT had discussions with Fujitsu, Hitachi, and NEC about doing joint work on VLSI under NTT's leadership. All three companies were part of NTT's so-called DenDen Family, the privileged tier of long-term suppliers to NTT. With visions of future NTT procurements dancing in their head, all three were interested in cooperating with NTT. NTT was in a hurry: without even waiting to sort out joint operations with the three companies, it fired up its VLSI effort that same month. In December, contracts were signed with the three companies specifying the distribution of intellectual property rights and the nature of the work that they would be doing, with research to begin in early 1975.

The launching of the NTT VLSI consortium sent shock waves

through the other major Japanese semiconductor and computer manufacturers, which were denied entry into the NTT group. Toshiba, Oki,
and Mitsubishi, in particular, which had a long history of cooperation
with the Japanese government in computer consortia, were afraid that
they would fall behind Fujitsu, NEC, and Hitachi if they had exclusive
access to NTT's research. NTT's labs were considered the best in Japan
in basic VLSI technology. However, when the excluded companies appealed to NTT to let them participate, NTT simply said no. Denied
access to the NTT effort, these companies turned to MITI and put pressure on it to help them, dramatically accelerating MITI's plans to
launch a VLSI consortium.

MITI and NTT's Fight for Control

Warning bells were going off all over MITI too. The NTT effort targeted technology vital for future computers and was being billed in the
Japanese press as ultimately leading to an "anti–Future System patri-
otic machine." From MITI's perspective, *it* controlled the Japanese
computer industry; NTT did not. MITI could not allow an NTT intrusion of this kind into the heart of the computer industry. MITI moved
to take control.

However, since the NTT project was already under way and MITI
itself had no program, MITI's hand appeared to be quite weak. One of
the things that one can pick up from the press reports at the time is that
as a first step, MITI wanted to stop the NTT project from going forward. As a MITI official told reporters in January 1975, "Now that the
computer industry has gotten strong, there is no need to develop a computer based upon NTT's specifications."[11]

However, this MITI stance did not get very far with NTT. MITI
could say what it wanted, but NTT was moving ahead. At that point,
MITI seems to have decided internally that if it could not stop the NTT
project, then at the minimum some joint effort between NTT and MITI
was desirable, so that MITI could exercise a degree of control. There
was no longer talk of ending the NTT effort; now MITI focused on
creating joint activities between MITI and NTT. The apparent result of
the extending of this MITI olive branch to NTT was announced by
Japanese newspapers in April: MITI, the Ministry of Post and Telecommunications, and NTT would cooperate on a joint VLSI consortium.

The degree of suspicion and hostility on the NTT side toward MITI
is indicated by NTT's reaction to these news reports. NTT vigorously
denied that there was any talk of cooperation and accused MITI of
planting a false story in the newspapers. Moreover, NTT continued to

deny access to the consortium to Oki, Toshiba, and Mitsubishi, believing that their technical capabilities were insufficient, and that too many companies in a consortium would make cooperation difficult.

Both NTT and MITI wanted there to be only one project. Since NTT had already launched its project, the NTT people felt they were in a good position to make that single effort theirs. But MITI had good support in the corporate world and deep political resources; it continued to press for some sort of "jointness." In May, for example, it publicly proposed a division of labor wherein NTT would work on memory devices and MITI would work on logic devices.

The result of the MITI lobbying efforts emerged, or at least *appeared* to emerge, in June. NTT's President Yonezawa told reporters on June 10, 1975, that NTT would "actively cooperate" with MITI. The words were quite important, for they indicated that the tide had turned. Rather than MITI cooperating with NTT, it was now NTT that would have to cooperate with MITI. MITI would be in charge—and in control. Thus, it appeared that NTT had folded its hand, that there would be a single project under MITI control.

However, when Yonezawa's statement was reported, unhappy NTT public relations people insisted that Yonezawa *had never said* that NTT would cooperate with MITI. They argued that the two projects were totally different and that the NTT consortium really had nothing to do with the effort to counter IBM's Future System—rather, it was building VLSI for an advanced telecommunications network.

Clearly, NTT had realized that the tide had turned against it, that it would lose control if there were to be only one project. It therefore accepted the idea that there should be two coexisting projects. But in the end this compromise did not satisfy the Ministry of Finance and the Liberal Democratic Party (LDP), the ruling conservative party, which believed that having coexisting overlapping projects was a waste of taxpayers' money. By fall 1975, NTT was forced to agree to participate in and cooperate with the MITI effort. So it was that the pitched bureaucratic battle between MITI and NTT over the destiny of VLSI R&D in Japan came to an end. In spring 1976, about a year and a half after NTT first got started on its VLSI program, a consortium of five computer makers—Fujitsu, Hitachi, NEC, Toshiba, and Mitsubishi—united with NTT in the MITI-led VLSI consortium.

The VLSI R&D Race

The unification of the MITI and NTT consortia was, however, little more than a public fiction. NTT had no interest in cooperating with

MITI; it was vexed and irritated that its program had been plundered by MITI. "MITI's plan was based upon NTT's proposal. They just incorporated it exactly as it was. . . . The name even was the same," complains an NTT manager.[12]

The disgruntled NTT VLSI research group did the necessary bare minimum to create the public appearance of cooperation, in line with the political mandate, but NTT had no genuine commitment to cooperation. NTT's consortium would continue on its independent path. As a senior NTT research manager describes it in the epigraph to this chapter, "The politicians didn't know that it was *tatemae* [a public fiction]. . . . we drew a picture that showed the MITI project. And, look, here is NTT cooperating with MITI. But it was just a picture." Defending this NTT gambit, he adds: "It was important to have two projects. It would have been an organizational mess [to combine them]. And two projects gave both sides a chance to test and verify the other's achievements."[13]

To demonstrate its commitment to "cooperation," NTT sent a representative to the board of directors of MITI's VLSI Research Association, and members of the two research groups had occasional meetings to exchange research results, but these meetings confined themselves to "extremely narrow technical issues."[14]

The public commitment to NTT/MITI cooperation was also belied by the competition between NTT and MITI to achieve technical breakthroughs and announce them to the press. When MITI announced a breakthrough in e-beam technology in March 1978, for example, NTT rushed out its own announcement that very same month, and claimed that its e-beam machine was both twice as fast and more accurate than the MITI consortium's.[15] The Japanese press often reported the *tatemae* of MITI and NTT cooperation, but at times it explicitly acknowledged the underlying competition between the two. A year earlier, when NTT announced development of a 64-kilobit DRAM prototype that relied upon existing optics technology, the *Asahi shimbun* had noted that while MITI's might be the larger VLSI effort, NTT appeared to be "one step ahead."[16]

Table 4 summarizes some of the key dimensions along which the MITI and NTT programs differed—from consortia time periods and budgets to participants, financing, and lab organization. In terms of *time periods* and *budgets*, MITI's project was about twice as large NTT's and ran for a shorter period of time. MITI carried out operations over four years, from fiscal year 1976 to fiscal year 1979. NTT launched a three-year effort with NEC, Fujitsu, and Hitachi in 1975,

TABLE 4

Comparing the MITI and NTT VLSI Programs

Category	MITI	NTT
Time period	1976–79	1975–81
Length	4 years	6 years
Budget (approx.)	¥74 billion	¥40 billion (est.)[a]
Number of corporate participants	5	3
	NEC	NEC
	Fujitsu	Fujitsu
	Hitachi	Hitachi
	Toshiba	
	Mitsubishi	
Financing	40% MITI/60% companies	100% NTT
Subsidies to companies?	Yes	No
Number of MITI/NTT researchers	Fewer than 10 MITI researchers	200-500 NTT researchers (varies over time)
Main research labs	Company "group" labs	NTT labs

[a] The NTT effort consisted of two three-year plans. The first three years were funded at ¥20 billion. This budget estimate assumes that the second three-year plan continued the funding levels of the first three years.

which was rolled over in 1978 into a second three-year effort that targeted higher levels of device integration.[17] In terms of *corporate participation*, NTT restricted access to its labs to just three firms, NEC, Fujitsu, and Hitachi, while MITI invited participation also from Mitsubishi and Toshiba.

Financing was also different. First, the companies contributed 60 percent of the funds to the MITI effort, while NTT entirely funded its joint work with the companies. Second, of the 40 percent of the funds that MITI provided to program financing, a large part went directly to the companies as subsidies for work in their labs. In contrast, part of the reason NTT did all of the funding was that it did not subsidize the three companies working with it beyond small sums to cover direct research expenses in building prototypes for NTT. Rather, the key in the NTT project was the flow of information and technology from the NTT labs to the companies, particularly with respect to what NTT's future procurement needs would be. NTT even built a production line in its Musashino lab in order to bring production in-house.

The organization of MITI's program was also quite different in form from NTT's, especially with respect to the number of government researchers and the main research labs. In the case of NTT, the bulk of the researchers were from NTT. At its peak NTT threw as many as 500 of its researchers into the VLSI effort, compared to under 10 from

MITI. The heart of the NTT effort was thus the activity at NTT's research labs, while MITI relied primarily on the five participating companies for research manpower, and most of the MITI consortium work took place within those company labs.

This separation in NTT and MITI efforts was also reflected in the way Hitachi, Fujitsu, and NEC, the three companies that participated in both programs, structured their interaction with MITI and NTT. NEC, for example, had researchers from three different groups—the R&D group, the Information Processing Group, and the Electron Device Group—participating in both consortia. However, in each of these groups, different research units worked separately either with NTT or with MITI.

NTT also pursued its independent course in its relationship with subcontractors. MITI called upon Nikon to develop a stepper; NTT in turn contracted with it for a projection aligner and for lenses for x-ray lithography. MITI worked with Hitachi, Fujitsu, and NEC on e-beam equipment; NTT used e-beam equipment from Hitachi, CSF-Thompson, a European firm, and JEOL, a Japanese supplier of semiconductor equipment.

Thus, despite the public appearance of cooperation between NTT and MITI, "the reality was different, of course." Adds an NTT manager, by way of explanation: "This way of doing things occurs all the time in Japan."[18] To this day, the public image of cooperation between NTT and MITI has been faithfully maintained. In 1991, NEC offered a prize to the research directors from both the MITI joint lab and the NTT lab for their accomplishments in the project. At the public award ceremony, the two spoke of how well they had cooperated with each other, but this was ceremonial politeness. "It was a public affair, so we had to say 'we got along well,'" observes an NTT R&D manager.[19]

The Supercomputer Consortium

For the drafters of Japanese industrial policy at MITI in the late 1970's, the supercomputer was just one of many options for the 1980's. Other possibilities included development of knowledge-based systems and machine translation, both topics that were integrated into the Fifth Generation computer program, and also advanced office automation systems.[20] The backers of a supercomputer project had to prove, not just that supercomputers were important, but that given MITI's limited manpower and resources, they were more important than these other options. Why should MITI focus on supercomputers?

The answer turned out to hinge as much on bureaucratic politics as on supercomputers' technical merits. Supercomputers were making news in Japan, and other agencies in the Japanese government were making that news. In August 1978, an institute of STA made headlines with the news that it had completed the basic research on a Cray-like supercomputer, which it expected to build by 1980.[21]

At around the same time, a researcher at one of STA's aerodynamics institutes (*kōkūgiken*) began to argue that Japan needed a supercomputer and proposed a research effort to STA and MITI. Although it had no plans for a supercomputer consortium in the works, MITI did not want this program to take place under STA auspices, inasmuch as it regarded the computer industry as its own domain. MITI quickly claimed jurisdiction and started a small-scale investigation within its aerospace group.[22] This planning languished in the aerospace group, politically one of the weakest parts of MITI, but it was eventually transfered to one of MITI's microelectronics sections after MITI suddenly increased the project's priority when a Japanese industry delegation was badly frightened by IBM's apparent advantage in Josephson junction (JJ) technology during a visit to IBM's Yorktown, New York, labs in 1979. (This visit and its aftershocks are described in Chapter 4.) Thus, the bringing of a supercomputer consortium proposal into MITI as a way to cut out STA ultimately led directly to the supercomputer project.

It is significant that when MITI responded swiftly to the above-mentioned IBM lab visit and began serious deliberations to create a supercomputer consortium that had Josephson junctions as a main device focus, this was done in a context of bureaucratic rivalry over JJ R&D. MITI saw MOE, STA, and NTT acting on JJ research, and given IBM's seemingly major advances toward commercializing that technology, it was important for MITI to lay claim to JJ R&D. Riken, an institute of the STA, which also had a program under way, announced in July 1980 that it had achieved a breakthrough in the production of stable, durable JJ devices suitable for mass production. STA was applying for both Japanese and U.S. patents on these devices, and was approaching Japanese manufacturers about licensing the technology to them.[23] MOE had also recently finished a three-year research-funding cycle that included work on Josephson junctions.

NTT, too, was extremely aggressive in pushing JJ technology forward. In fact, in the early 1980's, around the time MITI's supercomputer consortium started up, NTT claimed the largest number of Japanese patents in JJ technology.[24] And when ETL was the first to break the 10-picosecond barrier by producing a JJ device that switched every 7 picoseconds in April 1983, NTT's Electrical Communications Laboratory branch lab in Atsugi bested it a month later with a 6-picosecond device. With respect to device density, NTT's Atsugi was the best in the world, having developed a 1-kilobit JJ memory device ahead of everyone else. As regards Josephson junctions, "all the other companies are chasing" NTT, the *Nikkei sangyō* newspaper reported in 1984.[25]

Research competition was also going on between NTT and MITI's ETL in gallium arsenide, another of the device technologies pursued in MITI's supercomputer consortium. In mid 1980, for example, NTT's Musashino lab, an arm of the Electrical Communications Laboratory, announced a high-speed gallium arsenide device that switched at 30 picoseconds at room temperature and a little over half that when cooled by liquid nitrogen ($-196°C$).[26] Later that year, ETL made its own gallium arsenide announcement, which claimed higher speed and a cut in power consumption by a factor of ten. ETL argued that its gallium arsenide process was far superior to the method that had been used by NTT.[27]

NTT's gallium arsenide efforts, in turn, continued well after the launching of MITI's supercomputer consortium. Toward the end of 1982, for example, NTT announced the world's first 1-kilobit gallium arsenide memory, setting a standard for the Supercomputer consortium to beat.[28]

The Fifth Generation Consortium

Fifth Generation witnessed conflict between MITI and MOE over the participation of universities in the consortium's research. The flow of pre-launch deliberations also provides insight into disagreements of a much less public kind—internal divisions within MITI itself in the R&D area, which at times pitted MITI scientists at ETL against MITI career bureaucrats in Tokyo. These two areas of conflict and tension— (1) MITI versus MOE and (2) ETL versus MITI headquarters—are described below.

MITI Versus the Ministry of Education, Science, and Culture

Given its futuristic, highly speculative, basic-research orientation, the Fifth Generation project was a natural fit for universities. In the period leading to the consortium launch, all sides believed some role for the universities was both desirable and important, since universities, just as in the United States, specialize in basic research. The head of the MITI steering committee to plan Fifth Generation even expressed doubt early in the planning stages as to whether such a basic-research project was appropriate for MITI funding, and expressed his belief that Fifth Generation was clearly better suited to funding by MOE within a university environment.[29]

MITI was eager to do a futuristic project and welcomed university participation. It hoped to bring university and corporate researchers together to work on Fifth Generation, but it ran into a brick wall when it approached MOE about sanctioning university participation. As has been described earlier, MITI and MOE have never been able to cooperate in bringing together university and corporate researchers. When MITI asked for university participation, MOE said no.

This is not to say that university professors were totally uninvolved in the Fifth Generation program; in fact, they were well represented on the deliberation and advisory committees both before and during the Fifth Generation effort. A look at the steering and program committee membership and the papers presented at the three major international Fifth Generation conferences (in 1984, 1987, and 1992) reinforces this sense of academic involvement: members and papers were overwhelmingly contributed by academic environments. Companies were hardly represented.

There was even some small-scale work on Prolog targeted at Fifth Generation hardware at universities, particularly the Tokyo Institute of Technology, University of Tokyo, and Tokyo Science University. But what the universities could not do was directly participate in the Fifth Generation research program. "It was impossible."[30]

This lack of university participation had two major, negative consequences. Indeed, it might be said that it crippled the Fifth Generation program, because universities were clearly the more appropriate forum for such high-risk basic research.

The first, more obvious negative effect was to deny MITI access to a talented pool of university computer scientists who could have made significant technical contributions. A corporate research manager involved in Fifth Generation laments:

The biggest problem is conflicts between Mombushō [MOE] and MITI. There is a tremendous amount of scientific talent at national universities, but they can't participate in these national projects. For a university employee to work for a *zaidan hōjin* [a type of foundation or quasi-public corporation, frequently used by MITI to run its R&D consortia], for example, it's against the law. Why? Because of a turf conflict between MITI and Mombushō. National projects are under MITI's control. Mombushō doesn't want to let its scientists at national universities be susceptible to MITI's power. So it refuses to let university professors participate in MITI's projects.

This is a horrible waste—MITI has the money and the projects, so this prohibition means that, with the exception of a few really famous professors, the national universities are underfunded and can't get their research done, and MITI loses out on an exceptional talent pool. It's a horrible shame.[31]

Kazuhiro Fuchi, who headed the Fifth Generation research effort, echoes this concern—not as a complaint, but more with the air of one who has accepted an unfortunate fact of nature: Japanese bureaucracies cannot seem to get along. In an interview, he noted that the project faced a chronic shortage of technical talent, and that "a lot of people at universities who wanted to work with us" were denied the opportunity to do so directly.[32]

The second negative impact of MOE blocking MITI's access to universities is the flip side of the above: ICOT, the Fifth Generation research institute, had to rely upon company researchers. However, the companies were not at all suited to doing futuristic, speculative research of the Fifth Generation type. The companies' interests were in creating products to serve the marketplace. Unlike university researchers, they did not have any fundamental interest in research unlinked to the market that might be interesting or intriguing or contribute in some sort of global way to the building of new knowledge. Thus, denied access to universities, MITI was forced to turn to companies who were in many ways uninterested in Fifth Generation and ask them to provide the bulk of its engineering personnel.

This could not work well, and it did not. For one thing, companies held back on researchers; they also did not want their researchers to be at ICOT very long. "None of the participating companies want their best people following Fuchi down a blind alley for three years at ICOT. That's one reason it's hard for ICOT to get the people it needs."[33] As an NEC executive explained, "We can't keep our best people outside the company too long. It's impossible to meet 100% of ICOT's requests for qualified staff."[34]

In the face of company demands that their researchers not stay at ICOT's joint lab very long, ICOT could not maintain continuity in its research staff during the course of the consortium. It had to repatriate its existing researchers and then retrain and rebuild its organizational structure with new personnel every few years. In the end, only around ten researchers were at ICOT throughout the program.[35]

Edward Feigenbaum et al. describe ICOT's first large-scale rotation of personnel in 1985:

To a Western research manager, what they did was incomprehensible. On a single day, a highly trained team of (by then) forty-eight technical people, whose collective skill was ICOT's own knowledge base, and whose esprit de corps was built to a high level, evaporated and was replaced by new initiates. If they could survive this at all, it would mean slow going for the first year of Phase Two.[36]

And it was slow going—it could not but be. This personnel rotation system was like asking a company to fire most of its staff and bring in a totally new staff every few years. No company could long survive that process, and it clearly crippled ICOT.

The personnel rotation system in response to company needs was merely the most obvious organizational distortion resulting from reliance upon the companies. Since the companies had no real commitment to the consortium's R&D program, they could not be expected to give ICOT their full support in terms of manpower or resources and fought with ICOT about R&D priorities. This situation is described more fully in Chapter 5.

In sum, the conflict between MITI and MOE that blocked university participation in Fifth Generation deprived ICOT of its most willing and hence most valuable scientific manpower. The universities were eager to do ICOT-style futuristic basic research; the companies were not and *could* not. No company could justify such a large-scale effort on such a speculative technology venture.

MITI's Career "Generalists" Versus MITI Scientists

The launching of the Fifth Generation consortium was also complicated by tensions between different groups within MITI itself. The scientists at ETL have long had a strained relationship with the generalist MITI career bureaucrats in Tokyo. ETL is an elite scientific institution, and it is difficult at times for the ETL researchers to take R&D marching orders from MITI bureaucrats, who are largely drawn from nontechnical backgrounds. An ETL scientist admits that in many ways it is easier for ETL to work with foreign R&D labs than with MITI's central command.[37]

This is especially the case because of MITI's internal career and promotion structure. Put bluntly, within MITI there is a caste system that discriminates against those with technical backgrounds. There are a number of different layers and categories of employees within MITI; upon entering the ministry, each employee is assigned to a career group based on educational background, training, and entrance examination results. A MITI employee remains in that career group for his or her lifetime at MITI.

What is relevant to the discussion of ETL scientists and MITI gener-

alists is the differential treatment of the officials at the highest tier of the
internal career-ranking scheme, the so-called career officials, the small
group of bureaucrats drawn primarily from elite universities such as the
University of Tokyo who give MITI its reputation for eliteness and excellence. These are the men (for they are almost all men) who will run
MITI one day. Or perhaps one should say, *some* of these are the men
who will run MITI one day, for this group is broken into two categories: so-called *jimukan* (general officials) who have a shot at the top and
gikan (technical officials), who do not. The generalist *jimukan* make
up around 80 percent of this career group; the *gikan* who have degrees,
often advanced, in science and engineering are in the minority. ETL
scientists are, of course, part of the *gikan* group.

Unfortunately, being a *gikan* dooms an official's career. *Gikan* can
never reach the highest levels of MITI; outside of MITI's R&D arm, the
Agency for Industrial Science and Technology (AIST), their careers are
cut off at about two-thirds up MITI's management hierarchy, typically
at the level of *jichō* (deputy general director of a bureau).[38] The top
MITI positions are reserved for *jimukan*.

It is nothing short of perverse that in an increasingly technical age, in
which persons with technical skills are increasingly necessary and
highly prized in business and society, MITI maintains a system that
severely and deliberately penalizes officials with technical backgrounds. This is in sharp contrast to Japan's top electronics, engineering, and other manufacturing firms, where if you look to see the background of the president or chairman, you will usually discover that they
rose up through the engineering ranks and thus combine detailed product knowledge with a keen grasp of relevant technical issues. This division between *gikan* and *jimukan* forms the backdrop to friction
between ETL scientists and MITI headquarters, where the *jimukan*
hold sway.

These ETL/MITI headquarters divergences expressed themselves in
deliberations leading up to the Fifth Generation consortium. Upon
hearing about the Fifth Generation idea, there was an initial resistance
in ETL to, almost an instinctive desire not to cooperate with, the concept as floated by MITI's Electronics Policy Section (Denshi seisaku ka).

But getting ETL support, in particular Fuchi's support, was key to
winning approval for Fifth Generation, since ETL serves as MITI's
technical arm and internal technical watchdog, and Fuchi was widely
recognized as an expert in the field Fifth Generation aimed to tackle. A
MITI official, himself a scientist temporarily on loan from NTT (this
being a win-win situation for both NTT and MITI—MITI gets needed

scientific talent; NTT gets insight into MITI operations), was accordingly sent to lobby Fuchi to support Fifth Generation and to participate in a study group being held at JIPDEC.

Fuchi was skeptical, clearly thinking that this looked like another hare-brained *jimukan* technical fantasy. A key turning point in the meeting came when the visiting official leaned forward and said simply, "I'm a technical guy [*gikan*]." [39] The phrase was full of meaning. It said: this was not a Rube Goldberg machine dreamt up by a bunch of scientifically ignorant MITI bureaucrats out to pad their budgets and their careers. It said: this is real. I'm a scientist. You can trust me.

Fuchi agreed to join the JIPDEC study group and eventually came to head the ICOT effort. But Fuchi clearly had different goals for Fifth Generation than MITI's *jimukan*. MITI *jimukan* saw it as a way to break IBM's grip on the Japanese computer industry, to go where no man or company, and certainly not IBM, had gone before. But to Fuchi and his group at ETL, the issue was much more far-reaching than just overtaking IBM. They had a vision of breaking the von Neumann barrier and creating a pathbreaking parallel-processing machine. For MITI *jimukan*, the project was about competitiveness, but for Fuchi's ETL group it was about technology.

The TRON Consortium

TRON witnessed a conflict of interests between MITI and MOE in the specification of the BTRON computer as the standard computer for Japanese schools. TRON offered MITI the possibility of a fully Japanese personal computer, a windows graphical user interface for ease of use, and the end of NEC's nearly monopolistic control of the Japanese PC market, a situation that was stifling competition and market growth. For MITI, the PC-standardization decision was primarily industrial policy, a way to bring TRON to life as a new standard computer architecture.

On the other hand, for the Ministry of Education, the PC-standardization decision was education policy: to increase students' skills in computers and information technology, MOE was interested in putting computers into schools. These computers could be TRON or not TRON, as long as they were reasonable vehicles for the education of Japanese children in the use of computers. Thus, MOE did not share the industrial policy goals that MITI linked to the school PC-standardization decision, or at least gave these MITI goals secondary priority.

This divergence of interests came to a head in 1988 when the BTRON prototypes were being tested in various schools across the

country. For MOE's schools, the intended users of the TRON machines, the BTRON computers had two serious flaws. *First*, they were
totally incompatible with existing IBM-compatible, DOS-based PCs
and could run none of the DOS software. Since 80–90 percent of the
Japanese education market was controlled by NEC and its DOS-based
computers, this was a huge problem, because adopting TRON meant
asking the schools to throw away their existing investment in NEC machines and software.

Even worse, since the Japanese packaged software market for PCs
was underdeveloped (ironically, a situation MITI was in fact trying to
correct by imposing a standard TRON computer on the schools), a lot
of PC software had been *personally* written, requiring a mammoth effort, by Japanese teachers and the schools' computer personnel. They
were not going to give up their home-grown software, the fruit of their
long programming labors, without a violent struggle. And in fact
MOE discovered during the prototype testing period that the schools
did not like BTRON, because it was incompatible with everything that
they had.

Moreover, since BTRON was a brand new computer, there was essentially *no* software available for it. The Japanese software market
may well have been underdeveloped compared to that of the United
States, but there were nonetheless thousands of programs available.
The schools were being asked to buy thousands of new computers and
then have to wait while software companies decided whether or not to
write software for them and then wait again when the software was
being written. It seemed to the schools that it might take years before
software was widely available.

The *second* problem area was that BTRON was behind schedule and
did not perform well, a fairly fatal flaw when the whole sales pitch was
that it performed better than existing computers. BTRON development
was so far behind schedule that prototype testing slipped a year, from
1987 to 1988. And the performance problem was not that BTRON's
user interface was no better than existing machines. BTRON *was* better, theoretically at least. But the BTRON operating system software
was of poor quality. It was buggy; it crashed in the middle of programs.
The operating system had been written by Matsushita, a firm that had
never written a PC operating system before, and its inexperience
showed.

Given the expenditure of resources, time, and effort, the software
quality problem could be solved, although given the delays in delivering
even this initial buggy version of BTRON, it was not clear that this

could be done in a reasonable time frame. At any rate, it was clear in 1988 that BTRON was not ready for prime time, that if BTRON were adopted, it might mean imposing a flawed computer on the schools, something the conservative MOE was not inclined to risk.

As a result of these problems and the consequent revolt in the schools, by the end of 1988, MOE decided that it could not accept the BTRON solution that MITI favored. If BTRON were to go into the schools, it would have to be put into a computer that simultaneously had the ability to run NEC's DOS software. This was a solution that could not be to MITI's liking, for by specifying compatibility with DOS, it risked continuance of NEC's monopoly dominance of the PC market. Moreover, a dual computer that could run both BTRON and DOS would naturally be more complex, risking further delays in its introduction, and would certainly be more expensive. It would be a two-headed computer designed by a committee—MITI would get its TRON, MOE would get its DOS, and no one could be really satisfied.

As if the BTRON school decision were not already burdened enough by internal Japanese division, at this point an external actor also intervened. Suddenly, in late spring 1989, as MITI and MOE were trying to figure out how to reconcile their conflicting ambitions into a standardized dual BTRON–NEC DOS computer, the Office of the U.S. Trade Representative (USTR) issued a preliminary report that accused BTRON of being a trade barrier and asked the Japanese government not to make it standard in the school computer market. In June the Japanese government formally acceded to this request, and BTRON was dead as the Japanese standard school computer.

All sides in Japan expressed their regret at this "unfortunate intervention by the U.S. government in Japanese internal education policies," but it might be said that the United States's sudden objection rescued the Japanese government from a bad situation, and that compliance with the U.S. request was a face-saving way out. If there had been a consensus shared by MITI and MOE about standardizing on BTRON, it is doubtful whether the Japanese government would have given in so quickly, and it would likely have tried harder to figure out a way to get BTRON into the schools. Indeed, it was precisely because the two key bureaucracies, MITI and MOE, were divided on BTRON that the Japanese government was willing to scuttle BTRON standardization. Indeed, by the time the USTR objected to BTRON standardization, it did not look much like "standardization" in light of MOE demands that DOS compatibility be part of the standard. Since NEC DOS machines had all the advantages of (1) an existing user base with large investments in NEC machines; (2) a large software library; and (3) sales and distributor relationships with the schools, and the schools had already shown their hostility to BTRON, jointly specifying DOS with BTRON might very well have resulted in the schools using the computer's DOS functions and ignoring its BTRON functions.

Seen in this light, the USTR's demand was really little different from MOE's BTRON stance. The United States had demanded that Japan not lock out competing computers from the schools. Thus, both the United States and MOE believed that there should be no specification of a school PC that gave BTRON a monopoly. The difference within that shared point of view was that MOE was willing to tolerate a PC standard that included BTRON as long as it included NEC DOS compatibility, while the United States was against including BTRON at all.

It is significant that in the aftermath of the withdrawal of the BTRON standardization proposal, none of the Japanese computer manufacturers who had backed standardizing BTRON in the schools ever introduced a BTRON computer, hardly a ringing endorsement for the machine. From either the U.S. or MOE perspective, it was of course perfectly acceptable for any manufacturer to sell BTRON computers on an equal basis with every other computer, much the way Apple had successfully sold its new Macintosh computer into schools after its introduction in 1984. But without the guaranteed market provided by a BTRON school monopoly, no manufacturer had any confidence that BTRON computers would sell, especially given the problems that had led to BTRON receiving such a cold welcome during its prototype testing.

BTRON's only hope had been to get a protected start as the only PC allowed to be used in Japanese schools. But MITI/MOE conflict had made a BTRON-only standard impossible, a conflict that ultimately took the public shape of a dispute between the Japanese and U.S. governments, but whose outcome in many ways actually reflected MOE's own desires. The demise of BTRON thus foiled MITI's ambition to kill two birds with one policy: to create a Japanese standard PC and reduce Japanese dependence on U.S. suppliers and at the same time introduce competition into the monopolistic Japanese PC market through this common PC standard. In TRON, too, differences in interests between bureaucracies complicated MITI's industrial policy.

FOUR

A House Divided

MITI and the Companies

Most Japanese guys I talk to just want MITI to get out of
the way. They don't need MITI anymore.
                              American manager, Intel Japan

We joined TRON because we were asked to. But TRON
was the enemy—it competed with our products. We
never had any intention of promoting TRON, and we
never set up any group to do so. In true Japanese fashion,
we pretended on the surface to be a TRON backer,
because it was expected of us by MITI, but below the
surface we were totally uninterested.   NEC executive

There is a widespread impression, in both Japan and the West, that
Japanese high-tech consortia demonstrate a highly effective and cooperative government and industry relationship—a partnership of the
public and private sectors in the truest sense of the word. However, the
reality is that the MITI/company relationship is frequently marked by
conflicts over appropriate goals, funding profiles, and organization. In
fact, by the 1980's, more often than not, the major Japanese companies, the "makers" as the Japanese call them, did not even want to join
the MITI consortia, but for reasons of domestic politics, interfirm
competition, and public relations, decided that they could not turn
MITI down.

In the high-tech consortia examined here, the central tendency in the
MITI/company relationship is *minimal* cooperation. In the 1980's,
"grudging cooperation" or even sometimes "hostile cooperation" are
perhaps more accurate descriptions of the companies' attitude toward
MITI consortia. There were no cases of companies refusing to participate in MITI consortia, despite often having serious misgivings and privately not wanting to participate. And NEC acceded to MITI's demand
to develop a BTRON computer prototype, although it hoped BTRON
would fail.

However, the companies did their best to minimize the extent of their involvement with MITI when it did not serve company goals, refusing to contribute funds to MITI consortia and refusing to participate in the joint labs MITI called for. Or if joint labs were a nonnegotiable requirement on MITI's part, the companies made sure that the amount of activity at the joint labs was strictly limited, with most of the funds bypassing the joint labs and flowing to the companies themselves.

The VLSI Consortium

VLSI was clearly the most cooperative project in terms of the government/industry relationship. That is because the companies actually wanted to do it. The existence of a common external threat in the form of IBM, with all of the Japanese companies in a position of weakness, made them very active in seeking government support. Indeed, this is the single example of what might be called "private-sector-led government/industry cooperation." In contrast, Fifth Generation and Supercomputer were "government-led," with MITI, the driving actor, putting the squeeze on the companies to participate, and the TRON Association lacked a major government role. In the case of VLSI, the companies contributed most of the consortium's funding and agreed to participate in the joint lab, the two key dimensions where MITI sought and continues to seek corporate contributions to technology consortia.

However, it is important to note that the companies also resisted many of MITI's directives and forced MITI to compromise on certain key issues such as the size and structure of the joint lab. The extent of the common ground between MITI and the makers, and the tug-of-war that ensued when common ground was lacking, are described next.

Having seized control of the national VLSI effort from NTT (at least formally), in late 1975 MITI launched an intense planning effort and round of consultations with the companies it had decided to allow to participate. In designing the consortium, MITI planners seized upon an innovative idea: a joint laboratory mixing researchers from all the companies.There had been a number of joint consortia in Japan over the past few decades, but none of them had actually established a single physical location where all the participating companies could come together and jointly and (it was hoped) cooperatively do R&D. Three factors favored creating this joint lab, the first of its kind in the history of MITI's technology consortia.

First, the VLSI program was argued to be extraordinarily expensive, so a single effort would offer major economies by eliminating duplicated effort between the companies. (However, previous projects, particularly the 3.5 Generation program targeting the IBM 370 computer in the early 1970's, had been even more expensive, so it appears that issues of technology transfer and the political appeal of "cooperation" worked in tandem with this economy-of-scale issue.)

Second, in terms of technology transfer, MITI had enough experience working with the companies to know how secretive they could be, and it had frequently failed in the past to create the level of cooperation and harmonious interaction between the companies that it was felt was desirable. MITI believed that throwing together the companies into a single location would make the firms' researchers much more likely to cooperate. "What you learn when actually doing the research is different and deeper than what you can learn from magazines," explains a MITI official. "We wanted to encourage this kind of knowledge transfer while the researchers were drinking tea or watching high school baseball."[1] As a consequence, ironically, the VLSI joint lab concept was itself an expression of MITI's experience in failing to get the companies to work together. MITI was tired of funding "joint" projects where there was little "jointness"—establishing a central VLSI joint lab and making the companies send researchers to it was seen as a way to force companies to cooperate.

Third, also quite fundamental to the decision to create a joint lab was its political appeal. The joint lab would serve as a symbol of the VLSI effort; bringing together warring firms and having them create new technologies in cooperation would be popular with politicians and the public.[2] A joint lab would also reinforce the importance of MITI's role in computer R&D, since it was quite clear that the companies would never get together in a joint lab on their own.

For these reasons, MITI was totally committed to bringing its joint lab into reality. The companies were horrified. Perhaps "horrified" as it stands does not quite capture the intensity of their feelings. They were HORRIFIED, in big capital letters, full of shock and dismay. They thought this was one of the worst bureaucratic nightmares ever to emerge from MITI. The last thing, *the last thing*, they wanted to do was send their people to a joint lab. A MITI official remembers: "When MITI first proposed doing it to the companies, they all said 'Cooperative research with them? No way—it'll be a nightmare. There is no way that this kind of half-baked [*muchakucha*] project is going to succeed.' . . . Each maker said they had better technology than everyone else—if they participated in the project, their corporation would lose out. It was as if all the companies were sitting and waiting at a red light."[3] A company research manager who ended up heading one of the labs within the joint laboratory puts it this way: "The companies did not want to have joint laboratories. We were forced. . . . [We] wanted as little money as possible to go to the joint laboratories. . . . We were all forced by the government to cooperate and had no other alternative."[4]

In the face of this corporate resistance, MITI had to compromise. Although given its position of negotiating strength—it had the subsidy money the companies wanted—MITI was ultimately able to force the joint lab on the companies, it was in a very different form than it had originally hoped. The companies for their part were very frightened by the threat of IBM, and they desperately sought MITI's financial assistance in order to respond, so they had to come up with a way of fulfilling MITI's desire for a joint lab, yet doing everything they could to minimize its role in the project. They needed to make the joint lab not the central but a peripheral organ in the overall consortium program. And to a large extent they succeeded.

The companies first proposed that the lab not really be a research lab. It would do no actual research and have just a few engineers on site—no more, say, than 50. What would these engineers do? The consortium would buy lots of expensive foreign semiconductor equipment (Japan was importing around 70 percent of its equipment at that time) and move it to this neutral site, where company engineers would be able to examine it; they would take the foreign equipment apart and figure out how to build similar or better copies.[5]

This proposal was unacceptable to MITI. It insisted that the joint lab must actually do research. The companies were equally insistent: they did not want to participate in a joint lab. They saw little to gain. While they desperately wanted MITI's financial support, this was not at the cost of a joint lab: the other companies would just steal their technology.

It was Yasuo Tarui, a highly regarded semiconductor researcher from ETL who ultimately became the director of the joint lab, who forged the compromise that bridged the gap between MITI and the companies. Tarui's solution was to have the joint lab focus only on technologies that were both "common" and "basic." "Common" meant that the technologies would be useful to all participants, and "basic" meant that the technology would be sufficiently futuristic not to draw upon a company's existing stock of knowledge. If the joint lab worked with "common and basic" technologies, the companies would not have to be afraid of exposing proprietary information to their competitors.

Moreover, the Tarui solution also allowed for funneling funds directly to the companies' own research labs. If the joint lab was only to be a basic R&D lab, the important work in actually applying these technologies to competitive products would have to be done in the company labs. Here, too, there was a tug-of-war over the appropriate size and funding of the joint lab, and the companies won big. In the end only 15 percent of the VLSI consortium's funds were spent in the joint lab—the other 85 percent went to company labs. Moreover, the number of personnel in the joint lab was limited to 100, again only a small percentage of the total number of researchers. The companies had succeeded in keeping joint work small.

The companies also blocked MITI's efforts to promote more inter-company cooperation within the structure of the joint lab itself. MITI had originally thought that within the central joint lab there would be four sublabs, each with a mix of researchers from all five companies, and each working on a different research theme. The four research themes were: microfabrication equipment technology, crystal and wafer technology, device technology, and processing technology. In particular, the microfabrication lab was going to focus on direct-write e-beam equipment, where electron beams directly write integrated circuit designs onto the chip.

Here MITI ran into an insoluble problem. Hitachi, Fujitsu, and Toshiba were all well along in designing their own e-beam machines and absolutely refused to work with one another. They *absolutely* refused. Try as MITI might, it could not persuade them to agree to cooperate on this common technology. The result was that the original four-lab design expanded to six labs; instead of having just one microfabrication lab, there were three, one headed by Hitachi, one by Toshiba, and one by Fujitsu. NEC and Mitsubishi each had a few researchers in each of these three labs; since neither company had ongoing efforts in the technology, they were not considered competitors by Hitachi, Toshiba, and Fujitsu.

MITI also faced a problem in trying to mix researchers in each lab. If there were roughly equal numbers of researchers from each company in every lab, no company would feel responsible for the success of that lab's research. It was feared that the companies would not work together, and with the lab splintered, there would be no critical mass to get the research done. To overcome this problem, each of the six labs was put under the control of one of the five companies and ETL respectively, and most of the researchers in each lab were from that controlling company (with the exception of the ETL lab).[6] The problem here was that although MITI did create the critical mass it needed, when the joint labs' activities began, the researchers from the lead company would shut out researchers from the other companies. Controlling, or dominant, cliques and minority cliques thus emerged in the company-led labs.[7]

Companies also frequently refused to send their top researchers to the joint lab. One of the threads in the conventional wisdom about the VLSI consortium is that Tarui, who had long experience in basic semi-conductor R&D and was also considered a neutral party by the companies because he was a government scientist, handpicked the researchers from each company for the joint lab. This much is true. But what the conventional wisdom does not point out is that when Tarui went to a company and said, "Please send A-san to the VLSI joint lab," more often than not, he was refused.[8] The companies considered the joint lab as secondary to their own efforts, and in the main were not willing to give up their top people.

Within the joint lab itself, tensions between companies interfered with the smooth functioning of the lean, mean cooperative machine that it was meant to be. This will be described in greater detail later; suffice it to say here that a major effort was required of the VLSI consortium's management to try to create conditions in which the companies would interact with one another.

The Supercomputer Consortium

With the exception of research on Josephson junctions, it is quite clear that the major Japanese companies had little or no desire to participate in this consortium. The lack of a joint lab and of funding from the companies, both of which MITI requested and the companies refused, makes this quite clear.

IBM Shock II: IBM's Deep Freeze Computer

The one exception to the companies' reluctant participation was in the area of Josephson junctions, or "JJ's" as the Japanese called them, where at least the Big Three computer makers, Fujitsu, Hitachi, and NEC, felt very threatened by IBM.

In 1979, in an episode reminiscent of the Japanese acquisition of IBM's secret Future System plans and the president of NTT's visit to Bell Labs in 1974 that shocked NTT into approving a large-scale VLSI effort, Japanese visitors to IBM's Watson labs in Yorktown, New York, were frightened into action on Josephson junctions. JEIDA (the Japan Electronic Industry Development Association) had put together a group of powerful people from Japanese industry to tour the United States that year, and at Yorktown, they saw IBM's work in progress on

Josephson junctions, which promised huge performance improvements over conventional computer semiconductor devices. It was well known in Japan that IBM had had a major effort going on in Josephson junctions since 1965, and over those fifteen years had spent $100 million, with as many as 115 to 140 researchers working on them at its peak.[9] At the Watson labs, the Japanese visitors were shown what looked like a refrigerator and told, "This has several thousand times the performance of current computers. We plan on selling these in the 1990's."[10]

A supercomputer scientist close to the situation remembers: "The tour people totally panicked—they thought they had caught up [to IBM], and all of a sudden they were behind again. On their return to Japan, they went immediately to the director of MITI's Machinery and Information Industries Bureau [Kikai jōhō sangyō kyoku] and said, 'We're going to be done in—we have to do Josephson junctions now!' "[11] Suddenly, Josephson junctions became a huge priority within MITI. A joint R&D effort was started immediately between Mitsubishi, NEC, Fujitsu, Hitachi, and MITI's ETL, and the Supercomputer consortium planning was given a new emphasis and priority, taken out of the aerospace section and given to the Large-Scale Projects group within MITI's Agency for Industrial Science and Technology (AIST).[12] From there, the Supercomputer consortium was brought into reality. However, the full supercomputer consortium was achieved only after a major campaign and substantial compromise on MITI's part.

MITI's "Persuasion" Campaign

MITI pushed the companies hard to participate in the consortium. It had to, because the companies resisted hard. A senior academic on the MITI steering committee recalls: "They said, 'This isn't commercializable.' [They complained] that the plan was 'totally overspecified,' saying, 'We totally can't do this—it will never work.' So, we had to persuade them."[13]

The persuasion was not easy. For one thing, the supercomputer market was incredibly small; the Japanese companies were not interested in throwing money and people into a government project for a market that promised such a small return.[14] Furthermore, the MITI concept of the project that was being circulated indicated that it would tackle advanced devices such as Josephson junctions, gallium arsenide circuits, and other exotic, advanced semiconductors.

Hitachi, Fujitsu, and NEC were clearly interested in doing Josephson junction work, in part because MITI's ETL was thought to have the best technology in Japan in that area. Nevertheless, in the main the project's concept of aggressively pursuing exotic device technologies was problematic for the companies. One of the Big Three companies had decided in 1980, for example, that gallium arsenide was not going anywhere as a mass-market technology and was thinking of abandoning it altogether.[15] An engineer from one of the three second-tier companies (Toshiba, Mitsubishi, Oki) explains:

> To tell the truth, we never thought that these devices would ever be able to be the basis for a complete supercomputer. As you know, Josephson junctions and HEMT can only be used at low temperatures. . . . Trying to put them into supercomputers creates a mountain of problems. Making a whole supercomputer out of these new devices like gallium arsenide was in reality impossible, at least by the end of the project in 1990.[16]

The result was that the companies were not very enthusiastic about participation, although it appears that there were some differences in levels of resistance to joining the consortium. Oki, Mitsubishi, and Toshiba, for example, did not build large computers and had no plans to introduce a vector supercomputer, and they appear to have felt that they had correspondingly less to lose by participation. If proprietary technology were to leak out, it would almost certainly leak from Hitachi, Fujitsu, and NEC in their direction, rather than vice versa.

The Company That Sticks Up Gets Hammered Down: MITI Compromises, Divides, and Conquers

Ultimately, MITI employed a mixture of compromises and a divide-and-conquer strategy in mobilizing the firms, a strategy it frequently uses in trying to glue together joint consortia. Its concessions to the companies took three main forms. First, it abandoned the concept of a joint lab. Second, it funded the consortium 100 percent with government money. Third, it allowed the companies to specify very freely what they were going to do research on. These concessions are explained below.

No joint lab. "MITI always wants a joint laboratory because we believe it is more efficient to proceed this way—budget, equipment, researchers are used more efficiently," explains a MITI official involved in setting up the project.[17] Fujitsu, Hitachi, and NEC were especially unenthusiastic about the MITI proposal for a joint laboratory along the lines of the VLSI project, however. Not only were they suspicious of one another, they were convinced that their technology was superior to that of the other three participants, Toshiba, Mitsubishi, and Oki— after all, the Big Three were all preparing to introduce their own vector supercomputers within a couple of years. They viewed a joint laboratory as a place from which their technology would leak to the other firms and absolutely refused to accept one.[18] Unlike in the case of the VLSI consortium, MITI did not have the subsidies necessary to buy the companies' agreement to a joint lab.

No company financial commitment. MITI had initially asked for the companies to kick in funds, which MITI would match, in order to finance the consortium. This would have been akin to the VLSI project, where the companies ended up contributing just over half of the funds. However, this time, when MITI asked for money, the companies declined to supply it. If the consortium were to be created, MITI would have to fund it itself, so instead of the VLSI matching-fund approach, MITI switched to a contract-based financing system, where it paid firms to do research. This, of course, decreased the size and scope of the consortium, because MITI could not afford to finance a large effort on its own.

Company choice of R&D topics. Unlike in the case of the Fifth Generation consortium, which paid less heed to the concerns and criticisms of its corporate participants, in supercomputers MITI did give companies a substantial say in determining the research agenda. Thus, although the firms were largely unenthusiastic about MITI's decision to pursue supercomputer technologies, they at least could choose supercomputer-related research topics that they thought most relevant to their own endeavors. Each company made research proposals and for the most part got to work on these areas of interest.[19] None of the companies thought that ETL's data-flow machine, SIGMA-1, had much market potential, so ETL did it itself.[20]

In terms of the vector supercomputer, Fujitsu was interested in CPU research, while NEC had strengths in the CPU area and thus focused on memory. In contrast, Hitachi chose to concentrate on system software. Mitsubishi has historically been very strong in the space and defense markets, which offer potential applications for massively parallel processing (MPP) technology, so MPP was a natural choice for it, while Toshiba focused on a limited parallel machine that had the most immediate market potential. Oki chose to expand its offerings in display processing through the consortium research.[21]

In addition to making concessions, MITI employed a form of divide-and-conquer strategy to win company agreement. It hoped to get a few key companies to break ranks and agree to participate, and then to use their participation to force other companies to come along for the ride. With some firms participating, the nonparticipant firms would fear (1) that they might fall behind if the project achieved its technology goals, and (2) that they might be isolated if they did not go along, and would be psychologically pressured for being "selfish" and failing to contribute to a national effort. This might invite MITI retaliation and mean a blot on the company's image.

This is in fact what happened with the supercomputer project, as a MITI official admits:

> We succeeded initially in the persuasion of one or two of the companies. The others then agreed to participate. It was not so easy to persuade the companies. But it was easier than in the case of the Fifth Generation computer because, although the market [for supercomputers] was limited, the timing of the realization of the market was more certain than in the case of the market for artificial-intelligence-related computers [like the Fifth Generation computer]— perhaps the twenty-first century in the case of the latter.[22]

The key company to win over was whoever would be the main contractor for the consortium, which in this case was Fujitsu. With Fujitsu in line, the other companies would fall in. As a government scientist puts it, "Fujitsu was the main contractor. The other companies followed Fujitsu. Fujitsu was the most interested, so it would do the most work and have the most responsibility."[23] "[Our company] was not all that interested in this project," confirms an engineer from one of the Big Three. "It's always the main contractor who is most interested. . . . But [at the time we felt that] we really can't not participate. It's expected of us, since it's a big national project and we're a big company. It's kind of a custom [*kanshū*]."[24]

Ironically, even Fujitsu demonstrated a notable lack of enthusiasm for the project, underscoring how little basic support there was for MITI's consortium. Within Fujitsu, a division existed between some research scientists working on supercomputers and Fujitsu's top management. A group in Fujitsu who wanted to build a supercomputer "couldn't convince their own company to do it, but they figured that they could get company funding if there was a national project. So they came to MITI and said they wanted to do it."[25] MITI in turn approached Fujitsu's management. The tactic worked—MITI and Fujitsu reached agreement on participation in the project.

Lonely Labor: Isolation Within the Companies

With MITI pounding down their doors, the companies felt that they could not refuse. However, this halfhearted commitment to the supercomputer program under MITI pressure eventually led to tensions within the participating companies. Those engineers who had either volunteered for or been assigned to the government consortium could not count on support from other parts of their companies. If they needed extra lab space or personnel or help from the manufacturing group, they were likely to be turned down. As an engineer from one of the Big Three puts it: "The company's true work and the government project work are considered to be totally separate, so we don't get help from other people in the company, even from people working in the same [research] area."[26]

After spending a good part of the 1980's working on behalf of his company in the supercomputer consortium, this engineer was deeply frustrated about how he was cut off from the other researchers in his company, even those working on the same topics, a phenomenon that also seems to have existed in Fifth Generation: "Given the choice, I would much rather work on the company's own projects. To be in a company and work on one of these government projects is weird. You get treated differently. The company doesn't consider it part of its core business. It's hard to get cooperation from other people in the company."[27] Similarly, researchers from one of the three companies working on image-processing supercomputers thought that they had created a viable commercial product, only to discover that the decision makers in the product area had no interest in commercializing it.[28]

Perversely, it appears that some of the participating companies even had specific guidelines that prevented technology transfer from the consortium researchers to their counterparts doing "the company's true work." Says the engineer mentioned above:

The main reason is the company wants to make clear that information from the project is not being used in the company's own R&D. We're afraid of a lawsuit, so we wait until the end of the project. . . . we don't want to be accused of appropriating unreleased information, of taking stuff in the middle of the project. This is a reaction to the IBM spy incident—very severe restrictions were placed on information flow.[29]

The Supercomputer Consortium at the Midpoint: The Companies Lose Interest

The company/MITI divergence of interest did not end with the launching of the consortium. After several years' work, most of the companies decided that enough was enough and sought to scale back their consortium involvement substantially. MITI had to pressure them to continue. An ETL manager recalls:

The companies lost interest in the middle of the project. First of all, there wasn't a lot of money. ¥8.5 billion [at the time around U.S.$30 million] when divided up into a bunch of companies is hardly anything, not nearly as much as Cray, a single company, spends. Second, they had to give up the results of the project to others, because it was a government project. Third, there was a change in the research environment. When IBM quit Josephson Junctions, everyone else wanted to quit also. We told them, "Hey, you started this, you've got to finish it." [30]

Squeezed consortium finances were particularly to blame for Fujitsu's backtracking on what was intended to be a huge parallel vector supercomputer that showcased both the consortium's successes in parallel processing and exotic device technologies. The original plan was to create a 16-processor vector machine, but Fujitsu refused to build anything on that scale. "The problem in part was the budget. There was just ¥1 billion [at the time around U.S.$5 million] left for the final system, which is about three months' rent on a Fujitsu supercomputer, and they were supposed to build a big new supercomputer. It was clearly impossible," notes the ETL manager.[31] The Gartner Group has estimated the cost of designing and building a new supercomputer at $100 million; this means MITI's vector supercomputer budget was only around one-twentieth of what it would actually take to do the job.[32]

ETL pushed Fujitsu to be more ambitious, to do something adventurous and innovative, but Fujitsu ended up just doing a 4-processor system. Even with cutting back to one-fourth of the processors originally planned for, Fujitsu spent several times the money it received.[33] Of course, it was not clear at all why there was a need to do any system at all if it was just going to have four processors, since such a limitedly parallel machine would not advance the state of the art. The ETL scientists, who were interested in pushing the technology forward, found this awkward machine, born out of a public/private compromise that was more about budgets than about technology, difficult to understand:

It was strange—four is not enough to be [really] parallel. You really need at least eight processors to be parallel of any importance. But Fujitsu said, "We're just going to clear the 10-gigaflop goal." That's what they had signed up for, and they had neither the money nor interest to go further. . . . So we ended up with this strange four-processor machine that didn't really contribute anything to the state of the art.[34]

The Fifth Generation Consortium

The Fifth Generation consortium was marked by deep tensions and conflict between MITI, which demanded corporate participation, and the companies, which most decidedly did not want to participate, but did so reluctantly under MITI pressure. That corporate reluctance in many cases turned to bitterness over time, so that the managers at ICOT, the Fifth Generation research institute, found themselves in a constant struggle to get the companies to cooperate. Fifth Generation is the starkest refutation of assumptions of Japanese government/business harmony. In Fifth Generation, these notions are not just wrong— they are an absurd misunderstanding of a relationship between the electronics and computer companies and MITI.

The struggle between MITI and the companies began right from the beginning, when MITI officials first floated trial balloons about the possibility of doing a futuristic computer. The disagreements ran right through the more formal deliberations leading to consortium launch and through the eleven years of the consortium itself. The experience was for many participants on both sides deeply frustrating and at times quite ugly—yet in many ways, as argued earlier about the relationship between MITI and the Ministry of Education, it has to be considered an inevitable result of trying to lash together a highly speculative technology scheme with minimal potential for near-term applications and then ask companies, who are in the business of business, to be its prime backers. Major Japanese companies see their responsibilities as being to their customers, not throwing money after visions of technology breakthroughs. To understand the struggle between MITI and the companies, one must reflect back on the MITI/MOE struggle described earlier. Fifth Generation was a project the computer companies felt was not appropriate for them, but MITI was shut out of the university research labs by the Ministry of Education, so it decided to put the squeeze on the companies. This time, however, the ride was long and hard.

Fighting over What Is to Be Done: Consortium Launch

From the very first, the companies made it clear that they were not interested in chasing a Fifth Generation computer. In the very first meeting with a Japanese computer executive where a MITI official broached the possibility of Fifth Generation, four years before the consortium started up, the Hitachi executive just laughed. He didn't say anything else; it was just a laugh, and the conversation turned to other issues.[35] The signal to the young MITI official who was pushing the plan was clear: a laugh means no.

But for MITI, getting a no from companies on the first run through was not uncommon. The companies had after all said no to the idea of the VLSI joint lab, but MITI had pushed it through. The spurning of the Fifth Generation idea merely reinforced MITI's sense of duty and mission. It was vital to plan for the future, and if the companies laughed, then they were being shortsighted, thought the MITI bureaucrats, and MITI would have to take on the burden of planning for the future and guiding the companies.

During the following year, a MITI representative made the rounds of all the major computer companies to gauge their interest. There was no interest to gauge. None of the companies thought it was a good idea.[36] Nevertheless, MITI saw in Fifth Generation an opportunity to break IBM's lock on the computer world and continued to push hard. And when the companies were asked to send representatives to a committee formed at JIPDEC (the Japan Information Processing Development Center, a MITI-sponsored public/private association) to study the subject, they did not refuse, thinking their input might shape a MITI proposal more to their liking.

They were wrong. The JIPDEC study committee turned into a battleground between the companies and a group of ETL scientists who had the support of the Fifth Generation MITI bureaucrats. Their leader was Kazuhiro Fuchi, a brilliant ETL scientist who had made his reputation helping design the ETL Mark-IV computer. Fuchi is a man who radiates quiet power; in his presence you feel his intellect, his moral strength. He was an ideal leader for the pro-Fifth Generation forces (indeed, MITI had lobbied him precisely because of his significance)—he was brilliant, passionate, driven to excellence, and commanded fierce loyalty among his subordinates.[37]

The JIPDEC study committee was headed by Tōru Moto-oka, Japan's leading authority on computer architecture and a professor at the University of Tokyo. Under him were three subcommittees. The first studied "systematization technology"[38] and was headed by Hajime Karatsu of Matsushita Electric, the core company in the sprawling Matsushita group, the world's largest electronics manufacturer (but more widely known through its brand names Panasonic, Technics, Quasar, and National). Karatsu's systematization committee tried to project forward to understand what the user environment would be in the 1990's in order to better specify what kind of Fifth Generation computer was necessary.

It was between the other two subcommittees that the battles occurred. Fuchi headed the "basic theory" subcommittee, and a "computer architecture" committee was led by Hideo Aiso, also a brilliant computer scientist of high reputation. Professor and now dean at Keio University, one of Japan's top private universities, Aiso was chosen to succeed Moto-oka as the head of the Fifth Generation steering committee after Moto-oka passed away in 1985.

Although the theory committee and architecture committee were supposed to investigate different areas, this was yet another MITI division of labor that did not take place. Both committees took on the task of proposing a research program for the Fifth Generation consortium, and when the two subcommittees published their proposals in early 1980, they were in violent disagreement. The theory (Fuchi) group started out with the premise that the best bet was to move away from today's technology and start out on something completely new.[39] It called for a great leap forward to large-scale parallel processing, arguing that existing von Neumann schemes, with their single CPU's and limited processing power, would never be able to achieve capabilities such as humanlike inference and reason, understanding human speech, and so on. As Fuchi describes it:

I thought that it was possible to create a *new technology framework*. . . . Not just imitate the United States, do something possibly risky, something new. . . .
If we were to do a new project, there were two paths. One was to improve on existing technology. The second was to do something futuristic. . . . There were two groups [each supporting one of the two paths]. But for a national project, you should do things that the companies totally could not do, that was focused on the future. If they [the companies] wanted to improve existing technology, they could do it themselves.[40]

Based upon this reasoning, Fuchi's theory group advocated an aggressive and ambitious leap into the future. Not only that, but the theory group also proposed use of what was to the computer makers an obscure branch of computer science called logic programming. This was to be based upon a computer language called Prolog, which had been created in Marseilles in the early 1970's. For the computer makers, this was a discomforting choice: most of them—and, frankly, most of the academics—barely knew Prolog, let alone had experience programming in it.

The architecture group, half of whose ten members were from companies, came to reflect those company interests. They argued that the proper research direction was to build upon the current base of non–von Neumann machines, that to make this giant leap of faith into the twin unknowns of parallelism and logic programming was the stuff of dreams—bad dreams. It was unwise, unsound, and should remain unimplemented. As the architecture subcommittee argued in its 1980 report, "It is hard to believe that we can build a new computer from dreamlike new technology. Technology has a certain flow it follows, and the new computer will emerge as an extension of current technology."[41]

Rather, the companies argued, what was essential to future computers were the key concepts of *integration* (VLSI), *miniaturization*, *personalness*, *connectivity*, and *user interfaces*, all of which did turn out to be key trends of the 1980's. They thus proposed to use VLSI technology to make small but powerful personal computers and then encourage their widespread use. In addition, the architecture group advocated the creation of a central database and computation center that would store data that the public could access, and they would build connectivity into the new personal computers so that they could easily connect into the central database and to one another. Finally, they would create a powerful user interface to make computers more accessible to the average person.[42]

If any of these ideas seem similar to what emerged as the guiding vision of the TRON consortium, it should be no surprise that the founder of TRON, Ken Sakamura, was a member of the architecture subcommittee. When it became clear that the architecture group had lost its battle for control over the Fifth Generation vision, he quit the JIPDEC committee and started work on TRON.

With this vision, the companies in the architecture group argued they could bring together existing technologies in a new and innovative way, that they could build upon the best of the old without making their customers' existing investments in computer technology obsolete. The architecture group suggested a smooth transition to the future.

But what the theory group wanted was a sharp break. ETL's young researchers in the theory group had a real problem with the architecture group's proposal: "It represented at best the 4.5 generation, and would not be a path-breaking Fifth Generation computer."[43] As Fuchi notes above, this architecture group proposal did not seem to be sufficiently ambitious to justify a national project. If that was the agenda, the companies could do it themselves. For the MITI bureaucrats, too, this proposal was highly problematic. Increasingly worried about the trade tensions with the United States, they believed that doing something that had an obvious and close connection to current technologies would invite U.S. anger. If MITI were to launch a Fifth Generation program, it had to be much more futuristic. The desires of scientists who found excitement in building the latest and the greatest thus converged with MITI's need to avoid alienating the United States to form a Fifth Generation vision that was largely unlinked to existing technology trajectories.

In trying to reconcile the conflicting proposals of the architecture and theory groups, tensions worsened from the sullen hostility of early deliberations and exploded into open anger at meetings of the full committee. The companies thought that the scientists were a bunch of vapid dreamers, with no responsibility to create anything that anyone would actually buy. "The companies were not in the least intoxicated by dreams. For them, computers were products, and if they didn't sell, they weren't worth anything. It was much more important to sell a machine than try to seek out an ideal machine that was way off in the future. This was the reason that the companies had laughed at . . . [MITI's] proposal to build a non–von Neumann Fifth Generation computer. At the Aiso group, they didn't laugh, but their basic position was unchanged."[44]

For their part, the ETL scientists who formed the core of the theory group thought that the companies were wedded to their current money machines by greed and selfishness; they saw their own lack of concern with making money in the marketplace as precisely what allowed them best to pursue new technological directions.[45] The ETL scientists also had a great deal of confidence in their own intellectual and technical excellence—they were after all some of the finest computer scientists in Japan, victors in the harrowing academic competition of the Japanese education and employment system. ETL took only the best. Thus, when companies raised concerns about the theory group's proposed new machines' lack of IBM compatibility, this was met with derision:

We researchers usually win technical debates [with the companies]. Nonetheless, the companies were not convinced. The company technical people said "What you say may be true, but the reality is that IBM controls the computer industry, so we have to pursue an IBM-compatible path." That's why we didn't persuade them. For them, IBM compatibility was a kind of religious faith . . . people who don't get it, don't get it. That's why we chose a more ambitious path and said, "Let's do it. And please cooperate."[46]

In this ongoing struggle, it was ultimately Moto-oka who was the key vote that determined which path the consortium would take. Moto-oka was simultaneously the chairman, the senior member of the committee in a society that places tremendous emphasis on seniority, and Japan's leading authority on computer architecture. He had an immense network of contacts, with his former students populating companies and universities all over Japan. A go from Moto-oka meant GO. A no meant NO.

Moto-oka was extremely hesitant about the theory group's proposal, considering it speculative and more suited to funding by the Ministry of Education in a university environment. He did not know a lot about Prolog and was very reluctant to stake the consortium's future on it. Two things swung him toward the Fuchi camp. First, he had his graduate students at the University of Tokyo take Prolog for a test ride and do some programming in it. They liked it. It was powerful. It was interesting.[47] Second, it became very clear to Moto-oka that the key Fifth Generation decision makers in MITI were firmly in the Fuchi camp. MITI wanted something big, something new, something that would seize hold of the world's attention, something futuristic that would not anger the Americans. "It's a gamble," said a MITI official at a dinner with Fuchi and Moto-oka one night.[48] Moto-oka decided that if MITI wanted to gamble, he would not get in its way.

In March 1981, the final report of the JIPDEC study committee came out. It supported Fuchi's theory group. Resistance from the companies in the architecture group had been summarily crushed. There was no compromise, no careful "Japanese consensus." Fifth Generation would build parallel Prolog machines, with a vision of revolutionizing the computer industry. These would be computers radically new in form, computers that were one step closer to thinking and listening and understanding.

However, MITI had a major problem. It had snuffed out the companies' objections, but at the same time, because Ministry of Education antagonism blocked access to universities, it expected the companies to contribute half the consortium funding and most of the technical manpower. It was going to be difficult to ask companies whose opinions had been quashed to make major financial and personnel contributions.

To bring the companies on board, as it had done with the Supercomputer consortium, MITI used a combination of key concessions and a divide-and-conquer strategy, which was possible because the major companies were split between hard-liners and accommodators. The hard-liners thought the effort was doomed; it would crash and burn, a humiliating public failure for the Japanese computer industry. They publicly scorned Fifth Generation as "a game for academics."[49] The terms "resentment and hostility are hardly strong enough to describe the attitudes of [one such] firm's managers toward the Fifth Generation," Edward Feigenbaum and Pamela McCorduck observe. "They told us frankly that they had not wanted to participate and only under duress (whose nature we couldn't ascertain) did they finally contribute their researchers to ICOT."[50] Although in contrast to these hard-liners, the more accommodating companies continued to prefer the architecture proposal, they also saw some potential merit in the theory group's approach. They also realized that they really had little choice anyway.

MITI expected them to participate, and they thought they might as well enter with a positive mind-set and see what they could learn.

Just as with the Supercomputer consortium, these corporate differences of opinion gave MITI substantial leverage: once one company broke ranks and assented to participation, MITI could cajole and persuade the other companies. Fuchi is quite open about this:

That's Japanese society—if other people cooperate, we cooperate, too. . . . We may think differently about this, but then again we may learn something from doing it. If we alone don't cooperate, we could lose out. . . . Thus, while we are against that particular attribute of Japanese society, we ended up making use of it.[51]

A research manager confirms that his company's decision to participate had much to do with trying not to fall out of step with the other major companies:

The numerical computation market is much, much larger than that for logic programming. Logic programming is still very small. To that extent, in terms of market needs, we felt doing specialized machines for logic programming was premature . . . we felt doing something in tune with the downsizing trend, something in software, and integrating it into our technology would be a better approach. . . .

[But] saying that we're not going to participate? . . . to be honest, Japan is a *yokonarabi* world [literally, *yokonarabi* means "lined up side by side"], so the story is: if [other computer companies] are going to participate, then we also participate. . . . We decided to participate in part because of that reasoning."[52]

A good MITI negotiating strategy, however, was not enough to bring the companies on board. MITI also had to make substantial concessions to the companies in the areas of funding and the joint lab.

No company funding. Although there may have been some split in feelings about the merits of the consortium, the companies were united on funding. Or more precisely, the companies were united on *no* funding. No company had any desire to give a single yen to the consortium. Just as in supercomputers, if MITI wanted to do a futuristic project, MITI could fund it itself. The companies did not budge on this issue, so Fifth Generation ended up being 100 percent MITI-funded.

A small joint lab. Then there was the issue of setting up a joint lab, always a sore point between the companies and MITI. Of course, the companies were against it. The basic position seen in VLSI and supercomputers was unchanged: the companies did not want to send their researchers off to some place where they would mix with other companies' researchers. But given MITI's strong insistence on the need for a central lab to do common software development and computer-architecture design, a compromise akin to the VLSI consortium's joint lab was worked out.

There would be a joint lab, but it would be small. At its start it was only around 40 people, and grew to about 100 researchers at the end. So the companies only had to contribute a few researchers each to the joint lab. Moreover, most of Fifth Generation funding (approximately 80 percent of it in 1987) would go to researchers working on ICOT projects within each company's own private research labs. Thus, the bulk of the personnel and funds tied to Fifth Generation were not in the central lab but in the companies themselves. This was in keeping with the companies' desire to minimize the size and scope of the cooperative joint lab.

The Struggle Continues: Eleven Years of Fifth Generation

Relations between the companies and ICOT remained strained throughout the entire course of the consortium. This is unsurprising, given that the companies had never bought into the Fifth Generation proposal and were reluctant participants in the enterprise. As a Hitachi researcher revealed to a *Datamation* reporter in the middle of the project: "Passive participating in ICOT is the rule for companies with substantial research bases of their own. . . . We can cooperate, but our own independent research efforts are more important."[53]

While participation in ICOT research may have been passive, efforts by companies to drive the research agenda in directions more to their liking were quite active. As early as July 1983, only one year after Fifth Generation research began, the *Nikkei sangyō shimbun*, a daily newspaper in the powerful Nikkei group, featured a story on ICOT under the headline: "Fifth Generation Computer—Opportunity to Reevaluate Development Plan—Voices of Discontent in Industry—Leadership is Bureaucratic/Academic [and] Values Narrow and Biased Theory."[54] The *Nikkei sangyō shimbun* specializes in industry news, and its point of view tends to reflect industry's. It pointed out that the consortium was not a case of a San-Kan-Gaku partnership, where San is a *kanji* character representing industry, Kan is government, and Gaku academia. In fact, said the *Nikkei sangyō*, ICOT was more a case of the academic Gaku leading, the bureaucratic Kan supporting, and the hapless industry San being forced to follow.[55]

The article cited unnamed top company executives who insisted that they had no problem with academic leadership as long as it led to something useful, but that Fifth Generation was clearly not leading to anything useful. The companies were also bitter because MITI had signed a joint Fifth Generation R&D deal with the United Kingdom, primarily involving the British academic community, and the companies thought it was a waste of time. "Why should we cooperate with the British, who are weak in computer science?" they asked. They wanted to do something with the Americans, who with their strength in computers had more to offer.

Moreover, the companies were convinced that the reason that MITI could not get the United States to join the Fifth Generation consortium was that Fifth Generation was exactly what they, the Japanese industry, knew it to be: narrow and academic, with little to offer. They were angry that rather than trying to solve this fundamental problem, MITI had gone off and cut a deal with a group of British academics so that it could claim it was being internationally cooperative. The *Nikkei sangyō*'s conclusion was that clearly this situation could not stand: with industry up in arms, MITI was going to have to revamp the consortium.[56]

It was wrong—not about industry dissatisfaction, or the suspicion that the research would not end up making a substantial mainstream technology contribution. Rather, it was wrong in its assumption that a company revolt would result in change. ICOT was being run as a very tight ship. Straining under the huge expectations that had been created for it by the massive publicity campaign to secure government financing, and simultaneously facing a substantial lack of funds because the companies had refused to contribute any money, ICOT was barreling ahead, putting its hopes in pushing hard along a narrow front in order to create a technology breakthrough.

Thus, although the first few years of the consortium were supposed to be a period in which to investigate different technologies before choosing which areas to focus on for the rest of the project, the reality was that the major decisions had already been made: there would be a sustained, concentrated push to develop parallel-logic-programming machines, and no amount of company objections would stop that. A research manager from one of the Big Three firms remembers: "With the Fifth Generation project, ICOT constructed the basic technology story and made all the plans. . . . This may have been efficient, but if just a slightly different idea appeared, it was cut off."[57] A research manager from another company confirms that the various consultational committees made up of company and academic representatives essentially rubber-stamped ICOT's central policy decisions: "There were committees formed by companies. But their job was to confirm the direction set by ICOT. They were not places where policy directions were set." [58]

Thus, many of the companies had deep grievances about the way Fifth Generation was being run. But ICOT, too, was in a very difficult position. Short of funds, and with a huge mandate, ICOT in many ways had no choice but to pursue efficiency at the cost of consensus. This was especially the case because the companies showed little inclination to agree on a joint direction. One manager acknowledges that without centralized leadership, the project would have dissolved into bickering: there were "too many captains trying to guide the ship." [59] Thus emerged an authoritarian decision-making style. ICOT made the decisions. The companies' job was to follow orders.

This ICOT tendency to push aside alternative opinions and approaches was reinforced by Fuchi's experiences in an earlier MITI consortium, PIPS (Pattern Information Processing System), and his basic philosophical commitment to test the original proposition of the Fifth Generation program: that a concentrated focus on logic programming and parallel processing would produce a major breakthrough and that focus should be kept clear, without changes of plans or compromises or backup/secondary research projects to distract from the central goal. As Fuchi argues:

What was good about the project was the original plan, and that for ten years we worked hard to keep to the original plan. . . . We created a philosophy at the beginning of this project. People in Japan generally believe that it's better to compromise in these projects, but we were the opposite. We drew up our philosophy at the beginning, and even if people were against it, we did it.

Of course, if the philosophy were truly bad, we would have had to quit, but since there was a possibility that it was correct, for ten years we pushed forward. I would most like other Japanese projects to absorb this lesson from us. I think to have a big messy mix of things all thrown together into one project really is wrong. [60]

Fuchi's PIPS experiences during the 1970's had helped shaped this philosophy. Despite claims by some Western analysts that it should be considered a success, [61] in Japan PIPS was widely viewed as a project that had spun out of control, wasting talent and resources on a swollen conglomeration of thinly related research. Fuchi had observed PIPS from the inside, as a manager of one of the research efforts, and he did not want Fifth Generation to meet PIPS' fate. As one of the Fifth Generation researchers describes it:

Fuchi regretted what happened with the PIPS project. . . . PIPS was extremely diverse—its "center" became extremely diffuse. It included natural language processing, voice recognition, pattern recognition, computers, networks—all of information processing was included in PIPS. Fuchi saw all this. He wanted to create a project that had some centrifugal force and that had a clear goal. For that reason, he consciously chose to focus just on logic programming. He tried to prevent the inclusion of other research topics.[62]

Thus, the die had been cast: when the companies pushed for adjusting the research agenda, given a changing technology environment, Fuchi and ICOT stuck, consciously and tenaciously, to their original agenda.

Conflict over the research agenda occurred in two general areas: (1) whether to build *specialized or general-purpose* hardware and software; and (2) the relative effort to be put into *hardware or software*. With respect to the special-purpose or general-purpose debate, this was also a discussion that was going on in America in the early 1980's. At that time, it was felt by many in the American AI research community that general-purpose machines were too slow ever to be good engines for artificial intelligence, and that it was necessary to build specialized computers to run particular AI applications. Companies such as Symbolics Inc. sprang up to build specialized LISP computers and had booming sales and profits in the early 1980's. However, a new competitor emerged at that time that killed off these specialized computers. Ironically, Symbolics, which had made the same technology bet as Fifth Generation ("The future is specialized artificial intelligence machines!") declared bankruptcy in early 1993, the year ICOT ended operations as a MITI consortium after having been given a one-year extension.[63]

The new competitor was workstations: general-purpose workstations, built first by Apollo Computer and then by Sun Microsystems. Apollo was there first, but Sun had seized control of the market by the mid 1980's, bringing along with it a host of competitors. What the workstation makers sold was high price/performance and "openness." They used standardized parts to keep costs low and a standardized operating system, AT&T's UNIX, for ease of programming. There were a lot of flavors of UNIX, but moving software from one UNIX to another was fairly simple, at least by the standards of the mainframe and minicomputer worlds. Moving from UNIX to UNIX could take minutes or hours or days or, in the case of highly complex programs that had real hooks into operating-system internals, weeks. In contrast, in moving from proprietary operating system A to proprietary system B in the minicomputer or mainframe world, you usually started out in units of months or, more typically, years. Of course, that was more time than it was worth, so the general result in the proprietary mini and mainframe world was that you did not even try to move major software applications.

The result of workstations' standardized, low-cost approach was "killer" price/performance, and the introduction of new RISC (*Reduced Instruction Set Computer*) microprocessors in the mid 1980's confirmed that this killer price/performance had a glorious future, promising improvements of computing power that were nearly doubling every year in the late 1980's.[64]

By the mid 1980's, the Japanese companies in ICOT too had noticed that these general-purpose UNIX workstations were rapidly gaining market share and volume, that RISC microprocessors appeared to be the future of these workstations, and that ICOT's efforts in building a specialized Prolog computer had been overtaken and made obsolete by these new technological forces. The logical thing to do, the companies thought, was to abandon ICOT's effort to build a specialized machine, regroup, and refocus on UNIX and RISC workstations and perhaps the programming language C, which became hugely popular in the 1980's with the spread of UNIX-based computers. (The UNIX operating system itself is largely written in the C language.) ICOT said no. Fuchi cherished his commitment to the original philosophical premises of Fifth Generation: a no-compromise, no-holds-barred, aggressive push along the single, chosen technology path of specialized logic-programming computers. If companies wanted to do other things, the Fifth Generation consortium was not the appropriate venue. As Fuchi recalls:

Fundamentally, I believed that we could do just fine without any change of course. . . . People wanted to do things like workstations, do things that we can use within a short time frame. But they were already doing workstations themselves. It was not appropriate for a national project. That opinion nevertheless existed over the entire ten-year period. But that is not really a correct opinion.[65]

This perspective made many of the companies *very* unhappy. A corporate research manager recalls:

We suggested the use of languages other than Prolog, the use of RISC approaches—it was all ignored . . . we were strongly told: "This is the way we are doing things," and it was the specialized approach. This is the biggest source of dissatisfaction that we have. If you do research that is separated from business needs, when the research is over and you're told, "Go ahead and use it," the truth is, it's not usable.

What we're most disturbed about is the software that was produced at ICOT. When we bring it back to our company, it won't run on normal computers, it will run only on PIM or PSI [two special-purpose ICOT computers].[66]

A research manager from another company adds: "[A particular ICOT manager] was insistent. We wanted to build general-purpose machines. RISC and UNIX would have been better. But [the ICOT manager] thought that specialized hardware would be faster and overrode our protests. We did what we were told to do. We built the special-purpose machines."[67]

Having put down the companies' revolt against ICOT's special-purpose focus, ICOT did try to assuage them by having a version of Prolog it had developed, called ESP, ported to UNIX, theoretically making ICOT's software accessible to general-purpose use. But the effort was a failure, and in fact it seemed almost as if it had been designed to fail. Technologically, the problem was that ESP was not a parallel language—it was designed for existing serial-processor machines. And ICOT was washing its hands of ESP—having learned from its design experience with ESP, it was busy creating a new, *parallel* language that was substantially more sophisticated. In short, ESP was a technological dead end, which even its developer, ICOT, saw no future for. Of course, under these circumstances, there was no way potential users would be interested, and they stayed away in droves: Why should they commit resources to a language that was literally being phased out? Thus, the ESP port to UNIX turned out to be nothing more than a minor footnote in the Fifth Generation epic; it did not succeed because it could not succeed.

Years later, at the end of the project, however, ICOT, too, had come to realize that it needed to make genuine efforts to provide more general opportunities for use of its software: either that or its software would never be used. Thus, ICOT finally broke down and moved to port its parallel software to a UNIX environment, so that users of UNIX computers would have access to the software. In fact, this appears to be one of the major reasons for the extension of the Fifth Generation consortium beyond its initial 10-year time frame. The extension gave ICOT time to move its software to a general-purpose computing environment and provide opportunities for more widespread use.

This was a popular decision with the companies, but fundamentally the move was too little and too late. They mourned the years and opportunities lost by ICOT's fixation on specialized machines, feeling that ICOT had missed what one Japanese analyst called a "major paradigm shift" (*paradaimu no daihenka*) in the computer business—based upon the acceleration of "downsizing" (moving computing power to smaller machines); the erosion of brand loyalty based upon user demands for open, nonproprietary, unspecialized architectures; the move to UNIX workstations; and the introduction of RISC microprocessors—that was dramatically reworking competition in the computer industry.[68] Thus, ironically, a Fifth Generation program that had aimed to capture the future, to create a new kind of computer for the 1990's, seemed to have fallen victim to a future that it had not foreseen.

The unhappiness about the specialized ICOT approach spilled over into conflict about the relative emphasis the consortium should place on *hardware or software*. Given that the companies were not very happy with the specialized hardware being developed, and that manufacturing and materials costs typically make hardware much more expensive to develop, the companies decided that they would much rather focus their efforts on new software design. Japanese national technology consortia typically put a heavy emphasis on hardware rather than software development, not because hardware is a more appropriate R&D task, but because it allows the hardware to serve as a showpiece, a symbol of the government project. Software on the other hand is believed to be insufficiently solid and material to be well understood by the Japanese public.[69] The taxpayers and the Ministry of Finance, the guardian of the national purse, want to see something in metal in return for their yen.

ICOT, to its credit, has done the best job of any major Japanese national project in putting an appropriate emphasis on software R&D. To that extent it should be applauded, and the Japanese should hope that the precedent ICOT has set will continue into the future. Nonetheless, ICOT was not able to shake off MITI's hardware bias completely. It used its hardware as a PR tool and produced a dizzying array of machines over the consortium's lifetime, including PSI, PSI II, Multi-PSI I & II, PSI/UX, CHI and CHI II, Delta, Mu-X, and five versions of PIM. In all, ICOT built over 500 copies of these computers, a *huge* number for a research program; most U.S. university research projects build no more computer prototypes than can be counted on one hand, or maybe two hands if the project is incredibly well funded.

The particular difficulty with all of these machines was that building ICOT's research computers was not a mass assembly process—it was more akin to the craftshop approach that predated Henry Ford's assembly-line revolution. The companies begrudged all the manpower and effort required—building individual copy after individual copy of a computer and debugging its hardware and software to make sure it ran took a tremendous amount of resources, which the companies felt would be much better spent on other tasks, particularly developing advanced software that would have broader usability. "More than hardware, we wanted to place importance on software development in the project," says one manager. "The truth is, to put that much effort into building PIM, we were sort of against it. We wish PIM had been a smaller effort. . . . Why? Because we weren't really able to find any useful applications to run on the PIM machines. It would have been good to try to work on applications earlier."[70]

The corporate desire to focus more on software development has particular resonance given that the Japanese are widely regarded as being well behind the United States in software capability across the whole spectrum of computer software, from packaged PC applications to cutting-edge software in research environments. As Dr. David Kahaner, a highly respected U.S. Office of Naval Research scientist stationed in Tokyo, put it after attending the Japan Supercomputing '92 conference, right before the final ICOT conference in May 1992: "For the most part Japanese companies are behind those in the US in parallel computing hardware and Japan is far behind in software and tools development for parallel machines."[71] A Stanford University computer scientist who expresses admiration for Japanese hardware adds: "The Japanese are behind in software, way behind. I've never been able to figure out why, but they just are."[72]

But ICOT wanted the machines, and once again the companies had to toe the line. ICOT did compromise on the margins—for example, allowing the companies to do some work on expert systems software that was not particularly relevant to ICOT's core emphasis on parallel-inference machines. But in the main the companies failed to get what they wanted. One company manager speaks at great length about his feelings of frustration in working with ICOT and MITI:

It was a mistake to focus on the hardware. It was a waste of time, resources, and personnel. All of the manufacturers protested, but ICOT and MITI were insistent. They had set the public goal of a 1,000-processor machine and they weren't going to give up on it. Part of it was that careers were at stake—no one wanted to preside over a failure. Also they had committed to the Ministry of Finance at the outset that the project would produce a 1,000-device machine and so were insistent on meeting that commitment. . . .

[So] we suffered through PIM [the final ICOT computer]. It was ICOT's policy to do it . . . we didn't see such world-class technology there, so if you had to say, we suffered through it. We were strongly urged to do it [by ICOT], so we did.

While doing the project, [the companies] discovered that doing PIM was not important. More important was doing KL1 and ICOT's software environment. . . . We wanted to focus more on software. It clearly would have been a more valuable outcome if we had worked harder on PIMOS [the PIM computer's operating system software], etc., and made it easier to use. . . . Everyone came to understand this. If we had only done that. . . . If we had pursued the software on a broader basis, for example, if we had put it on top of the personal computers that everyone has. . . .

It would be best for ICOT's technology results to be usable not only to re-searchers—everyone came to realize this in the middle of the project. But the final project was not this. It was to build a specialized machine. Thus, ten years after the start of the project, if a Japanese citizen wants to use ICOT's tech-nology, what can he do? Nothing but actually go to ICOT's building.[73]

Part of the problem for the companies was that in many ways, ICOT and MITI were unsympathetic to their situation. The view of the com-panies as selfish and technologically timid private interests that needed to be prodded and controlled carried on from the early struggles be-tween the architecture and theory groups. "From the beginning and to this day, industry has been dissatisfied," Fuchi said in 1992. "They are not being asked to do things that directly relate to their own self-interest, so they are even now dissatisfied. . . . Industry doesn't really have much confidence. They just have confidence in the things that they normally do."[74]

ICOT managers saw company researchers protest when their com-panies tried to call them back from their ICOT stints. Some of these researchers even left their companies. This reinforced ICOT's sense of the essential rightness of its mission. If the companies were so smart, why couldn't they hold onto their researchers? Fuchi himself spoke out publicly on this issue: "Young people run away because the companies are not doing much basic research. Corporations should reflect on their own shortcomings."[75]

"ICOT was constructed for the benefit of the nation, not the benefit of the participants," a MITI official adds.[76] But the companies could not be satisfied with this response. This was a computer consortium. They were the country's top computer makers. If this consortium did not benefit them, then *whom* did it benefit?

Given these attitudes, when ICOT faced conflict from the middle managers who oversaw company participation and were pushing for changes in ICOT policies, rather than negotiate to resolve differences, ICOT managers sometimes went over the manager's head and com-plained directly to his superiors. This embittered the company manag-ers. "ICOT's top people or sometimes MITI would go to the top tech-nology people of each company and say, 'We'd like more cooperation. Your people are constantly resisting,'" says one manager. In classic Japanese understatement, he continues, "When they go above you [to your superiors] and say, 'We'd like more cooperation,' it's a form of pressure."[77]

ICOT was under pressure, so it put the companies under pressure. It was a pressure-filled decade in the Fifth Generation consortium.

The TRON Consortium

The primary conflict in TRON's BTRON educational personal computer effort was between MITI and NEC. MITI's goal of creating a new desktop computer standard through BTRON was anathema to NEC, since a new computer standard would mean breaking NEC's grip on the PC market. NEC knew this, MITI knew this, and all the other Japanese computer manufacturers certainly knew it. Despite all of Sakamura's idealism about demonstrating Japanese creativity, breaking the unfair monopolistic hold of Intel and Microsoft, and making a uniquely Japanese contribution to the world of computers through an open computer standard, from the perspective of NEC and the other Japanese makers, TRON in its BTRON desktop form was primarily about breaking NEC's near-monopoly on PCs in Japan.

NEC had a huge incentive to try to stop this, because NEC made *huge* profits on its PCs in the 1980's. When the BTRON standardization process was in full swing in late 1987, NEC had a proprietary version of DOS with which it controlled 70 percent of the Japanese PC market and 90 percent of the market for higher-end machines (at the time these higher-end PCs were based upon an Intel microprocessor called the 80286 that could process 16 bits of information at a time— today, most new PCs process 32 bits simultaneously).

One indication of the monopoly rents NEC was extracting is the size of its price reductions in early 1993 in the face of the first major competitive threat NEC had faced in PCs since grabbing the lion's share of the Japanese market in the early 1980's. The competitors were low-priced PCs from the United States and Taiwan using a version of DOS, DOS/V, that allowed unmodified IBM-compatible PCs to handle Japanese characters.

The low-price attack was launched by Compaq in the fall of 1992, and IBM and Dell, among others, swiftly followed. NEC unsuccessfully tried to convince Japanese PC users that NEC's high prices meant high quality and the U.S. makers' low prices meant low quality, but its PC sales plunged. So in early 1993, NEC cut prices on its PCs on a price/performance basis by as much as a factor of four. Yet, even with its new prices, NEC machines were priced higher in Japan than the low-priced U.S. and Taiwanese PCs that were storming ashore.

With these kinds of profits, NEC executives wanted to see BTRON succeed about as much as they wanted to cut their own throats. The idea that it might devote any engineering resources to building a BTRON computer was laughable. MITI, however, was not laughing. Without the participation of NEC, Japan's largest PC maker, it would be hopeless to try to create a new desktop standard based on TRON. When throughout 1987, NEC refused to submit a BTRON prototype to the Center for Educational Computing (CEC), the trilateral MITI-MOE-industry group that was making the school PC standardization decision, MITI decided it needed to make itself understood. The showdown occurred on October 5, 1987, when MITI officials met behind closed doors with NEC executives. The newspapers reported the result the following day: NEC had decided to make a BTRON prototype and submit it as a candidate for the Japanese school PC standard. MITI had won.

Or had it? MITI had forced NEC to submit a BTRON prototype, but it could not change NEC's fundamental interest in seeing BTRON fail. In 1992 an NEC executive recalled, in an admission that forms one of the epigraphs to this chapter:

We joined TRON because we were asked to. But TRON was the enemy—it competed with our products. We never had any intention of promoting TRON, and we never set up any group to do so. In true Japanese fashion, we pretended on the surface to be a TRON backer, because it was expected of us by MITI, but below the surface we were totally uninterested.[78]

During the next few years of the BTRON standardization process, NEC continued to fight a rearguard action, trying to delay the standardization decision as much as possible. It figured (correctly) that time was on its side, that the more BTRON was delayed, the greater NEC's software advantage in terms of available applications would be and the more opportunity NEC would have to improve the functionality of its own machines to rival that of the TRON computer.

The decision to abandon the BTRON standardization effort in June 1989 must have been met with whoops of joy in NEC's mammoth postmodern headquarters in Tokyo. Although MITI had tried to make NEC pretend otherwise, "TRON was the enemy."

FIVE

Enemies in the Same Boat

Companies as Competitors Within Japanese Joint Technology Consortia

> My great interest in the organization was the human problem: how to coordinate the researchers from different companies and make them interact. I wanted them to become good friends, communicate to each other, and open their hearts. So what I did was the typical Japanese way: All I did for these four years was to drink with them as frequently as I could.
>
> Masato Nebashi, managing director
> of the VLSI consortium

> There was a lot of suffering on that project. . . . The problem with doing stuff that is close to the market is that it's a pain to try to make it happen. The backstabbing starts immediately.
>
> Fujitsu executive, about the Supercomputer consortium

An old Japanese expression, *goetsu dōshū* (enemies in the same boat), aptly describes the uncomfortable position companies are placed in when MITI drafts them into joint technology consortia with their chief Japanese competitors. The feelings of intercompany hostility and suspicion were somewhat ameliorated in the earliest consortium analyzed here, VLSI, because all of the firms faced a common enemy, IBM, and could find common ground in their effort to protect themselves from a perceived IBM technological juggernaut.

But even in the VLSI consortium, the fundamental reality that the five participating Japanese firms were competitors being asked to cooperate could not be papered over, and the companies fought MITI attempts to bring them to cooperate in a significant and tightly linked way. Even in VLSI, in many ways the peak of cooperation for MITI high-tech consortia, deeply rooted competition and conflict coexisted uneasily with the cooperative premises and structures of the consortium. Moreover, by the launch of the Supercomputer and Fifth Generation consortia in the early 1980's, the specter of mighty IBM no longer held the same frightful sway over the Japanese computer firms, and it became impossible for MITI to force cooperation upon the companies.

The VLSI Consortium

Despite all of the public rhetoric about the "cooperative nature" of the VLSI consortium, as with all of the consortia investigated here, genuine intercompany joint R&D was the exception that proves the rule: Japanese firms do not like to cooperate under government mandate, and despite all MITI's efforts to try to force them to do so, they largely do not.[1]

That the VLSI consortium was not a model of intercompany harmony is unsurprising, for outside the MITI-made world of the VLSI consortium, the five companies remained vicious competitors. The *Nihon keizai (Nikkei)* newspaper wrote in October 1976, several months after work began in the VLSI consortium, that all the major Japanese semiconductor companies had "bloodshot eyes" as they grimly sank huge investments into new semiconductor production facilities.[2] Every firm was driving up its production volume in an attempt to create economies of scale and have the lowest-cost production.

NEC, Hitachi, and Toshiba, in particular, were locked in a three-way battle for leadership of the semiconductor market, with the three firms' monthly semiconductor sales tightly packed at ¥7.5 billion, ¥7.0 billion, and ¥6.5 billion respectively. The *Nikkei* went so far as to worry that with demand for CB radios, calculators, and color TVs slowing, there did not seem to be sufficient end-market demand for semiconductors to warrant the firms' investment and production frenzy and that a vicious semiconductor price war might well soon ensue.[3]

The Uphill Battle: Promoting Cooperation at the VLSI Joint Lab

To begin with the centerpiece of the VLSI consortium, even in the joint lab, which was both quite small and focused only on basic and precompetitive technologies to lessen company fears of leaking proprietary information, MITI still could not generate a substantial level of joint R&D between researchers from different companies. MITI had originally planned on having four sublabs working on different R&D topics, but in one of the areas, microfabrication technologies, Fujitsu, Toshiba, and Hitachi were all working on similar technologies and refused to participate in any research that involved the other companies. So MITI had to expand that particular sublab into three different sublabs, headed by Hitachi, Fujitsu, and Toshiba respectively, and each including researchers from Mitsubishi and NEC. Why did the three companies tolerate Mitsubishi and NEC? First of all, MITI insisted. Second, Mitsubishi and NEC were not a competitive threat. As a senior researcher put it: "Mitsubishi and NEC were not competing companies in this technical field. Even if Mitsubishi and NEC scientists took the information acquired in the joint laboratory back to their companies, this would not pose a problem."[4]

Creating an environment conducive to even a small amount of co-operative R&D took Herculean efforts from the consortium's management. Some of the tactics were quite clever and continue to be standard practice in MITI high-tech consortia. For example, before starting up the consortium's R&D, all of the companies had their participating engineers write up their relevant proprietary knowledge on their consortium R&D topics. These huge stacks of paper they sealed and lugged over to MITI or the VLSI Association offices, where they were stored. This sealing of prior intellectual property claims was designed to promote broader sharing of technical knowledge: if you had written it down, at the end of the consortium, you could claim it as your prior knowledge and the intellectual property would belong to your company, not the consortium. It was hoped that this would allow engineers to participate freely in joint R&D without risking their companies' intellectual property claims.

Sealed intellectual property claims or no sealed intellectual property claims, however, the company researchers were suspicious and hostile when joint lab research began in 1976. Masato Nebashi, the VLSI Association's managing director, who had been sent from MITI, was furious one day when he discovered that researchers at some of the sub-labs were blocking entrances to their labs with equipment to prevent other researchers from entering. "Why is this equipment here?!" Nebashi bellowed, and the offending equipment was removed. But within a week or so, in violation of fire regulations, the equipment was back, and the doors were blocked again.[5] "Things were difficult at first in terms of cooperation," Nebashi remembered. "By the time I arrived there were a number of agreements made, but they were mostly words, not reality. Everyone was carrying around the particular concerns of their company. There was not a single person there with an open mind. Clearly, they were all there to do research for their company."[6]

Nebashi and Tarui knew that such hostility would poison the atmosphere of the joint lab. They quickly seized upon opportunities to create more exchange between the researchers, including regular technical meetings and an internal lab newsletter. Other attempts to create a sense of community were more social in nature, including setting up sports clubs and Nebashi's tactical use of liquor. Nebashi would gather up researchers and they would go out drinking together, night after night. In Japan the nightly journey to the watering hole, where workers frequently drink heavily and release the tensions of the day with co-workers or the boss (more tension is typically released when it is co-workers!) is still common practice, although it is receding over time. This custom can invite a measure of concern or disapproval from Americans, but the plain fact of the matter is that Japan is more tolerant of the social consumption of alcohol than America is. The greater avail-ability of mass transit also makes drunkenness a great deal less deadly in Japan, if decisively more public.

On these evenings, Nebashi hoped to break through the walls that separated the researchers. Some of the researchers called his approach "management by whiskey."[7] Nebashi explains: "My great interest in the organization was the human problem: how to coordinate the re-searchers from different companies and make them interact. I wanted them to become good friends, communicate to each other, and open their hearts. So what I did was the typical Japanese way: All I did for these four years was to drink with them as frequently as I could."[8]

The combination of these seminars and other less formal exchanges, Nebashi's social gatherings, and changes in the technology environ-ment created a much less tense atmosphere by the second two years of the project. Technical change was critical in this respect: "In the first two years of the four-year project researchers [in the first three joint laboratories] were very nervous about sharing information because we brought our own company technology. After two years the information flow increased because the advance of technology was so rapid; almost all the technology was new after two years."[9]

Thus, by the end of the consortium in 1980, relationships formed through shared experiences had created a truly congenial atmosphere at the joint labs, in stark contrast to the sullen suspicion of the opening days. Indeed, when the farewell party was held to celebrate the end of the joint lab in March 1980, the attendees linked arms and sang "Dōki no sakura" (literally, cherry blossoms of the same cohort), a song about falling cherry blossoms and the death of Japan's young World War II *kamikaze* pilots, a song that celebrates a close-knit group sacrificing themselves for the good of the nation. Years later, a number of the joint lab researchers still get together every year on the anniversary of that day to renew old acquaintanceships and talk about old times.

This VLSI joint lab experience can thus be seen as a triumph of con-geniality over corporate suspicion, but in a deeper sense, it failed to achieve its more fundamental goal of creating large-scale joint R&D activities between the firms. The analysis of patent applications from the consortium reveals that R&D continued to be largely confined to single companies, despite the presence of all the researchers from other companies. They may have become friends, but they were for the most part not allies.

Fifteen Percent Full or 85 Percent Empty?: Analyzing Joint Lab Patent Data

Despite these efforts and despite the presence of a mix of personnel from various companies in all the sublabs, a look at patent data reveals that rather than being joint patents between different companies, most of the patents at the joint lab were created by individual researchers or a team of researchers from a single company (see Figure 2). The VLSI joint lab research director, Tarui, has argued that the approximately 15–16 percent of patents that were jointly created at the joint lab indicate substantial cooperative R&D activity.[10] I argue below, however, that this 15 percent figure overstates cooperation between competitors. Moreover, it is clearly open to debate whether even the full 15 percent of patents being jointly generated warrants description as "substantial cooperation." So the question becomes: was the cup 15 percent full or 85 percent empty? The answer is: both, depending on one's baseline for what qualifies as "substantial" cooperation.

Tarui is right that the 15 percent of joint patents constitute a truly remarkable achievement compared to preceding and subsequent MITI

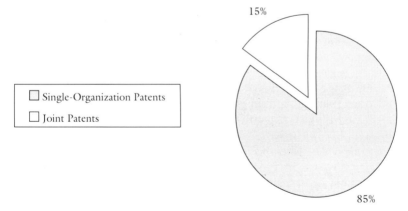

2. VLSI Joint Patent Registration Versus Single-Organization Patents. (Data from Fransman 1991)

projects. In the VHSCS consortium (1966–72), for example, a catch-up effort that produced only 39 patents, there was no joint lab and very little sharing of technology, and none of the patents were jointly held.[11] Similarly, in the Pattern Information Processing System consortium (PIPS) (1971–80), there was again no joint lab, and of 365 patents, only 7 were jointly held, but the two corporations involved were both from the Hitachi group, Hitachi and Hitachi Metal, so it was not really a case of competitive companies doing joint R&D.[12] Furthermore, as we shall see, there were no joint lab and no joint patents in the Super-computer consortium, and although it is difficult to track, intercompany joint patents would appear to be minimal or nonexistent in Fifth Generation as well.

So by the standards of MITI consortia, Tarui is quite right that joint R&D in VLSI was exceedingly high, and Tarui and Nebashi did a remarkable job in inducing the cooperation that they did. But in the end, exceedingly high by MITI standards as this was, this is little more than saying: "Getting the firms to cooperate is almost impossible. To the extent that we even got 15 percent cooperation, it was a great success."[13]

Furthermore, even the approximately 15 percent of joint patents in the VLSI joint lab were less cooperation between competitors than meets the eye. First of all, around a fifth to a quarter of those patents were joint R&D between company researchers and researchers from ETL, the MITI central research institute, so they were not instances of MITI bringing together competing companies. Thus, intercompany patents appear to comprise 12 percent of all joint lab patents at best.[14]

In addition, a close look at the intercompany patents reveals that over 40 percent of them were patents shared between Mitsubishi and another company (see Figure 3). Why would Mitsubishi command such a great share of joint R&D? Mitsubishi was the weakest techno-logically of the five semiconductor companies and had originally been left out of the consortium for that reason. It got in through effective lobbying. Since Mitsubishi was a weaker player, like ETL, it did not pose as much of a competitive threat to the other four companies, and thus joint R&D was seen as less threatening. Even if there was leakage of know-how to Mitsubishi, Mitsubishi was less likely to be able to make effective use of it in the marketplace. It may well also have been the case that Mitsubishi's weaker technological position made it rela-tively more eager to cooperate with, and thus learn from, other firms, so it may more aggressively have sought out R&D partners.

In sum, even at the small joint lab, where MITI put tremendous effort

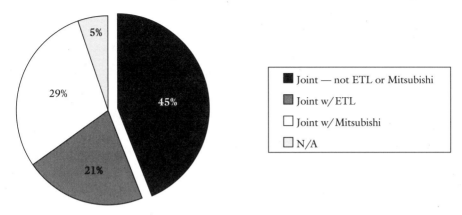

3. Breakdown of VLSI Joint Patents by Organization. (Data from Fransman 1991)

into the design and promotion of a setting conducive to joint research, it was extremely difficult to get researchers from competing companies to work together. Patent data reveal that joint research was minimal. We turn now to the even less cooperative R&D at the group labs.

The "Group Labs" as *tatemae*

Even more so than in the joint lab, in the group labs, cooperation or "jointness" was largely *tatemae* (the public face or public fiction, as opposed to *honne*, the inner reality). The group labs were substantially larger than the joint lab, with about 80 percent of the funding and manpower in the consortium. This was in keeping with the intent of the companies to minimize the size of the joint lab.

The group labs were divided into two, with the Hitachi-Mitsubishi-Fujitsu joint venture, CDL, and the NEC-Toshiba joint venture, NTIS, each managing a set of labs. While MITI described them as actual joint R&D operations, in reality these two joint ventures served primarily to funnel funds to individual company labs. While there was some degree of information exchange about R&D projects within the joint ventures, actual R&D was conducted separately in company labs, and joint patents were nonexistent. To this extent, it might be said that the group lab structure served as a *tatemae* cover of joint R&D over an underlying *honne* reality of independent company efforts.

The CDL and NTIS joint ventures had been set up under orders from MITI, originally as part of MITI's response to IBM's 370 computer in the early 1970's. MITI set up three of these "computer *keiretsu*":

Fujitsu-Hitachi, NEC-Toshiba, and Mitsubishi-Oki. Oki's later decision to leave the computer business created a dilemma for MITI as to what to do with Mitsubishi. Hitachi-Fujitsu & Mitsubishi-Oki had been doing computers compatible with IBM systems, and NEC-Toshiba did non–IBM compatible machines, so the natural solution for MITI was to move Mitsubishi into the Hitachi-Fujitsu camp. It was decided in 1975 that beginning with its participation in the VLSI consortium, Mitsubishi would join the Fujitsu-Hitachi group.

Like most MITI efforts to create cooperation between competitors, these anti–IBM 370 *keiretsu* failed to fulfill their mission as cooperative ventures. Oki abandoned its effort with Mitsubishi fairly quickly. Hitachi and Fujitsu fought with each other. Toshiba largely abdicated control to NEC because of a corporate decision to focus on other sectors.

Under MITI orders, Hitachi and Fujitsu divided up the market for large IBM-compatible computers, so that each firm would produce machines for separate performance levels. MITI's notion was that by keeping each company from producing equivalent machines, the Japanese computer industry as a whole could economize on development costs and at the same time manage to field IBM-compatible computers with a broad spectrum of performance levels. Unfortunately for MITI's grand design, Hitachi and Fujitsu were less than willing players in this scheme, and appeared to be at least as concerned about stealing market share from each other as they were from IBM.

Thus, Hitachi and Fujitsu did not perform the joint R&D that MITI expected them to, doing little more than agreeing on software compatibility standards, which were largely predetermined by IBM anyway, since they were pursuing an IBM-compatible strategy. Hitachi and Fujitsu then went off and did their own R&D. And the original MITI-led agreement on dividing up the market broke down when Fujitsu introduced a machine that had performance characteristics of the kind that only Hitachi was allowed to produce. Hitachi retaliated by bringing out a machine that moved into Fujitsu's assigned performance territory, and in the ensuing atmosphere of bad blood and mutual suspicion, any hopes of R&D cooperation were history.[15] Yet the joint Hitachi-Fujitsu organization, which became CDL when Mitsubishi joined it in 1975, continued to exist. Why? Because MITI wanted it to, and Fujitsu and Hitachi were receiving MITI subsidies and protection and did not want to offend MITI.

NEC-Toshiba relations were much more cordial, but that was because Toshiba had decided to de-prioritize its computer business, eventually pulling out of it in the middle of the VLSI project.[16] Toshiba was thus happy enough to let NEC take the lead in the joint venture company. An American analyst who conducted a series of interviews with NTIS managers concludes that the intention of the two companies "was never to combine the technological resources of NEC and Toshiba by pairing up to develop a computer system or its components jointly"; rather, the joint venture was seen "as a way to maintain good government-industry relations, receive government funds, and possibly divide up a product line."[17]

The companies in NTIS and CDL, when asked to manage the company labs in the VLSI consortium, assumed that they would adhere to past patterns—namely, provide an umbrella for independent R&D. The use of NTIS and CDL would give MITI the putatively cooperative structure that it wanted. And the companies would make occasional technical exchanges under these umbrellas in order minimally to fulfill MITI's demand for cooperation and receive MITI subsidies. But joint R&D was out of the question, and in the NTIS and CDL group labs, it did not occur.

A quick look at the group labs' organizational structure reveals the underlying reality. All of the group labs were always described by MITI and in the VLSI consortium literature as being CDL Lab 1, NTIS Lab 3, and so on, promoting the public relations goal of an appearance of joint ownership by CDL and NTIS. However, each of the CDL/NTIS labs were actually the private labs of the participating companies, as can be seen in Table 5. CDL's three labs consisted of a Hitachi lab, a Fujitsu lab, and a Mitsubishi lab, in which each company separately

TABLE 5

MITI VLSI Consortium Lab Structure

Lab	Company	Site
Joint lab	VLSI association (all 5 companies + ETL)	NEC Kawasaki
Group labs		
CDL 1	Fujitsu	Kawasaki
CDL 2, CDL Central	Hitachi	Musashino (Tokyo)
CDL 3	Mitsubishi	Itami (Osaka area)
NTIS	NEC	Sagamihara (Tokyo area)
NTIS	NEC	Tamagawa (Kawasaki)
NTIS	NEC	Fuchū (Tokyo)
NTIS	Toshiba	Horikawa-chō (Kawasaki)
NTIS	Toshiba	Komukai (Kawasaki)
NTIS	Toshiba	Ōme (Tokyo)

SOURCE: Laboratory locations are from *Chō LSI Gijutsu Kenkyū Kumiai* (VLSI Technology Research Association) 1990.

did its own work. NTIS had six labs, three for Toshiba and three for NEC, each also doing their own R&D.

This is not to say that no information exchange occurred. Again, the argument here is not that *no* cooperation occurred; rather, it is that cooperation was highly limited. As at the joint lab, each umbrella group, CDL and NTIS, had monthly technical meetings, where each company would describe what research it was doing with the funds allocated to it by CDL or NTIS headquarters. But this level of information exchange was a far cry from a truly cooperative relationship involving shared facilities and joint R&D. As one senior researcher puts it: "They had open conferences and produced thick reports. But of course the reports did not contain all the relevant information about know-how."[18]

This technical exchange appears to have been conducted with more openness and to a greater extent between NEC and Toshiba than between Fujitsu and Hitachi in CDL. While NEC and Toshiba had no interest in doing joint R&D together, they did hold review meetings at NTIS headquarters once a month and explained their projects to each other. The two companies viewed each other as competitors, but nonetheless exchanged "extremely detailed information."[19]

The basis for this greater information exchange was both historical and market-driven. First, historically NEC and Toshiba had a relatively amicable, if passive, relationship in NTIS, in contrast to the storms that rolled through Fujitsu and Hitachi's CDL. Thus, unlike that of Fujitsu and Hitachi, NEC and Toshiba's relationship was not poisoned by mutual suspicion, which had been aggravated in the former case by the two companies' grievances against each other during the early CDL years.

The market-driven reason for greater NTIS amicability is tied to this historical one. NEC and Toshiba were simply not competitors to the same degree as Fujitsu and Hitachi. NEC and Toshiba could be more amicable because their companies' strategic businesses did not overlap to nearly the same extent as those of Hitachi and Fujitsu, who were going toe-to-toe in the IBM-compatible mainframe market.

This divergence of strategic focus was reflected in their R&D assignments within the VLSI consortium—they focused on different markets, so they did different R&D. Figure 4 shows that CDL companies took on the same R&D tasks in three of their four assigned R&D areas, and Fujitsu and Hitachi did so in two areas, whereas the NTIS companies overlapped in none. In memory devices, Toshiba was the only participant that did not do DRAM (*Dynamic Random Access Memory*) R&D; instead, it focused on SRAMs (*Static Random Access Memory*),

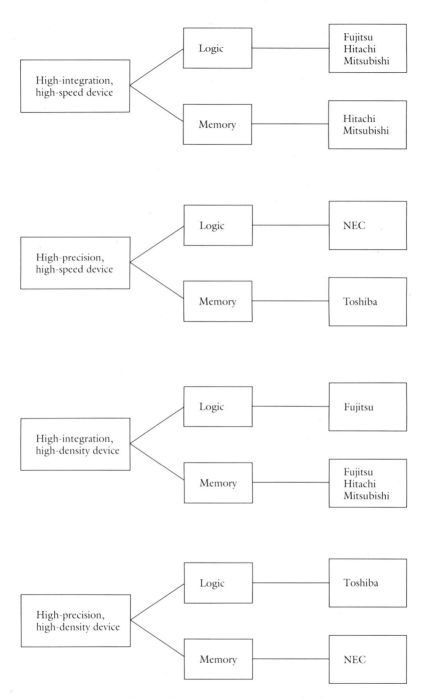

4. VLSI Joint Lab: Device R&D Division of Labor

a different kind of computer memory device, which is faster and more complicated in its internal structure, and thus more expensive than DRAMs. (Today, SRAMs tend to be used for small, fast specialized memory in computers, while the cheaper and slower DRAMs serve as main memory.) Toshiba did not put major energies into developing future DRAM products until the tail end of the consortium, and published reports had Toshiba even considering withdrawing from the DRAM business and getting supplies from NEC in 1979–80. With Toshiba focusing on developing markets for SRAMs and NEC focusing on DRAMs, they were not nearly in the same competitive conflict as Hitachi and Fujitsu, who were both focusing on DRAMs. Similarly, in the logic area, Toshiba withdrew from the mainframe business in favor of NEC in 1978, so they were not competing in that field either.

In reality, the elaborate division of labor shown in Figure 4 had two aspects. The first and central purpose was to separate out the research activities of all of the firms, so that they would each work on a separate area and all of them would then share the results. Toshiba, for example, was assigned "High Precision, High Speed Memory" and worked on fast SRAM memory—the other companies did not.

But the very minuteness of the division of labor reveals a second, ironic aspect, entirely contradictory to the first. This second purpose was to describe essentially identical tasks as being somehow different, therefore allowing different firms to work on the same technologies *under the appearance of a division of labor*. What was the difference between "High Precision, High Density Devices" and "High Integration, High Density Devices"? In the case of memory: nothing. They were both DRAMs. A corporate researcher explains: "There was no need to subdivide this up so carefully, but MITI did so out of fairness considerations. Every company [except Toshiba] wanted to do DRAMs. Thus, you could do it under 'highly integrated, high density' memory or you could also do it under 'highly precise, high density' memory."[20] In other words, sometimes the divison of labor was intended to separate R&D activities, and at other times it was supposed to disguise the *lack* of separation in R&D activities. This was yet another example of surface appearances in MITI high-tech consortia belying the underlying reality.

To sum up the CDL/NTIS group-lab story, the CDL and NTIS organizations largely served to funnel funds from MITI to the participating companies. In response to MITI's demands, they did do a certain amount of information exchange within each group, but the companies were not interested in actually doing cooperative R&D, and so they did not. They were a far cry from the "joint R&D organizations" that MITI intended them to be and described them as. Once again, the underlying reality was quite different from the public story.

The lesson here is that competitors within the VLSI consortium did not share information readily and certainly did not willingly do joint R&D together. When they were forced together into the joint lab, there was some joint creation of patentable technology, but for the most part the company researchers worked with other researchers from their own companies. When they interacted with researchers from different firms, they were typically from a weaker, less competitive firm, such as Mitsubishi.

And in the CDL/NTIS joint ventures, the major sites for VLSI consortium R&D, and where cooperative, applied R&D was supposed to take place, it did not. Although they were more likely to share information than Hitachi and Fujitsu, which considered each other to be major competitive threats in core business lines, companies that did not view each other so strongly as direct competitors, such as NEC and Toshiba, nonetheless guarded proprietary knowledge and refrained from joint R&D.

Even so, VLSI was, as we shall see, the peak of cooperative interaction between the companies. From VLSI onward, MITI faced increasing obstacles to the creation and effective management of its joint high-tech consortia. In VLSI, MITI may not have gotten the large joint lab that it wanted, it may not have gotten joint R&D in the NTIS/CDL group labs, it may not have gotten more than minimal joint research activities in the joint lab itself, but at least it got substantial corporate commitment to the VLSI consortium. MITI would soon discover, however, that the 1980's were the beginning of a new era, and it was not an era sympathetic to MITI-led technology initiatives.

The Supercomputer Consortium

As described in Chapter 4, the companies were not very interested in the supercomputer consortium and successfully resisted MITI's efforts to force them into a joint lab. Lack of a joint lab essentially meant that the companies would not be doing joint R&D, and indeed the patent data for the consortium show no intercompany joint patents.[21] Failing to achieve its first priority of a joint lab, MITI fell back onto a division-of-labor strategy for the consortium. The idea was that instead of cooperatively developing technologies through joint R&D, each company would do totally separate technologies, and then all companies would share their results.

The division-of-labor strategy was of course not new; MITI had tried to do the same in the group labs of the VLSI consortium. Also not new was the failure of the strategy. In the consortium's device research, companies frequently went ahead and did whatever related R&D they wanted, whether it adhered to the division of labor or not. In some of the device R&D and in the two cases of system development, the division of labor was maintained, but at the expense of knowledge sharing. MITI did manage to channel the companies into different research areas, but then was unable to get them to share information.

In addition to this division-of-labor strategy, MITI employed a number of other mechanisms to try to promote cooperation and information sharing. First, there was the *tōroku seido* (registration system), which was also used in VLSI, where company researchers recorded all of their relevant technical knowledge before beginning consortium-financed R&D. MITI also had the companies publish reports on their research activities, although strangely these reports did not seem to go to the other participating companies, an odd outcome for a putatively joint R&D consortium.[22]

MITI further used the steering committees that oversaw the consortium's technical progress to promote information flow. An ETL participant describes how this system worked:

> ETL people sit on the committee and ask questions. Basically, we force the company scientists to reveal their research by asking highly focused technical questions. Representatives from the other companies are sitting in the room as observers, waiting for their turn. The company guys don't necessarily want to answer in front of the other companies, but they have no choice, because they are being directly questioned by ETL people. So they answer, and all the other companies learn what they are doing and what their approach is.[23]

There were limits to what information could be gleaned in these brief and occasional interrogations, but in the absence of a joint lab, there were not a lot of other options for prying open often-secretive company R&D activities.

One final aspect of MITI's approach was its now-familiar public stance on cooperation within the consortium. MITI went to considerable lengths to promote the appearance of joint R&D, which obscured the fact that there were separate companies doing separate research within the consortium. The final conference report on the consortium in 1990, for example, lists participating firms as a group under each research category in the table of contents, creating the impression that the particular research area has been jointly investigated. Turning to any section that corresponds to a particular research category, however, one discovers that each research topic within that research area has a separate subsection, and these subsections frequently have different fonts and layouts. They have in fact been written separately by the companies that oversaw that work, but in the research descriptions no company names are ever mentioned. Not only have all company names been purged, but *sentences frequently have no subject*, so it is left unspecified as to who performed the research. Leaving out subjects in Japanese is grammatically possible. "In 1983 developed high-speed device" is a perfectly acceptable sentence in Japanese, and sentences like this appear everywhere in the conference report. As a consequence, seeing the table of contents, and given no evidence to believe otherwise in the report details itself, the unknowing reader is likely to assume that these research tasks were the joint work of the companies cited together in the table of contents, when in fact they were not.

Similarly, where consortium activities are described in English in the conference proceedings abstracts, again there are no company names. Since in English the dropping of the subject in the active voice results in bizarre headless sentences, the passive voice is almost always used. Alternatively, "we" is occasionally thrown in. In the case of a separately published English-language analysis of the project results, the favored phrase is "a group."[24] A group did X. A group did Y. A group also did Z. The reality is that these "groups" were in fact companies: Fujitsu did X, Hitachi did Y, and rarely did the twain meet. It would clearly be relevant and useful to know which companies were funded to do what research within the consortium, but explicit acknowledgment of who "we" were and who "a group" were would undercut the notion that MITI had led a "cooperative" R&D consortium.

We turn now to the saga of the constrained cooperation, competition, and conflict in the areas of devices, the image-processing supercomputer, and the vector supercomputer, the consortium's showcase "final system."

Ignoring the Division of Labor: Device Technology

For device research, MITI established a division of labor that had two conditions: (1) each company would work on a separate area; and (2) as they went along, they would share information about what they were learning on that topic with the other companies, which would similarly report on their own results. Both conditions went largely unfulfilled, because the companies had little interest in fulfilling them. They would take the MITI money and do their own research.

Like Herman Melville's Bartleby, the companies preferred not to co-

TABLE 6

The 1982–1983 Speed Race:
Major Josephson Junction and HEMT R&D Breakthrough Announcements

Date	Announced switching speed achieved (faster = better)	Organization	Type of device
3/29/82	20 picoseconds	ETL	Josephson junction
4/1/82	16.7 picoseconds (at room temperature) 12.8 picoseconds (at −196C)	Fujitsu	HEMT
4/9/82	10.8 picoseconds	NEC	Josephson junction
4/83	7 picoseconds	ETL	Josephson junction
5/83	6 picoseconds	NTT [Atsugi lab]	Josephson junction
9/83	5.6 picoseconds	Hitachi	Josephson junction

operate, because cooperation was an unnatural act. The companies were fierce competitors outside the consortium. When a survey of three participating firms in the mid 1980's asked them to rate the intensity of competition they felt toward their fellow participants, with 1 being "not competitive" and 5 "intensely competitive," all three scored 5 in each case.[25]

One aspect of this competition can be seen in Table 6, which shows device announcements in 1982–83. All the major players in low-temperature, high-speed computing devices on both the corporate side (Hitachi, Fujitsu, and NEC) and the public sector (MITI's Electro-technical Laboratory [ETL] and NTT's Electrical Communications Laboratory [ECL]) were active in pushing their device technology to world-class speed levels, and were very aggressive in promoting their own efforts over those of their technological competitors. Notice, for example, the period in late March–early April 1982. ETL started things off by announcing on March 29 that its Josephson junctions, cooled to the temperature of liquid helium (−270°C) could switch at 20 picoseconds, second in the world to IBM's 13 picoseconds.

Two days later, Fujitsu responded by announcing that it had bested both ETL and IBM with a HEMT device that at the temperature of liquid nitrogen (−196°C) could switch at 12.8 picoseconds. (HEMT, a type of gallium arsenide semiconductor that got extremely fast when cooled, was a Fujitsu innovation, and it believed quite strongly in the early 1980's that given the manufacturability advantages and less need for expensive cooling, HEMT was going to prove much more viable than Josephson junctions.)[26] *Eight days after Fujitsu,* NEC jumped into play, announcing that it had bested ETL and IBM and Fujitsu with a

Josephson junction that switched at 10.8 picoseconds. Over the next year and a half, NTT, Hitachi, and ETL all proceeded to make further public announcements of world record speeds in Josephson junctions.

This competing for media mind share is a common practice in Japan, where companies and research labs vie fiercely for top honors in technology advances. Following a major announcement of a technology breakthrough by one company or research organization, if you look carefully at the newspapers in the next few days, you are almost certain to see coverage of announcements by competing organizations declaring that they too have made a breakthrough in the same area.

It was in this competitive environment that MITI failed to achieve a joint lab and settled for a cooperative division-of-labor approach. MITI's device division of labor in shown in Table 7. In coaxing them into joining the consortium, MITI had given the firms latitude in deciding what research they would do, so this R&D division of labor reflected the companies' research interests. Nonetheless, companies appear not to have hesitated to poach on the R&D territory of the other companies and do their own research in that area also. "In the case of devices, a number of companies did the same research, the exact same research," observes one consortium participant.[27]

In Josephson junctions, for example, Fujitsu was supposed to do high-speed logic and Hitachi high-integration logic, but some of Fujitsu's devices were more integrated than Hitachi's and some of Hitachi's ran at faster clocks than Fujitsu's. An ETL manager acknowledges:

Josephson junctions on the surface looked like a division of labor, but the truth was it was competition. Each company had its own technology and own agenda for what they wanted to do. We divided everything up to be different— different densities, different speeds—but the results looked about the same.

TABLE 7

Supercomputer Consortium: Breakdown of Device R&D Division of Labor

Device	Research task	Company
Josephson junction	High Speed Logic	Fujitsu
	High Integration Logic	Hitachi
	Memory	NEC
Gallium arsenide	High Speed Logic	Toshiba
	High Integration Logic	NEC
	High Speed Memory	Hitachi
	High Integration Memory	Mitsubishi
HEMT	HEMT	Fujitsu
	Reverse HEMT	Oki

The speed people worked on density, the density people worked on speed, and they all ended up around the middle.[28]

Similarly, in gallium arsenide devices, research was broken up into separate logic and memory efforts, but since the logic R&D performed was on a particular technology called "gate arrays," which has a very uniform layout and is thus "technologically not very different" from memory devices, the firms were working on much the same issues, despite the apparent distinction between "logic" and "memory."[29] While the gallium arsenide division of labor between "high speed" and "high integration" appears to have been formally maintained between Hitachi and Mitsubishi in memory, the lines were sufficiently blurred that one of the participants doing system work in the consortium mentioned in an interview that his company had taken on R&D in the area that actually had been assigned to the other company.[30] In the logic area, Toshiba and NEC ran all over each other's assigned domains. Toshiba was to do high-speed logic and NEC high-integration logic, but some of Toshiba's devices had higher gate densities than NEC's, and NEC returned the favor by building devices that had substantially higher clock rates than Toshiba's.

The companies also failed to cooperate on information exchange. Martin Fransman notes that there was a "consensus" among those he interviewed that knowledge sharing was minimal.[31] For Josephson junctions, there was some joint activity at the beginning of the consortium, because all of the companies considered themselves far behind IBM and pooled some of the information they learned about U.S. JJ activities. However, when actual R&D began, the companies went their separate paths.[32] And in HEMT devices, Oki and Fujitsu "did not cooperate at all—they just exchanged information for the past six months," much of which was already available in the public domain, having been published by the researchers.[33]

Three Companies + Three Computers = One Supercomputer?
The Graphics Supercomputer

The joint development of the consortium's special-purpose supercomputer for image processing by Mitsubishi, Oki, and Toshiba would seem to be a textbook case of MITI-coordinated cooperation that worked smoothly and well. In contrast to the struggles between Hitachi, Fujitsu, and NEC that will be described in the next section, the three second-tier companies in the Supercomputer consortium got along quite well. During the long design period for their graphics supercomputer, they had many joint meetings, typically at least once a month, and it is generally agreed that these meetings took place in an atmosphere of openness and cooperation.[34]

During the final year of the consortium, when the integration of the three companies' subsystems took place, researchers from all of the companies got together in a room that had been arranged by Toshiba right near the Kawasaki JR train station and successfully brought all of the pieces together into a functioning whole. During that time, researchers from all three companies frequently went drinking together in the evenings, creating what one researcher described as a *nakama ishiki* (loosely translated, "a buddy mentality").[35]

However, this rosy picture of gentle cooperation hides as much as it reveals. In the first place, the "image-processing supercomputer" that the three companies developed was actually three different computers, each independently designed and built by the respective companies. Toshiba built a 16-processor computer specializing in numerical computation, Mitsubishi built a massively parallel computer with several thousand processors, and Oki built a specialized graphics computer. The cooperative design meetings and the cooperative final integration effort were all focused on designing a high-speed *communications channel* that could connect these three machines, so that at the end of the project, the three computers could be connected together and declared to be a single, jointly developed computer. One participating engineer describes this process as typical of MITI projects, where all the companies do their own work and then at the end try to come up with a combined system "that's not strange."[36]

In linking these three computers together, the three companies knew that the key was satisfying MITI's requirement to create something that was both "joint" and "not strange," so there was no need for the system to be particularly fast (even though that is in fact what supercomputers are supposed to be).[37] The machines just had to be able to work when connected together, and that the companies managed to do just fine.

Because the three companies, unlike Fujitsu, Hitachi, and NEC, were not rivals in the supercomputer area and moreover were working independently on their three machines and merely had to discuss the proper way to interconnect them, discussions could proceed fairly smoothly. "There was our own technology that as a company we could not reveal to them, did not reveal to them, but with respect to the interface, the discussions were 100 percent open," says one researcher.[38] An engineer from a different company confirms that his company did not fear any leakage of proprietary knowledge to the other two firms either, because after all the only thing they were creating jointly was the communications interface.[39]

In sum, the Supercomputer consortium's image-processing supercomputer is not a case of the cooperative development of a single computer but rather a story of three firms working on their separate machines and doing some cooperative make-work at MITI's demand to give their efforts a sense of "jointness." This loose linkage of efforts is in striking contrast to the tight integration of effort demanded by MITI of Hitachi, NEC, and Fujitsu in the case of their vector supercomputer "final system," which typifies what can go wrong when MITI takes its own rhetoric about creating cooperation between competitors seriously.

"The Companies Just Don't Trust Each Other": The Mammoth Vector Supercomputer

The effort to create the world's fastest supercomputer was the showpiece of the Supercomputer consortium, and the top three Japanese computer makers, NEC, Fujitsu, and Hitachi, were assigned to the job. This so-called "final system" absorbed most of the funding for systems development. It was also a miserable failure, both in terms of the design process and the final technical result. The final system was a headache for all parties, most especially Fujitsu, which had the final responsibility for successfully completing it and was given neither the funds nor the cooperative partners to do so.

The vector supercomputer started out with a number of strikes against it. First, it brought together NEC, Fujitsu, and Hitachi, companies that were vicious competitors in the supercomputer market and deeply suspicious of one another. Second, the vector effort had a high level of integration and more of the characteristics of a single computer than the "three machines connected together and described as one computer" developed by Oki, Mitsubishi, and Toshiba. Fujitsu was in charge of the CPU subsystem and systems integration, NEC of the memory subsystem, and Hitachi of the "compiler" software, which translates higher-level software code written by programmers into the 1's and 0's that computers can understand. Thus, a high degree of cooperation was demanded of the three companies.

Third, again unlike the image-processing supercomputer, which was made up of more futuristic experimental systems, the vector supercomputer was much closer to the marketplace, largely using existing technologies. In fact, existing Fujitsu supercomputers were the basis for Fujitsu's CPU subsystem. Thus, in order for NEC and Hitachi to best integrate their subsystems with Fujitsu's CPU subsystem, Fujitsu was called upon to provide detailed, highly proprietary information on an existing product to its main competitors, something that it ultimately could not bring itself to do. Vicious competitors, demand for tight integration, use of existing technologies—three strikes, and the vector final system was out.

But in the planning phases of the Supercomputer consortium, none of these problems were seen as insurmountable. MITI thought the companies would work together, because they had told MITI they would work together, and it was *their job* to work together. And in fact in the final evaluation of the Supercomputer consortium in 1990, the MITI-sponsored evaluation committee said the vector supercomputer project met all its goals and called it a success. This (inaccurate) statement will be taken up later in this book; what follows here looks at the period up to the finishing of the final system and describes the deep strife and conflict that occurred.

Self-Help in the Development Years, 1984–1988

Coordination of the three subsystems for the vector supercomputer proved to be a nightmare. None of the three companies had much interest in helping the others, clearly a problem when the final system depended so much on tight integration of the three efforts. Most of the burdens fell on Fujitsu, which as the main contractor for the vector supercomputer, ultimately had to shoulder responsibility for it and thus was the only company truly motivated to make the system happen. But even Fujitsu appears to have been torn by an internal struggle between those who were trying to make the Fujitsu consortium effort successful and other Fujitsu managers who were against Fujitsu doing anything to promote the consortium effort if it risked leaking Fujitsu proprietary information to NEC and Hitachi. This internal Fujitsu struggle had implications for the degree of cooperation it received from NEC and Hitachi, since it resulted in restrictions on the flow of information from Fujitsu to the other two, a situation that hardly invited decisions on NEC's and Hitachi's part to be highly cooperative.

"Companies did the absolute minimum of information exchange," recalls an ETL scientist. "In fact, Fujitsu, the main contractor, was upset that they weren't getting much information from the other companies."[40] A Fujitsu executive who was not an official participant, and thus watched the goings-on from the sidelines, confirms: "There was a lot of suffering on that project. . . . The problem with doing stuff that is close to the market is that it's a pain to try to make it happen. The backstabbing starts immediately."[41] The problem was that the other two companies had never really been interested in the consortium and had been roped in by MITI. Stuck in the consortium largely against their will, they considered it Fujitsu's baby—after all, Fujitsu was the main contractor. NEC and Hitachi were thus unwilling to devote more than the bare minimum of personnel and resources to the effort. "It's true we as a company had other things to do," a researcher from one of the two companies admits. "People are valuable, and we didn't help Fujitsu that much."[42]

It is important to be clear that this lack of active cooperation among the company researchers was more a response to the needs of corporate middle managers than to the desires of the researchers themselves. As in all of the other consortia studied here, researchers who were assigned to the consortia efforts were torn between their two roles: their first and primary identity as an employee of a particular company, and their secondary identity as a member of the consortium effort. As consortia participants, most of them had every desire to do the best job that they could.

Even in the case of the vector supercomputer, the researchers themselves were perfectly willing and able to get along. For example, during the final year of integration, when Fujitsu forbade the NEC and Hitachi researchers to ride on the Fujitsu company bus from the train station to the plant, the Fujitsu researchers showed their solidarity by joining their colleagues from Hitachi and NEC in taxis to the plant. "The researchers themselves really tried hard and worked really well together," says an engineer from one of the other two companies.[43] It appears that left to themselves, the researchers might well have cooperated fully and harmoniously.

In contrast to company *researchers*, company *managers* had a standing preference *against* research cooperation. The companies' managers ran businesses in extremely fierce and competitive markets, however, and they considered their researchers extremely valuable resources, proprietary to their companies. The managers therefore tried to make sure that the researchers' roles as "company men" were not compromised by cooperative research in the consortium.[44]

It was in this context, then, that Hitachi, Fujitsu, and NEC squabbled over the sharing of information about the interfaces between Fujitsu's CPU subsystem and the other two subsystems. Fujitsu itself was not forthcoming with access to the supercomputers it was using for its CPU subsystem, so both Hitachi and NEC were *forced to build simu-*

lators of how they thought the Fujitsu CPU's would function, based upon the much more general information Fujitsu was willing to make available. Thus, during the development of their own subsystems, NEC and Hitachi never had an opportunity to test their interaction with the actual Fujitsu CPU's—all development was done using the simulators, which NEC and Hitachi built separately.

The degree of dependency between subsystems was highest between Hitachi and Fujitsu, since Hitachi was writing a new parallel programming language and a compiler that targeted the Fujitsu CPU's. Here Hitachi and Fujitsu clashed not only on the subject of access to Fujitsu's CPU and CPU specifications, with Hitachi ultimately building a simulator of Fujitsu's CPU. They also faced off on the appropriate target for Hitachi's compiler. Hitachi naturally expected that if it was going to write a compiler, it would target Fujitsu's CPU and produce software code (so-called binaries) that would run unaltered on the Fujitsu subsystem.

However, to allow Hitachi to write binary software that would automatically run on the Fujitsu subsystem would have required providing extremely detailed information on the inner workings of the Fujitsu CPU, which Fujitsu did not want to do. Instead, Fujitsu created a higher-level interface layer for Hitachi's compiler to write to. The output of Hitachi's compiler would be so-called "source code," which could not run on the Fujitsu machine until Fujitsu's own compiler translated it into binary code that the Fujitsu CPU could actually run. This resulted in a bizarre two-compiler compilation process.

Hitachi in turn retaliated by not porting its compiler to the Fujitsu CPU subsystem. The official reason given was that Hitachi had run out of time and could not do it by the end of the project, but this was obviously *tatemae*.[45] The compiler was largely written in Pascal, and despite some differences between Fujitsu and Hitachi flavors of Pascal, it could have been moved quite easily. The real reason was that "if we converted it so that it ran on Fujitsu's machine, then Fujitsu would be able to just go off and use it, and we basically didn't want that to happen. That reflects the tension that existed between the two companies."[46] This was yet another bizarre outcome: the compiler that targeted the Fujitsu machine could not itself run on the Fujitsu machine and had to be transferred from the Hitachi machine via a communication channel. This conflict between Hitachi and Fujitsu resulted in a software product that was highly compromised, a perverse manifestation of the lack of cooperation between the two.

On-Site at Numazu, 1989: The Final (Dis?)Integration

With the 1990 deadline for the end of the consortium closing in, Hitachi, NEC, and Fujitsu got together in 1989 to integrate their disparate subsystems.[47] The location for this work was Fujitsu's Numazu works, about one and a half hours' drive southwest of Tokyo in the direction of Mount Fuji. Numazu was the vector supercomputer's tragicomic denouement.

Fujitsu had real problems with the idea that engineers from its bitter rivals were going to be coming to one of its factories, and it took measures to "protect" itself. This was not the first time this had happened in a MITI consortium. The VLSI joint lab had been at NEC's Miyazawa-dai works, and NEC built a separate entrance and a separate cafeteria for the joint lab researchers to prevent them from seeing other parts of the site. In Numazu, Fujitsu took a page from NEC's VLSI playbook and went to great lengths to restrict the movements of the NEC and Hitachi engineers.

For the convenience of its employees, Fujitsu ran a bus at frequent intervals from the station for the bullet train from Tokyo to Numazu, but NEC and Hitachi engineers were not allowed on it, for fear that they might overhear Fujitsu secrets along the way. Instead, they had to take taxis, thirty minutes in each direction, twice a day, for six months.

When the NEC and Hitachi engineers arrived at the Fujitsu plant, they were escorted to their rooms. Hitachi had one room, and NEC had another. They were to stay in their rooms, unless they had to go to the bathroom, which was nearby. The Hitachi and NEC engineers were not allowed to use the cafeteria, again for fear that they might overhear Fujitsu secrets there. Instead, food was brought to them in their rooms.

Access to the vector supercomputer prototype itself was restricted. "We weren't allowed to use the Fujitsu [subsystem], or even see [it]," a Hitachi engineer recalled in 1992. "We had to ask a Fujitsu person to take the programs we wanted to run to the machine. That person would disappear and go run it, and then come back and give us the results. The first time we were allowed to see the final system was the public unveiling ceremony at the end of the project."[48] He repeatedly emphasized that he was not singling out Fujitsu for criticism. "This isn't just Fujitsu's problem," he said. "The same thing would have happened if our company had been in charge. The companies just don't trust each other."[49]

The Fifth Generation Consortium

The intercompany conflict that arose with Supercomputer was not nearly such an issue in the case of Fifth Generation. This was for two reasons. First, the size of the Fifth Generation joint lab was limited, with most of the money going to work done separately at the company's private labs; moreover, outside the joint lab, Fifth Generation did not call for nearly the degree of cooperation that Supercomputer's vector supercomputer did. Second, ICOT, the Fifth Generation research institute, did basic research in the most basic sense of the word. As described earlier, many of the companies thought that ICOT was sorely off-track, pursuing obscure technologies in such a specialized way that it had little hope of creating anything directly relevant to the computer market. Ironically, the sheer irrelevance of ICOT to near- or midterm competition thus made it possible for the companies to allow the few researchers they had at ICOT's joint lab to work together—it could do no harm. These two reasons for lessened intercompany conflict are examined in more detail below.

Keep It Small: ICOT's Joint Lab

In size and nature, ICOT's joint lab was in many ways quite similar to the compromise that had been struck between MITI and the companies over the VLSI joint lab. First, ICOT's research staff was limited in size, starting off at a little over 30 researchers and growing to just 100 by the end of the consortium. Moreover, ICOT had a substantially larger "in-house" research staff than the VLSI lab, which had a few researchers from ETL and was almost entirely staffed by the five participating companies, which contributed on average around 20 researchers apiece. In contrast, by the end, ICOT appears to have had on the order of 20–25 researchers on its own payroll and got contributions of researchers from 18 organizations.

The number of researchers any one company sent to ICOT was thus quite small. From interviews it appears that the major firms contributed 5–10 researchers apiece to ICOT, with the peak period being the mid 1980's. In contrast, these companies typically had three or four or five times as many engineers doing their own ICOT-funded work independently in their own company labs. The funding situation mirrored this distribution of personnel: in 1987, for example, 80 percent of the funds went to the companies, who did contract work for ICOT.[50]

ICOT and the companies also had a division of labor similar to that which had existed between the VLSI joint lab and group labs. In the main, ICOT focused on software development and more basic research. ICOT developed the system software for all of the ICOT computers. Hardware development and the actual implementation of this system software on those hardware platforms were, however, done entirely by the companies at their private labs.

Intercompany collaboration on building these computers was minimal in the early period, and it declined from then on. As regards ICOT's very first hardware, PSI and CHI, there was some collaboration on the "firmware" (software that is permanently stored in memory hardware) between Oki and Mitsubishi on PSI, but Mitsubishi did the hardware itself and NEC also did CHI alone.[51] Work on ICOT's final computer, PIM, was done independently. Says one corporate researcher about the PIM development process:

There is almost no information sharing between the firms. ICOT contracts *separately* with [the three companies that did the initial PIM work] and so there is no discussion between the firms. . . . In the initial stage—in building the 10 processor parallel system—we had some cooperation because this was the very early stage. But in the second stage, 100 processors is a large system and so we don't like to share knowledge. . . . The companies want to do their research inside the company.[52]

PIM came in five different versions, each built by a separate company, and each slightly incompatible with the others because of different hardware architecture, different microprocessor instruction sets, and so forth. ICOT put the best face it could on these five disparate PIM computers, declaring that the differences allowed for innovation in design.

There was a certain truth to this, although it was also true that the range of innovation was quite constrained, given that all five machines are based on ICOT's PIM architecture. ICOT's PIMs were five machines that were "mostly the same, but slightly different." Since this slight difference came at the cost of software compatibility, it was a fairly heavy price to pay.[53] At any rate, it is likely that the real reason that the five PIM machines were different was that it would have been impossible to get the companies to agree on common specifications.

The Companies Resign Themselves to ICOT's Research

To proceed to the second reason for the lack of intercompany warfare in Fifth Generation, the whole enterprise appeared to its corporate participants to be so speculative and futuristic that no company really perceived any potential competitive threat emerging from the project. As one Japanese observer presciently observed before the consortium started up, "No one knows if there are really big markets for these projects; only if big profits seem apparent will they [the companies] start to fight each other."[54] In the end, no big profits loomed, and no fighting began. ICOT was not torn by the suspicions and conflict of the Supercomputer consortium or even the VLSI joint lab in its early years—there was a consensus among those interviewed that within the ICOT joint lab itself the researchers interacted in a cooperative way. One company manager notes, "It was pretty cooperative over at ICOT. After all, it was basic R&D."[55]

Nonetheless, again reminiscent of VLSI, despite the cooperative atmosphere, an examination of ICOT publications suggests that most in-depth cooperation between researchers from different organizations took place, not between companies, but between researchers from companies paired with ICOT researchers. While joint publications between company researchers do exist, they are few and far between. Even when the walls between companies appear to have been broken down, company researchers tended to seek "neutral parties" in their choice of joint R&D partners.

The TRON Consortium

In truth, TRON is more of a standards-setting organization than an R&D consortium. Participating firms agree on common interfaces and then go off and do their own work. This can be seen by looking through the papers presented at international TRON conferences since 1987: there are hardly any joint papers between firms. Joint publications between NTT and its suppliers for CTRON—a very different kind of interfirm interaction than that between competitors—are the exception. This is not to say that there are *no* instances of joint activity between competing firms, but the few papers that have been jointly produced typically focus, not on development issues, but on more general activities, like creating a common bus specification or standardizing performance benchmarks.

One would expect that given its private nature, there would be more inherent interest in TRON than in the explicitly MITI-led Fifth Generation and Supercomputer consortia. But, in fact, in addition to NEC's violent opposition to BTRON, there was a considerable amount of half-hearted participation among other companies. Toshiba, too, seemed to be quite reluctant to participate, joining only after all of the other major firms were on board.

It is unsurprising, then, that in the TRON consortium there was a general lack of cohesiveness between members because of differences in interests: Matsushita wanted to do BTRON, Hitachi and Fujitsu were more interested in the TRON chip, NEC in ITRON, and so on. As a result, one finds a surprising lack of interdependence between the TRON subprojects—the BTRON software that Matsushita wrote, for example, did not target the TRON chip. It targeted Intel microprocessors, the sworn foe of the TRON chip developers. In turn the TRON House and TRON Building plans made use of non-TRON computers and microprocessors. ITRON also runs on top of a number of different microprocessors other than the TRON chip—some companies want it on top of Intel, some on top of Motorola microprocessors. And, of course, in the specific case that we focus on here, BTRON pitted NEC against all of the other top Japanese manufacturers.

The TRON chip that was left out of the BTRON specifications is the sorriest tale of a lack of coordination between the TRON members, since there was such an obvious commonality of interest. All of the TRON chip makers needed to band together to create enough critical mass to overcome the market advantages of Intel, Motorola, and to a lesser extent the new U.S. RISC (*R*educed *I*nstruction *S*et *C*omputer) microprocessor firms.[56] TRON was a brand-new architecture, and no software existed for it. It faced a daunting uphill battle to penetrate microprocessor markets. This was the same battle that U.S. RISC makers fought, but the U.S. firms managed to turn their weakness into strength. Being too small to create new microprocessor markets alone, they turned to alliances with large multinational semiconductor vendors, including all of the Japanese firms in the TRON consortium. To create critical mass, the U.S. RISC firms made sure that the microprocessors within their particular family of RISC chips—Sun Microsystems' SPARC, the Mips R series, Hewlett Packard's Precision, Digital Equipment's Alpha—were standardized.[57] Thus, a customer buying a SPARC chip from, say, Fujitsu, would know that it was strictly software-compatible ("binary compatible" is the term the industry uses) with a SPARC chip made by Cypress Semiconductor.

This is a sharp contrast to the TRON chip producers. Even though each TRON vendor is supposedly producing standard TRON microprocessors, their chips are in fact incompatible. This incompatibility exists in both the microprocessor's internal "instruction set" and its external packaging. (The number and formats of a microprocessor's instruction set are the primary determinants of compatibility and interoperability. If different microprocessors use different instructions, software written to make use of one microprocessor's instructions cannot

TABLE 8

TRON Companies' Incompatible TRON Microprocessor Designs

Category	Mitsubishi	Hitachi	Fujitsu	Oki	Toshiba	Matsushita
Microprocessor instruction count	92	122	135	102	93	93
Microprocessor Layout ("Packaging")	135-pin PGA 152-pin QFP	135-pin PGA	178-pin PGA 208-pin SQFP	176-pin PGA	155-pin PGA 144-pin QFP	144-pin PGA 148-pin QFP

SOURCE: TRON Association 1992: 36–38.

run on top of a different microprocessor. The software will assume the existence of instructions that exist on the first microprocessor but not on the second.) In the case of the TRON chips, Table 8 shows that the instruction-set counts are different, so we can know by definition that software that makes complete use of each TRON microprocessor's different instructions will not run on the other TRON chips.[58] Ergo: the supposedly standardized TRON chips are in fact software-incompatible.

Moreover, the "packaging" or physical configuration of the microprocessors is also incompatible. The TRON chips come in different standard shapes and with different "pin counts" (meaning the number of "pins" or interconnections necessary to connect the chip to a computer board). This is not nearly as much of a problem as the software incompatibility created by different instruction sets, but different packaging means that a computer manufacturer that wants to switch from one TRON chip to another has to redesign its computer board to accommodate the different chip layout. This can be expensive. Standardizing packaging would probably have helped the TRON chip break into the microprocessor market by promising customers lower switching costs and vigorous competition without design lock-ins. In short, given the TRON chip's weak market position as a late entrant into the 1980's microprocessor wars, if the TRON consortium had been truly interested in creating a unified, standard family of chips, the companies would have standardized both instruction sets and packaging.

Even within the G-Micro group of TRON makers, which was set up to resolve these standardization differences, Hitachi, Fujitsu, and Mitsubishi remain incompatible. This is truly pathetic. There is no other word to describe it. Here were all of these companies trying to create a new standardized architecture—they needed every advantage they could get in order to try to appeal to potential users. Yet, their incompatibilities fragmented the market and blocked achievement of any kind of critical mass as a platform for software development.

TRON also created internal company discord. There were primarily two types of battles: (1) between existing PC groups and TRON PC backers and (2) between TRON chip and RISC chip groups. These battles took their toll on Fujitsu's TRON effort. When Fujitsu was considering joining TRON, Fujitsu systems people did not want Fujitsu to do TRON software. They saw TRON as consuming resources that would be better used on existing Fujitsu system software. These anti-TRON forces won the battle to have Fujitsu focus solely on the TRON chip—Fujitsu treats TRON as primarily a semiconductor project, not a computer project. Similarly, in the TRON versus RISC battle, despite Fujitsu's work on the TRON chip, Fujitsu's RISC microprocessor division continues aggressively to promote its Sun Microsystems–based SPARC microprocessor designs. And Mitsubishi announced its support for DEC's Alpha in March 1993, so all of the major Japanese companies who are ostensibly still backing TRON have lined up with U.S. RISC microprocessor designs. The TRON chip seems to be on the ropes.

To sum up, rather than there being a unified group of companies backing TRON, it is more accurate to describe the consortium as a loose-knit group of companies, brought together under a single banner, but disagreeing about goals and priorities. NEC fought with the other manufacturers about BTRON, and intercompany and internal company battles continue to plague the TRON program.

SIX

What Went Wrong? What Went Right?

Success and Failure Among Japanese High-Tech Consortia

> TRON is not a project. TRON is a religion. It is a
> question of fundamental belief—some people believe in
> it, some people do not.
> > Gerhard Frieder, dean of the School of Engineering,
> > George Washington University

> Fifth Generation didn't anticipate changes in the com-
> puter world. . . . The bureaucrats build a ten-year plan,
> then they don't change it. The world changes and the
> bureaucrats don't change the plan. They stick to the
> original goal.
> > Industry member of the Fifth Generation
> > planning committee

As we have seen, of VLSI, Supercomputer, Fifth Generation, and
TRON, it is only the VLSI consortium that can be considered a genuine
success. This is more because of the effectiveness of MITI subsidies in
signaling and triggering corporate investment than for the reasons typically given, such as the efficiencies of joint R&D.[1] In contrast to VLSI's
success, Supercomputer and Fifth Generation largely chased exotic
technologies that did not pay off, and technical problems and divergences of opinion between first MITI and the Ministry of Education
and then the Japanese and U.S. governments killed off the TRON PC's
chance to become the new PC standard in Japan's schools.

In analyzing VLSI, Supercomputer, Fifth Generation, and TRON,
the primary measure of success is whether or not the consortium met
its stated goals. This is natural: when a government agency proposes a
plan that promises certain outcomes and then consumes money, years,
and human talent implementing that plan, the first step is to figure out
whether or not the agency achieved what it said it would achieve.

In addition, where they loom important, I also look at *spillover effects*, consequences of consortia activities, perhaps unanticipated, that
are of a broader or longer-term nature.[2] These spillovers can be either

positive or negative. An example of a potential positive spillover is the training of engineers: when the consortium is over, engineers take their consortium knowledge with them, potentially to put it to use in their companies' future products. Finally, I examine potential *opportunity costs* (in simplest terms, the costs of missed opportunities): were there, for example, approaches or technologies that would have had better payoffs than the ones chosen?[3]

The VLSI Consortium

The VLSI consortium was successful (1) in meeting its goals; (2) in having an important spillover effect in promoting Japanese production of semiconductor equipment; and (3) in minimizing potential opportunity costs.

VLSI Goals and Achievements

MITI essentially stated three VLSI goals: (1) to cushion Japanese companies against trade liberalization; (2) to catch up to IBM; and (3) to promote VLSI technologies as a core element in computers, a strategic industry. The consortium succeeded on all three counts. Nonetheless, it is important to point out that the existence of the government-sponsored VLSI consortium was far from sufficient to ensure the triumph of the Japanese companies in DRAM computer memory and their rapid advance in other semiconductor technologies. After all, the historical evidence is abundant that pumping government money into losing companies or industries frequently just means turning low-cost bankruptcies into costly ones.

Rather, the consortium can be considered a success in the sense that MITI and NTT VLSI efforts gave companies with existing technical and manufacturing strengths the financial incentives, and more broadly speaking, the confidence, to aggressively target VLSI technology. With an estimated 85 percent of the funds flowing to the companies' private labs, the companies got money that they desperately needed. This, not any efficiencies from joint R&D, was the most important element of the VLSI consortium. MITI provided the firms with large-scale financial subsidies at a time when they were in financial crisis, and the companies were able to apply these funds directly to market-relevant, competitive technologies in their own private R&D labs.

In this regard, it is important to understand the context for the establishment of the VLSI consortium, for it was a response to a much more fundamental and far-reaching MITI policy decision that took place at the same time. The most important MITI policy in 1975–76 in the

Japanese computer and semiconductor industries was emphatically *not* the VLSI consortium, although the VLSI effort seems to get all of the publicity and analytical attention. Much more decisive was the full liberalization of the computer and semiconductor markets in 1975–76, a decision made by MITI in response to U.S. pressure. MITI had finally succumbed to U.S. pressure in 1973 and set up a timetable for liberalization of these industries in 1975–76, giving MITI and the Japanese firms several years' warning and time to prepare for the new competitive regime.

Thus, the setting up of the VLSI consortium was explicitly seen by MITI and Japanese industry as in part a response to this more fundamental market-opening decision. Through ventures such as the VLSI consortium, MITI reaffirmed its commitment to the Japanese firms that it was not cutting them loose to perish under the barrage of foreign competition. MITI was with the firms, and the ending of MITI-supervised protectionism did not mean the end of MITI policies of support for the industry.

The liberalizing of the Japanese computer and semiconductor markets had far-reaching implications, ones that are a quite natural consequence of the end of protection as described by classical economic theory. There were two major implications. *First*, as a natural consequence of the increased competition from the United States, which continued to command substantial advantages over a broad array of computer and semiconductor technologies, Japanese firms had to compete harder and smarter. They could no longer count on MITI using import controls to keep superior U.S. products out of the Japanese market and had to learn how to compete head-to-head with the Americans or risk losing control of their own turf.

The most obvious consequence of this was that Japanese firms had to invest extremely heavily in more advanced equipment, to upgrade their facilities and processes to world-class levels. It also called upon the Japanese to increase their R&D activities substantially, so that they could bring new advanced products to market at the same time as the U.S. firms. In the past, if the U.S. firms were first to market, MITI would simply block their sales into Japan while the Japanese firms either licensed the U.S. technology or figured out how to copy or better it without licensing. This was now over.

The *second* major effect was that liberalization of the Japanese market forced the major Japanese firms, for the very first time, to seek export markets for their semiconductor products. In the past, while it was a disadvantage for Japanese firms to sell only into the small (but growing) Japanese semiconductor market, since they could not achieve the vital economies of scale for low-cost semiconductor production and to amortize the costs of advanced R&D over a larger sales base, it was not particularly significant, since they could sell to Japanese customers behind MITI's wall of protection. However, with the dismantling of these walls in 1975–76, the Japanese firms realized that being small producers for the Japanese market would cripple them in competition with U.S. firms that achieved economies of scale by selling worldwide. Japanese firms therefore began to set up overseas sales operations for the first time. They had to export or die.

This gives new meaning to the shock of IBM's secret Future System documents. Not only did IBM appear to be poised to smash its Japanese competitors with VLSI technology that far outstripped the Japanese capabilities, it was going to be able to bring this technology to bear on the Japanese market without MITI being able to protect the Japanese firms.

The Japanese firms were thus both facing impending market liberalization that would forever end their protected hold on the Japanese market and simultaneously forced to invest hugely to upgrade technologically for what was believed to be the coming U.S. onslaught. They had every reason to believe it was coming. Texas Instruments (TI), the only foreign semiconductor firm with manufacturing facilities in Japan, was in the mid 1970's prone to starting price wars to grab market share. The Japanese firms bled red ink every time TI did so, and they believed these kinds of attacks would accelerate dramatically after market liberalization.

To ready themselves for this onslaught of more technologically sophisticated U.S. firms, the Japanese semiconductor firms had to invest hugely, but they had very little money to do so. When MITI locked Japan into the liberalization timetable of 1975–76 in 1973, it had no way of knowing that the following year OPEC would plunge the industrialized world into a terrible recession. More dependent on imported oil than any economy in the world, Japan reeled under the blow of soaring oil prices. Economic output plummeted for the first time since World War II—inflation surged to 18 percent, the highest in the industrialized world. Every Japanese semiconductor company was losing money. With word of the IBM Future System, they were desperate for help. They believed they needed government money to survive.

The funding that came through the VLSI consortium was, in fact, HUGE. Table 9 shows that at its peak, VLSI consortium funding paid for around three-quarters of *total* R&D in the semiconductor industry,

TABLE 9

TABLE 9

VLSI Consortium Spending Compared to Total Japanese
Semiconductor Industry R&D and Capital Investment

(unit: ¥ billion)

Year	R&D spending	Capital investment	VLSI consortium budget	VLSI budget /R&D spending	VLSI budget /R&D and capital investment
1976	24	35	7	29%	12%
1977	24	22	17	71%	37%
1978	88	46	20	23%	15%
1979	55	84	14	25%	10%

SOURCE: Industry data from *Nihon handōtai nenkan* (Japan Semiconductor Yearbook) 1985: 101.

with around 40 percent of those funds coming from MITI. Financing on this scale was clearly significant in easing the transition of the companies into the brave new world of liberalized competition.

Another way of putting this is that the key to the success of the VLSI consortium was *not* the joint lab.[4] It was the work done in the companies' private labs (the so-called group labs) with MITI funds. The joint lab represented what might be called the "joint R&D effect" of the consortium. It aimed at creating common and basic technologies for application by all of the participating manufacturers, above all to the 1-megabit generation of DRAMs. This joint R&D effect was not nearly as significant as the VLSI funding for work in the independent labs, for despite contributions, particularly in crystal technology, overall joint-lab R&D did not pay off very well.

The main problem was that the major effort of the joint lab, which half of the sublabs concentrated upon, was in microfabrication technology, the development of new production techniques for the greater device density of future generations of integrated circuits.

Here the joint lab guessed wrong. It did not guess badly, for the assumptions it made about future technology trajectories were entirely reasonable and were shared by most, if not all, of the industry worldwide. Nonetheless, the bet it made turned out to be terribly wrong. It bet almost entirely on e-beam lithography, in which electron beams write device patterns directly onto silicon. It was widely believed that the optical methods used up until the mid 1970's were going to hit a wall—that because of the coarseness of the lines they produced, the 16-kilobit generation of DRAM computer memory was probably going to be the last optically fabricated generation. It seemed clear that an entirely new technology was necessary.

The joint lab management decided, as did most of the world semi-conductor industry, that this new technology was going to be e-beam lithography. They were all wrong—the prophesied new technology was in fact not necessary. Today even the 16-megabit generation, five generations after 16 kilobits and a thousand times denser, is still being produced with the same optical techniques—more advanced, of course, but fundamentally the same—as those seen as obsolete in the mid 1970's. MITI's joint lab thus put most of its effort into a technology bet that was reasonable, but ultimately wrong. Optical technology improved, allowing it to be used to create finer lines on denser chips, and the direct-write e-beam equipment that the joint lab's three sublabs created proved inferior to the improved optical approaches.[5]

Why was the joint lab's e-beam equipment unusable for production of semiconductor chips? Although it worked perfectly well, it was orders of magnitude slower than optical equipment, because it required the electron beams to write minute circuits one by one, whereas the photographic method used in the optical approach allowed semiconductor producers simultaneously to process the design of *the entire chip*, not just one of the many thousands or millions of circuits, which the e-beam approach was limited to. Optical techniques could thus do in a few steps what e-beam lithography did in thousands or millions of steps, depending upon the storage density of the chip.[6]

Spillover Effects

The key secondary effect of the VLSI consortium was the promotion of the Japanese semiconductor equipment industry. Japan's dependence on imported semiconductor equipment dropped from 70 percent of total demand at the time of the launching of the consortium in 1976 to around 30 percent in 1983.[7] There is no question that the VLSI consortium played a role in this surge in strength in the Japanese equipment industry.

However, the reality of the strengthening of the Japanese equipment suppliers was very different from the account tendered by the conventional wisdom. Although there were instances of VLSI consortium funding helping to win company acceptance for equipment projects, such as the effort at Nikon to build a "stepper" (semiconductor production equipment that places desired circuit designs on chips in a sequential, layer-by-layer, stepwise process), it was the spillover of the consortium's contribution to a world-class semiconductor industry, rather than its specific technological outputs, that benefited the Japanese semiconductor equipment makers. The equipment producers were long-term suppliers to the semiconductor industry—they benefited from the surge in revenue growth and capital investment in semiconductors that the VLSI consortium helped precipitate.

In fact, technology transfer from the consortium to the equipment makers was minimal. The main equipment research that took place at the joint lab was on direct-write e-beam equipment, but since (as we have seen) this technology bet proved to be misplaced, the results had scant impact on the state of the art in Japanese semiconductor equipment. In any case, the equipment makers were not even allowed into the consortium as members and were relegated instead to peripheral roles as occasional subcontractors, limiting the extent of any potential knowledge transfer. An executive at one of Japan's leading crystal suppliers is quite explicit in stating that he believes the consortium benefited more from the information his company was able to provide on U.S. semiconductor firms than any information that his company got from the consortium.[8] Furthermore, the Japanese equipment firms clearly did not benefit from any significant direct financial subsidies. One estimate has equipment purchases making up around 20 percent of the VLSI budget, but the bulk of that money went to American firms, not Japanese ones.[9]

Opportunity Costs

The main opportunity cost of the VLSI consortium was probably its abortive e-beam work. However, three factors minimize the negative opportunity costs of the e-beam failure. First, the funding of the joint lab that did the e-beam work was only a small part of the budget, so the drain on the overall VLSI consortium was small. Second, the VLSI consortium management allowed for a wide variety of approaches to integrated circuit manufacturing, and the choice of the e-beam technology did not preclude investigating these alternatives. Third, there was widespread expectation that e-beam would be the technology of choice for VLSI semiconductor production, so it is difficult to blame the VLSI consortium for pursuing it. It was a reasonable attempt at developing a likely future technology. It would have been far more dangerous to do no e-beam research at all, which would have risked missing out on the next major breakthrough in integrated-circuit manufacturing.

Before turning to discussion of the 1980's consortia, it is important to note that the major effect of the VLSI consortium, its stimulus of investment through large-scale MITI funding, could not have occurred in the following decade. As will be explained in greater length in Chapter 7, with the declining size of MITI R&D budgets in the face of huge corporate R&D and capital-investment increases, MITI's ability to fund significant R&D efforts declined precipitously. As of the 1980's, MITI could not count on the subsidy/investment stimulus effect that had worked so well in VLSI. Rather, it had to hope that its technology choices and any efficiencies from joint R&D would pay off. As we shall see, this hope turned out to be misplaced.

The Supercomputer Consortium

In contrast to Fifth Generation, where there is a certain controversy *in retrospect* about what exactly the goals of the consortium were, there has been no such controversy in the case of the Supercomputer consortium. MITI included specific technical goals in its original Supercomputer plan. And in its 1990 final report, MITI concluded that these clearly specified technical goals had all been met and declared the consortium a success.[10] These goals are shown in Table 10.

Closer examination reveals an outcome decidedly less rosy than this MITI description. Some of the technical goals were indeed met, but many were not. These failures were obscured, and as described below, in one case a major performance test was even rigged to generate the desired technical performance. Moreover, it was not just with respect to narrowly specified technical goals that the consortium encountered problems. Technical success in the sense of the broader objectives of the

TABLE 10

Performance Targets of the Supercomputer Consortium

Research project	Performance target
SYSTEMS	
Vector "final system"	
Computation speed	10 gflops
Memory transfer speed	1.5 gbytes/second from 1-gbyte memory subsystem
Image-processing (graphics)	0.1 gflops
Computer	
DEVICES	
Logic (computational) devices	
Delay time	10 picoseconds/gate (low temperature)
	30 picoseconds/gate (room temperature)
Integration	3,000 gates/chip
Memory devices	
Access time	10 nanoseconds
Integration	16k/chip

SOURCE: MITI 1990: 3.

consortium was not achieved. The consortium aimed to create super-fast supercomputers well beyond the state of the art. But by the time its operations ground to a halt in early 1990, existing supercomputers out-performed and outclassed the "final system" vector supercomputer that was the showpiece of the Supercomputer consortium.

The Supercomputer consortium had cast its net relatively wide, sponsoring research in a number of different areas. Table 2 shows the research division of labor, which spanned two research areas, systems and architecture and devices, with three subprojects in each. The fol-lowing evaluates the results in each of these research areas, beginning with the systems projects, with particular attention to whether or not the results met the consortium's stated goals as listed in Table 10.

The Mammoth Vector Supercomputer

The huge vector supercomputer project that MITI assigned to the Japanese computer industry's Big Three, Fujitsu, Hitachi, and NEC, was the showpiece of the supercomputer consortium. It was the main "final system" that would bring together all of the technical advances in software, computer systems architecture, and device (i.e., compo-nent) technology in a single awesome package. This supercomputer was to meet the following technical specifications: (1) it was to have a computational speed of over 10 gigaflops per second (10 billion computations per second); and (2) it was to access a huge computer memory subsystem of over 1 gigabyte at a speed of 1.5 gigabytes per second. In accomplishing these narrower technical goals, the vector su-percomputer was also to accomplish the two broader aims of the con-sortium: (1) it was to be the fastest computer in the world; and (2) it was to incorporate the exciting and exotic new device technologies, HEMT, gallium arsenide, and Josephson junctions, that the consortium was also developing.

How well did the consortium do in reaching these two technical and two broader objectives? The short answer is, not well at all. It failed on all four counts. This should not be at all surprising, given (1) the im-mense amount of backbiting between the three firms and (2) the ten-sions between Fujitsu and MITI over the small budget for the vector supercomputer. The original plan for the vector supercomputer had called for 16 CPUs. However, the actual vector supercomputer only had 4 CPUs, because MITI ran out of money to pay for the additional processors. Fujitsu was already sinking several times more money than it was getting from MITI into the project, and it refused to increase its stake. As a consequence, the final system was supposed to meet the original performance specification of 10 billion computations per second with only one-quarter of the CPUs that were called for.

And it did. Or so MITI said in its final report.[11] How did they achieve this amazing accomplishment? It was quite simple: the final performance evaluation was rigged. To achieve the goal of 10 billion computations, a tiny software program was written solely for the purpose of generating the absolutely highest speed measurement for the computer. The program was so small that it only took one-and-a-half seconds to run—1.498199 seconds, to be exact.[12] At the end of *a decade's* effort on a *national* R&D project, the final major computer system was thus evaluated on the basis of a single, specially concocted, *one-and-a-half second* program. And in that tiny instant, this specially written software program did manage to record a computational speed of 10.9 billion computations per second, clearing the goal of 10 gigaflops per second.[13]

Of course, on any real program, the computer could not achieve anywhere near that speed.[14] The MITI final report itself mentions that on a different performance benchmark, the final system only achieved around 1.8 billion computations per second. Even this number is suspect. An ETL scientist who participated in the consortium suggests that in any real application, the vector supercomputer could achieve at best 1 billion computations per second—10 percent of the speed officially claimed to have been met.[15]

The researchers who participated in Supercomputer were both totally embarrassed by and extremely critical of this phoney benchmarking. An ETL scientist avers, "It was incredibly trivial software. . . . We invited criticism from university professors for doing such a trivial benchmark. It was ridiculous to do."[16] A company researcher describes the benchmark as "meaningless software" that was "totally artificial."[17] Nonetheless, MITI apparently could not tolerate failure on this key measure of the consortium's success. The rigged performance benchmark went through.

The same sort of suspect performance evaluation also seems to have been the case with respect to the second technical goal: to achieve a transfer speed from memory to CPU of 1.5 gigabytes per second. The MITI final report claims to have exceeded this goal, but a separate report by the NEC team who actually built the memory subsystem openly admits that they fell short of the MITI performance goal, achieving 1.0 gigabytes/second, only two-thirds of the 1.5 gigabytes/second goal.[18]

The point here is not that 1.0 gigabytes/second is inadequate: depending upon the specifics and difficulty of the performance benchmark, it may be reasonably good. Rather, this appears to be once again an instance where there were substantial pressures to inflate the official stated performance artificially so that MITI could avoid having to admit failing to meet its originally specified goals.

Turning to the broader objectives of the vector supercomputer project, by the time the final system was tested in late 1989, given its true capabilities of around 1 billion computations per second, it was well behind the performance of other supercomputers. Top supercomputers at that time were in the 3–4 billion operations per second range. The consortium's final system was not in their league.

Moreover, in terms of testing the consortium's device-technology R&D, the vector supercomputer can also be considered a failure. Of the three new devices—HEMT, gallium arsenide, and Josephson junctions—Josephson junctions were not used at all, and HEMT and gallium arsenide components were used in only a few places and never as part of the main CPU system. In the end, the vector supercomputer was a conventional silicon-based machine with a few non-silicon components thrown in.

The Graphics Supercomputer

Frankly, it is very hard to evaluate the three different smaller machines that were linked together to form the consortium's graphics supercomputer. Numbers are reported for performance, but since the details of the performance benchmarks are not available, it is hard to know what to make of them. I shall therefore not try to evaluate this smaller system here, since the graphics supercomputer was a secondary effort in the consortium.

Even without a thorough performance evaluation, however, we can know two things about this graphics supercomputer effort. First, it was clearly more successful than the vector supercomputer effort, in the sense that the companies were left alone to develop technologies independently rather than being forced into a time and talent-consuming tug-of-war. In fact, an ETL supercomputer scientist contends that the Oki display machine is "as a graphics machine, one of the best in the world."[19] Moreover, Mitsubishi actually used some of the technology commercially. Demonstrating some use of the consortium's technology, a slightly reworked version of the Mitsubishi machine was commercialized as part of a larger multicomputer system, with around 50 machines sold in its first year.[20]

Despite some successes, the graphics venture thus had only a limited impact. Absent a stunning breakthrough, this was as much as could be hoped for, given that the effort was small in terms of both manpower and funding. The Mitsubishi and Toshiba machines were both quite conventional. Mitsubishi's computer was "not particularly new or interesting," and was slower than a U.S. Thinking Machines CM-2 computer that was being commercially sold at the time. The Toshiba computer likewise was "not really a contribution." An ETL supercomputer scientist concluded in 1992: "In [computer design and] architecture we didn't do much—it would have been fine if the project had never existed."[21] In terms of commercial applications, the Toshiba system was never commercialized. When the group of Toshiba engineers who had built the Toshiba system for MITI proposed to management that Toshiba market the computer, they were told no.[22]

The Data-flow Supercomputer

The consortium's data-flow machine was both a success and a failure. It was a success to the extent that an extremely small team of ETL researchers, fewer than five, built the most advanced data-flow supercomputer in the world. There is no question but that ETL pushed the edge of the technology envelope in this novel form of supercomputer architecture, and did so remarkably efficiently, given the very small size of the research team.

But in taking data-flow architecture to performance levels that had never been seen before, it became clear that the data-flow concept needed to be modified, because these performance levels could not match those being achieved with other massively parallel computing architectures. It turns out that there were certain complexities and performance problems inherent in data-flow approaches, making other supercomputer architectures more promising. Thus, the consortium's data-flow effort did not achieve its goal of demonstrating the viability of data-flow technology. This is not to say that ETL's implementation of data-flow architecture was not excellent, because it was. But it had bet on the wrong horse: data-flow approaches turned out to be the wrong choice for high-performance parallel supercomputing.

Device Technologies

Here again the consortium failed to meet its broader goals of jump-starting the commercial use of non-silicon computer component technologies: HEMT, gallium arsenide, and Josephson junctions (JJ's).

The Josephson junction results were the most negative. IBM had abandoned JJ's in 1983, declaring that they were difficult to build and that advances in silicon technologies were eroding the JJ performance advantage. In the face of the IBM decision, the Supercomputer consortium continued to fund JJ's, although it switched its research effort to a new alloy based upon niobium, as opposed to IBM's efforts based primarily on lead alloy.

The new niobium alloys failed to pay off, however, since they proved to be extremely difficult to manufacture (one reason, in fact, that IBM had not pursued them). IBM turned out to be right: given the rapid advances in silicon technologies and the cost and reliability problems associated with JJ's, they would not find a place in computers anytime soon.

Amid the MITI group's struggle to create usable JJ devices, another blow fell, once again delivered by IBM. In 1986, the discovery of new high-temperature superconductors by IBM scientists in Zurich (unrelated to IBM's original JJ effort) completely wiped out the consortium's prior JJ efforts. They had been working entirely on so-called low-temperature JJ devices, which when cooled by liquid helium to nearly *absolute* zero ($-459.67°F$) could achieve superconductivity and thus high computing speeds. But cooling computing devices that much was extremely expensive: it meant that you had to have the equivalent of an unbelievably cold refrigerator around every JJ component. Not only was it expensive, but it was incredibly stressful on computer components to be cycled between room temperature and hundreds of degrees below zero. The JJ components encountered the same phenomenon that had doomed the key component that failed in the space shuttle *Challenger*: as the components expanded and shrank under the influence of these huge temperature changes, they developed cracks and were prone to failure.

The announcement of the discovery of superconductors that functioned at higher temperatures thus meant that the consortium had largely to abandon its previous JJ research approach and try again, this time with high-temperature devices. But even with these, it is apparent that JJ's are not dense enough and reliable enough to replace silicon devices, and they may never be. U.S. scientists who visited Hitachi's central research lab in 1990 were told that with MITI's consortium funding ending, Hitachi was planning on reining in its Josephson junction research, and that "practical application of this technology may be 10 to 20 years away."[23]

As a final indicator of the problems MITI encountered in its JJ research, it is instructive that none of the machines produced by the Supercomputer consortium included any Josephson junction technology. Given the huge priority that MITI gave to demonstrating these new devices in the consortium's computers, their lack of inclusion is a telling statement of their immaturity as computing devices.

In the case of HEMT and gallium arsenide devices, MITI similarly discovered that progress was difficult to achieve. The problem was that the HEMT and gallium arsenide researchers were chasing a moving target: silicon computer components got ever faster, denser, and cheaper through the 1980's and continue to advance on all three fronts to this day. In this respect, the non–silicon device story is quite similar to the problems the researchers encountered in the VLSI joint lab working on e-beam equipment. Both consortia prematurely predicted the demise of status quo technologies—the VLSI consortium, photolithography; the Supercomputer consortium, silicon computer components. As a result, both overinvested in a future that was not to be.

Although the HEMT and gallium arsenide devices met their specific technical targets, the consortium thus failed to achieve its broader objective: to produce non-silicon devices that could replace the reigning silicon components. In one sense, this was a contribution to the body of knowledge about computing devices: the consortium found out that these devices were not yet ready for prime time—that even with a major R&D push, they could not achieve the price, performance, and reliability necessary to unseat silicon. However, this negative finding, contribution though it was, was a far cry from the ambitious, positive goals that the consortium had originally laid out.

We should note that these problems with non-silicon components were not unique to Japan. Seymour Cray was experiencing the same difficulties in trying to design his newest supercomputer, the Cray-3, based on gallium arsenide. Difficulties in manufacturing the gallium arsenide components kept holding up the delivery schedule, and Cray Computer finally got its first Cray-3 machine out the door in May 1993. This is not to say that gallium arsenide is unused in the computer world—Convex Computer, based in Texas, and Fujitsu, have marketed computers that use these chips. But they are the exception that proves the rule: silicon continues to be the most reliable and cost-effective technology, even in the rarefied and highly cost-insensitive world of supercomputing.

We turn now to a brief discussion of the spin-offs and opportunity costs in the Supercomputer consortium. In terms of spin-offs, it is believed that Josephson junctions may have some application outside of computers in sensor technology, and gallium arsenide and HEMT appear likely to play some role in communications and microwave transmission applications. However, these are relatively minor and narrow applications of technologies that were hoped to achieve broad application in computers.

An opportunity-cost analysis is similarly severe, although we have to be careful here not to impose too negative a judgment based on hindsight. We have information today that those making the decisions in 1981 obviously did not have. In retrospect, with the vector supercomputer in disarray, data-flow architectures revealing their inherent limitations, and the non-silicon devices not being able to outpace silicon, it appears that the Supercomputer consortium funds could have been better spent elsewhere.

However, just because certain technology bets did not pay off in retrospect, it does not mean that those bets should not have been made. So the question becomes: were these good technology choices as of 1981? Unfortunately, even here considerable doubt exists. That the companies resisted joining the consortium and objected to its R&D agenda on the grounds of its speculative nature and the limited commercial prospects for its targeted technologies suggests that even from the beginning, this may not have been a research agenda with good potential payoffs. An engineer from one of the three second-tier companies (Toshiba, Mitsubishi, and Oki) explains:

> To tell the truth, we never thought that these devices would ever be able to be the basis for a complete supercomputer. As you know, JJ and HEMT can only be used at low temperatures . . . trying to put them into supercomputers creates a mountain of problems. Making a whole supercomputer out of these new devices like GaAs was in reality impossible, at least by the end of the project in 1990.[24]

In sum, the Supercomputer consortium was unable to achieve its goals of creating new systems and new device technologies that would leapfrog the status quo. The problems came in three forms: (1) the chosen technology path turned out to be inappropriate for mainstream commercial computers (data-flow and the three non–silicon device technologies); (2) the consortium's effort was behind the technology curve (the vector supercomputer final system), and the evaluation process was distorted to hide this inconvenient fact; or (3) the research effort was on so small a scale that it could not hope to have much of an effect on computer technology trajectories (the graphics supercomputer).

The Fifth Generation Consortium

Fifth Generation was a tragedy for MITI and for Japan. The consortium got its public start in a publicity stunt that succeeded all too well, creating tremendous pressures and overly high expectations that when unmet led to whispered pronouncements of doom that dogged the consortium for its entire lifetime. Fifth Generation had to struggle through over a decade of rancorous relations with participating companies, and at its final conference, in May 1992, it found itself on the defensive against widespread charges of failure, which MITI and ICOT did their vigorous best to squelch.[25] Despite aggressive marketing of the consortium's claimed accomplishments, it could not shake the perception that Japan and MITI had gotten their comeuppance: Fifth Generation had not created the machine to end all machines, the Japanese computer revolution that was going to make modern computing, Western computing, *American* computing, obsolete in a single decisive stroke.

This is not to say that the Fifth Generation researchers did not do world-class research: in certain areas of software development, in particular within the tightly focused technology target of logic-programming systems for knowledge processing, there is no question that ICOT, the Fifth Generation research institute, is the best in the world. Nonetheless, these more narrow technical results were both increasingly distant from computing's mainstream as the 1990's began and a far cry from the grand vision of "thinking machines" with which Fifth Generation had exploded upon the world scene in 1981.[26]

Fifth Generation was meant to be visionary and revolutionary, Japan's creative blockbuster in world computing. The problem, however, was that MITI had trouble funding such a radical scheme. In the context of a general budgetary retrenchment in the early 1980's, the Ministry of Finance was trying to cut, not increase, spending, so in the midst of a MITI–Ministry of Finance budgetary tug-of-war, Fifth Generation's MITI backers decided in 1981 to hold an international symposium to drum up publicity and support for the idea. If Fifth Generation generated a lot of press coverage, they reasoned, there was no way the Ministry of Finance would be able to deny it funding. It would look tightfisted or, even worse, out of step with the future.[27]

As a public relations gambit, the conference succeeded brilliantly— in fact, *too* brilliantly. In retrospect it was a Pyrrhic victory, tactical genius that paid a heavy strategic price. MITI's conference did not merely get local publicity, a few column inches in Japanese newspapers. In the fall of 1981, it ignited a frenzy of worldwide speculation about "what the Japanese were up to." On top of the acceptances from overseas guests invited to the symposium, requests *for* invitations poured in from all over the world. MITI's VLSI consortium had awakened Japan's overseas competitors. Every major company wanted to have people present to hear the latest plans from MITI, that scourge of the Western computer industry.

When the multitudes gathered in Tokyo for the Fifth Generation conference in October 1981, what they heard shocked and confused them. The Japanese were thinking big, very big. They proposed a research agenda that would sweep away the "archaic" concepts of traditional von Neumann computing. They proposed the creation of machines that could infer, could perceive, could reason. Some in the audience thought the Japanese were crazy. Some thought that they could do it. Some thought both.

One of the Western experts on artificial intelligence who had been invited to the conference, Edward Feigenbaum from Stanford University, was part of the group that thought that the Fifth Generation plan had every chance of succeeding. He returned from the conference convinced that he had to spread the alarm and help mobilize a decisive U.S. response, without which, he felt, the Japanese were going to seize control of the global computing industry, and hence global power. To lay out the nature of the Fifth Generation threat, Feigenbaum and Pamela McCorduck, a journalist who had written extensively on AI issues, co-authored *The Fifth Generation: Artificial Intelligence and Japan's Computer Challenge to the World* (1984), bringing MITI's plans to the attention of a broader audience of policy makers and the public, not just in the United States, but also in Japan, where a translation was a best-seller.

Western governments geared up for a response to Fifth Generation. If what was at stake was truly control of global destiny, no government could afford to do anything but respond. In the United Kingdom, the Thatcher government bent its anti-industrial-policy inclinations (this was, after all, a *national security* issue) and launched the Alvey program. The European Community as a whole sponsored its Esprit counterpart. In the United States, the Strategic Computing Program took shape in the Defense Advanced Research Projects Agency (DARPA, now ARPA). These were all programs costing hundreds of millions of dollars and targeting AI technologies. If there was to be a thinking machine, these governments were going to try to get there first.[28]

Fifth Generation's Goals and Achievements

This assessment of Fifth Generation begins with the 1981 conference and the worldwide reaction to it, because an understanding of just what was proposed at that conference is critical to evaluating the Fifth Generation consortium, its goals and its achievements. For in that 1981

TABLE 11

The Fifth Generation Research Agenda Announced in 1981

Basic application systems	(1-1) Machine translation system
	(1-2) Question answering system
	(1-3) Applied speech understanding system
	(1-4) Applied picture and image understanding system
	(1-5) Applied problem-solving system
Basic software systems	(2-1) Knowledge base management system
	(2-2) Problem-solving and inference system
	(2-3) Intelligent software system
New advanced	
architecture	(3-1) Logic-programming machine
	(3-2) Functional machine
	(3-3) Relational algebra machine
	(3-4) Abstract data–type support machine
	(3-5) Data-flow machine
	(3-6) Innovative von Neumann machine
Distributed function	
architecture	(4-1) Distributed function architecture
	(4-2) Network architecture
	(4-3) Database machine
	(4-4) High-speed numerical computation machine
	(4-5) High-level man-machine communication system
VLSI technology	(5-1) VLSI architecture
	(5-2) Intelligent VLSI CAD system
Systematization	
technology	(6-1) Intelligent programming system
	(6-2) Knowledge-base design system
	(6-3) Systematization technology for computer architecture
	(6-4) Database and distributed database system
Development of supporting	
technology	(7-1) Development support system

SOURCE: Moto-oka et al. 1982: 37.

conference, an extremely detailed research agenda was proposed (see Table 11).

This was an awesome research agenda. Its size was matched by its ambition, its scale by its scope. It spanned software and hardware, system-level efforts and component efforts; in each of the seven categories of research, there was not just one, but frequently several hugely ambitious tasks. And in the 26 separate subprojects that Fifth Generation proposed, the R&D agenda was equally specific about R&D content and the "targets and specifications" in each of these areas. This was not just vague handwaving about unspecified forms of futuristic computing—this was a clearly laid out research plan, a research agenda with teeth. Table 12 shows one of the 26 subproject plans to give a sense of the level of detail.

In setting forth these goals, the research agenda mentioned almost casually that Fifth Generation intended to accomplish tasks that had confounded Western computer scientists for decades, things like enabling computers to communicate with people through spoken language. The applications envisioned for Fifth Generation gave a sense of the sweeping vision. There were to be: (1) a computer that could translate from English to Japanese and vice versa; (2) a computer that could answer questions posed to it in spoken language about various specialized areas of knowledge; (3) a computer that could understand human speech; (4) a computer that could process pictures and images—that could, for example, find a picture of the Tokyo Tower from a library of 100,000 images; and (5) a "problem-solving" computer that could both solve sophisticated problems and, as a second goal, play the Japanese game of Go at an expert level. In short, explained the Fifth Generation planning group's 1981 report, "in these systems, [computer]

TABLE 12

R&D Plan for a Fifth Generation Machine-Translation System (1981)

R&D area	*Basic-application system:* "A basic application system representing functions like hearing, speaking, seeing, drawing, thinking, and problem solving will be studied and developed."
Specific R&D subproject	*Machine-translation system:* "Results of researches [*sic*] in documentation techniques and artificial intelligence for knowledge utilization will be combined together to research and develop an integrated multi-lingual translation system."
R&D details	(1) "Designing a machine translation system and its core."
	(2) "Development of the grammars for the languages."
	(3) "Development of sentence generating grammars."
	(4) "Development of an integrated machine translation system with room for operator intervention."
	(5) "Development of a specialized terminology data base (knowledge base)."
	(6) "Development of a machine for the specialized terminology data base."
	(7) "Development of high-level word processing techniques."
R&D targets and specifications	(1) "Number of words to be handled: 100,000 words."
	(2) "Machine must assure 90% accuracy, and the remaining 10% is to be processed by the translators."
	(3) "The system must serve general purposes computerizing all the jobs including text compilation to printing of translated documents."
	(4) "Translation cost must be 30% or less than that [done] by translators."

SOURCE: Moto-oka et al. 1982: table 4-3.

intelligence will be greatly improved to approach that of a human being."[29]

These, then, were the goals of Fifth Generation: sweeping in their ambition, precise in their specification, laid out clearly before the world in the fall of 1981. Were these goals met? In a word, no. In retrospect, it is fair to say that the goals were so hopelessly ambitious, particularly in terms of the targeted applications (human speech understanding, translation, etc.) that they could not possibly have been met.

It is also clear that Fuchi, who at the time of the 1981 conference headed a planning committee but became the top research manager at ICOT, the Fifth Generation central lab, was unhappy about the 1981 proposal. Given Fuchi's emphasis on a focused attack on the technology area of parallel inference, for him the research agenda was totally out of control. The 1981 plan was a classic product of "committee thinking": the 26 subprojects that were included covered technologies from microprocessors to supercomputers—each technology "interest group," each group of technology advocates had managed to get its particular R&D proposal included. As Fuchi explained, looking back in hindsight in 1992:

> I have heard that there is a proverb in the West that goes, "The horse designed by a committee will turn out to be a camel."
>   The preparatory committee for this project had a series of enthusiastic discussions for three years before the project's launching. I thought that they were doing an exceptional job as a committee. Although the committee's work was great, I must say that the plan has become a camel. It seems that their enthusiasm has created some extra humps.[30]

Not only that, but the 1981 plan emphasized spectacular goals such as enabling computers to understand human speech, which it was felt would be easy for people to grasp and would sell the project to the public, the politicians, and the bureaucrats. Many Fifth Generation researchers knew that achieving the goals specified at the 1981 conference would be highly problematic, but they accepted the need to sell the program, even at the cost of exaggeration.[31] They wanted their opportunity to blaze new technology trails and were confident that they could achieve important results, and the promise of concrete applications helped sell Fifth Generation to the Ministry of Finance, to the Japanese public, and even to MITI itself. Whereas the idea of building a "parallel inference machine" lacked pizzazz and had little hope of generating government funding, Fifth Generation's concrete proposal to develop a thinking machine—thinking *in Japanese*, no less—drove the funding of, and excitement about, the project. In short, it was the applications of Fifth Generation that struck fear into Western computer firms and Western governments.

However, these major applications were nowhere to be seen at the final Fifth Generation international conference in May 1992. They had been abandoned by the consortium, because they were not achievable. Fuchi and other top ICOT managers emphasized in 1992 that they should not be bound by these earlier commitments. Indeed, they argued that in fact no commitment had been made, that the 1981 plan had not been a plan, but merely a set of public musings about potential future technology paths. Fuchi spent considerable time disavowing the 1981 conference plan in his keynote speech at the 1992 conference. In summarizing the accomplishments of the Fifth Generation program, he noted:

When this project started, an exaggerated image of the project was engendered, which seems to persist even now. For example, some people believed we were trying, in this project, to solve in a mere 10 years some of the most difficult problems in the field of artificial intelligence (AI), or to create a machine translation system equipped with the same capabilities as humans.

In those days, we had to face criticism, based on that false image, that it was a reckless project trying to tackle impossible goals. Now we see criticism, from inside and outside the country, that the project has failed because it has been unable to realize those grand goals.

The reason such an image was born appears to have something to do with FGCS '81 [Fifth Generation Computer Systems 1981]—a conference we held one year before the project began. At that conference we discussed many dreams and concepts. The substance of those discussions was reported as sensational news all over the world.[32]

Fuchi is clearly correct that the 1981 conference proposal had everything to do with creating the public image of Fifth Generation as a hugely ambitious effort to rework all of artificial intelligence. And this was clearly an unfortunate burden for Fuchi to carry as the consortium's research director throughout the eleven years of ICOT. The burden must have been all the heavier given Fuchi's deep commitment to the Fifth Generation concept, the Fifth Generation *philosophy*, and his disagreement with the compromise, "everything but the kitchen sink" R&D agenda that the 1981 plan demonstrated.

Nonetheless, to call the 1981 research plan merely "dreams and concepts" is, plain and simple, revisionist history, perhaps understandable given the terrible predicament ICOT faced in 1992—results that fell far short of the announced 1981 goals—but nonetheless revisionist history. As Tables 11 and 12 help show, the 1981 plan was, in fact, a clearly laid out, highly detailed R&D proposal. It ran for nearly 300 pages, with a point-by-point breakdown of how each R&D subcomponent was to be realized, complete with time schedules and performance targets. It was *the plan*.

That this plan was presented to the attendees at the 1981 Fifth Generation conference as the "Fifth Generation research plan" is precisely why so many were shocked and frightened by the prospects of the Japanese actually achieving their proposed technology targets. Not only that, but the 1981 proposal had been developed over three years of consultations with the companies and used to secure first internal MITI approval and then Ministry of Finance and, ultimately, legislative budgetary approval. Moreover, this research agenda in its broader outlines was reproduced in a MITI document that appeared in the spring of 1982, right before the launching of the Fifth Generation consortium.

Nonetheless, Fuchi went on to argue at the 1992 conference that much of the 1981 plan had been scrapped by the time the consortium was launched in April 1982, about five months after the plan's announcement in late October 1981: "Our plans had become much more modest by the time the project was launched. For example, the development of an application system, such as a machine-translation system, was removed from the list of goals."[33]

Unfortunately, the available evidence does not seem to confirm the specifics of this claim, although there is no question in my mind that Fuchi was clearly in favor of such a pruning of the 1981 research plan. However, Fuchi was part of a *group* decision-making process, and his personal preferences were subsumed in building a coalition in favor of Fifth Generation. Moreover, it was precisely the stunning reach and appeal of the huge 1981 plan, with its portents for radically changing the future both of computing and of everyday life, that were critical in winning the consortium's funding.

As a result, far from abandoning the epochal applications proposed for Fifth Generation in 1981, ICOT clearly had a comparably aggressive R&D plan, *including machine-translation* applications, well into the early years of the consortium. In April 1983, one year *after* the consortium had started, ICOT itself published an *Outline of Research and Development Plans for Fifth Generation Computer Systems*, which among its "Research and Development Themes" includes "New Application Fields: The knowledge information processing systems realized by the Fifth Generation Computers are expected to expand extensively the fields where computers are applied . . . VLSI CAD, machine translation, and consultation systems are chosen to develop as the model systems to apply the basic Fifth Generation software as well as to prove and assess the basic software system. The development of these application systems is planned in the intermediate and later stages."[34] That ICOT was working on machine-translation applications in its first *four* years is also made clear by the fact that it spun off this machine-translation effort into a new entity, the Japan Electronic Dictionary Research Institute (EDR), in April 1986.[35] Even as late as 1989, ICOT leadership was claiming vast future applications for its Fifth Generation computers in medicine, education, business (for example, voice typewriters), and manufacturing.[36] To illustrate these claimed applications and their "social impacts," it used illustrations and text that were largely unchanged since 1984.[37] The language in 1989, too, continued to be grandiose: "The goal of ICOT's project is to create a knowledge information processing system that can help humans solve problems in their exploration of the unknown, and significantly extend the scope of their intellectual activity."[38]

What had changed by 1989, however, was the degree of linkage between the Fifth Generation consortium's R&D activities and the breathtaking future to be based on Fifth Generation. Although it works hard to describe the monumental potential of Fifth Generation computers, a careful reading of the 1989 text makes it clear that nowhere does it say that the consortium is, in fact, *working* on these applications. Rather, the applications appear to be merely illustrative. Indeed, notes of caution appear in various places. "There is no guarantee that all goals can be attained within the 10-year period of the project," ICOT now conceded.[39]

In sum, ICOT's scope underwent what might be called "creeping shrinkage," but the consortium's central research focus—specialized, logic programming–based parallel-inference machines—remained essentially unchanged. Over the years, as it became clearer and clearer that the original 1981 plan had been too ambitious and unsustainable, and that the program *continued* to be too ambitious and unsustainable, the more ambitious parts of it were abandoned bit by bit, leaving behind the original central focus on specialized parallel-inference machines that made the industry people unhappy. From the beginning, Fuchi had wanted a leaner, more focused research plan, but that was not what the committee- and consensus-oriented decision making and funding and lobbying process had given him. At the end, the research plan had been whittled down by circumstances, rather than design, and Fuchi was left to defend it against the inflated expectations created in the 1981 publicity blitz to win funding for the consortium.

Thus, as one of the three measures of consortium success—whether the originally stated goals were met—it seems fair to use the original 1981 research plan as the baseline goals of the Fifth Generation consortium, since it clearly was the original plan, and then undertake a broader assessment of spillover effects and opportunity costs in order better to assess the program's achievements.

Using the 1981 plan as a baseline for judging Fifth Generation's results also sheds light on a problem broadly afflicting the Japanese government R&D funding system: the need to overcome technological conservatism and skepticism on the part of the funding agencies. The standard approach to doing this has become a kind of technological bait and switch: promising excessively ambitious achievements and then delivering what one can, and either declaring that the original goals *unmodified* have been met, even if they have not (as with the Supercomputer consortium), or retrospectively reworking the original goals so that accomplishments far less significant and glamorous than original claims can be said to have matched the original goals (as with Fifth Generation and TRON).[40] As a U.S. scientist in Tokyo observes: "Everybody knows that this is the game. At some level every project is going to save the world. To get funding, MITI and MOE researchers have to overblow the significance of proposals. . . . [Even] the head [of the most recent major MITI effort] told me that he exaggerates stuff when he presents to MITI."[41] When there are systematic, structural incentives to make exaggerated claims both at the beginning and at the end of R&D efforts, it is clear that the problem lies in the decision-making apparatus that creates those incentives, and not with the scientists and researchers who have to work the system to secure funding.

Based on its original 1981 goals, then, one cannot call Fifth Generation a success. Reaching the same conclusion is the most thorough existing assessment of the Fifth Generation consortium, undertaken in the summer of 1991 by an arm of the powerful Nikkei publishing group, the (Japanese-language) publication *Nikkei AI* (*Artificial Intelligence*), which in a 70-page special issue devoted to evaluating Fifth Generation concluded that it had "clearly not met expectations. It is not just that the image of a Fifth Generation computer that was the proclaimed as the original goal has been almost entirely unfulfilled, but also that the project's main achievement, PIM [the *Parallel Inference Machine*], is nothing but 'an experimental parallel-processing machine.' "[42]

The latter charge, that PIM was still "experimental," got to the heart of the problem of a lack of applications. PIM was far from ready for commercial use to solve real-world problems. Although Fifth Generation had promised to solve concrete problems of immense complexity in order to bridge the gap between man and machine, it had come up with computers as confusing and complicated to the layman as any computer out there—*more* confusing, in fact, than new PCs with windowing interfaces.

This criticism of Fifth Generation for having failed to deliver usable hardware and software was echoed by the participating corporations, as described in Chapter 5. And even Stanford's Ed Feigenbaum, who had spread the alarm about Fifth Generation a decade earlier, was pointed in his judgment on what it had actually achieved: "They had some real success on a technical level; that's why they can have this impressive seminar. But they haven't produced applications that will make a difference."[43]

Spillover Effects

Fifth Generation had a number of important repercussions. I shall focus on three of them here: (1) the effect on Japan and MITI's international reputation; (2) the triggering of an AI boom; and (3) the training of engineers.

The most interesting repercussion was on Japan's international scientific reputation and on MITI's reputation as an effective architect of industrial policy. A deep cleavage exists here. Fifth Generation clearly played a role in enhancing Japan's stature *within the academic AI research community* as a place where exciting, leading-edge basic research was being done. Over the course of the consortium, Fifth Generation scientists received hundreds of visiting scientists from abroad at ICOT's headquarters, along with sponsoring conferences in 1981, 1984, 1987, and 1992 whose cumulative overseas attendance numbered around 1,000. These academics had different expectations of Fifth Generation and were less disappointed when it failed to achieve the breakthroughs it promised. In fact, a survey of foreign computer researchers carried out by MITI in early 1992, primarily focusing on the AI research community, found that around three-quarters of the respondents had a favorable impression of Fifth Generation.[44] Leaving aside for the moment the problems of credibility and methodology when one conducts a survey to evaluate one's *own* activities, at a minimum the survey confirms the existence of an opinion group of overseas scientists who support Fifth Generation. A member of the Fifth Generation planning committee from a computer-user company is highly critical of the consortium. Yet, he admits that "university professors are satisfied with the result—they did an interesting experiment with interesting results."[45]

In stark contrast to this enhanced reputation within the academic research community, Fifth Generation *damaged* Japan and MITI's reputation in the mass media and the world business and policy-making communities. Newspaper headline writers around the world had a lot of fun writing Fifth Generation puns after its final May 1992 conference. "'Fifth Generation' Became Japan's Lost Generation" headlined the *New York Times*.[46] "Japan's Fifth Generation Fails the Artificial Intelligence Test," added the English *The Independent*.[47] Negative assessments in headlines were carried through in articles. *The Times* of London wrote that "most agree [it] has been a gigantic flop."[48] The *New York Times* also expressed this consensus opinion, noting that "a bold 10-year effort by Japan to seize the lead in computer technology is fizzling to a close, having failed to meet many of its ambitious goals or to produce technology that Japan's computer industry wanted."[49] In short, Fifth Generation's reputation is split: positive within the narrow community of AI researchers, negative among the public at large.

A second repercussion of Fifth Generation was the worldwide AI boom it launched. The Western government response has been described above. Within Japan itself, a private sector *AI būmu* was also ignited by Fifth Generation.[50] At its peak in the mid 1980's, artificial intelligence was the hottest topic in the Japanese computer press. Hundreds of companies launched their own AI ventures so as not to be left behind in the new age of thinking machines. By the end of the 1980's, however, the *AI būmu* had collapsed. Both governments and companies came to realize that achieving genuine advances in computer intelligence was much more difficult than expected. AI ventures were either not renewed or shut down.

Fifth Generation thus did have a signaling/trigger effect similar to that of VLSI, which stimulated increased work in Japan on VLSI technology, but unfortunately in the case of Fifth Generation, this increased activity was in an area that was not nearly as fruitful as VLSI.

The third spillover effect of Fifth Generation was the training of engineers. One argument in support of Fifth Generation is that even if it did not produce usable advances, it "trained hundreds, perhaps thousands, of engineers in advanced computer science."[51] However, this argument is problematic. In the first place, no more than several hundred engineers directly worked on Fifth Generation over its twelve-year lifespan, so it is hard to know who the "thousands" might be. And these hundreds of engineers are spread over hundreds of groups in different organizations in a nation with hundreds of thousands of engineers in the computer industry. The Fifth Generation engineers are thus too dispersed to form a critical mass to foster Fifth Generation development. Moreover, training is only as valuable as the concepts that are acquired, and it is fair to say that much Fifth Generation work is barely relevant to commercial realities, and the education and technologies will be difficult to apply.

Opportunity Costs

The opportunity costs of Fifth Generation were clearly very, very heavy. Company complaints about the technology choices have already been laid out in detail in Chapters 4 and 5, so I shall just summarize them here. The essence of the companies' charge against Fifth Generation was aptly put by a manager from a computer-user company who had served on the Fifth Generation planning committee: "Fifth Generation didn't anticipate changes in the computer world. . . . The bureaucrats build a ten-year plan, then they don't change it. The world changes and the bureaucrats don't change the plan. They stick to the original goal."[52]

This intransigence in the face of change resulted in Fifth Generation computers that used specialized hardware and software when the computer world had long since embraced open architectures for software portability and ease of software development. It resulted in a focus on minicomputer and mainframe-type architectures when microprocessor-based PCs and workstations were cheaper and had substantially better cost/performance.

ICOT, of course, denies this. In a paper given at the 1992 final conference, a top ICOT research manager devoted a section to "Comparison of [ICOT's] PIM hardware with commercially available technology" and asserted that a single PIM processor with a capability of computing 500 *thousand* logical operations per second was as fast as a RISC processor capable of 50 *million* instructions per second—at the time a mid-to-high-performance RISC chip—because the ICOT PIM machine computed more complex instructions. He further emphasized that in practical application, the greater software code size inherent in RISC microprocessors would slow them down relative to the PIM processor.[53] When one considers that PIM machines were built to house as many as 512 separate processors (or 1,000 processors in a more loosely coupled configuration of several PIM machines), the implications of ICOT's claims are clear: PIM machines' performance can outclass RISC workstations several hundredfold.[54] A separate MITI report says the final PIM machine's performance is *one hundred million* "logical operations per second" (LIPS)—a hundred times better than that of today's mainframe computers.[55]

Unfortunately, these performance claims are highly problematic, and ICOT does not provide evidence to back them up. For example, key to ICOT's comparison that PIM is superior to commercially available mainframes or RISC workstations is the assertion that executing *one* PIM instruction is equivalent to a non-ICOT, numerically based computer computing *100* instructions—in other words, before comparing PIM machines to a non-ICOT computer, divide the other computer's measured performance by 100. ICOT claims that the PIM machines are processing "logical inferences" that are substantially more sophisticated than the numeric instructions processed by workstations, making this hundredfold adjustment necessary.

However, the number 100 is pulled out of thin air—ICOT never explains why 100 is the proper number to divide workstation performance by. It stands as a mere assertion. Why 100? Why not 50? (Which obviously would reduce the relative performance of ICOT machines by one-half . . .) Or 20? Or 2? Without any data or analysis to buttress this ICOT-advocated adjustment, it is frankly *impossible* to evaluate ICOT's relative performance claims.

This is symptomatic of a more general problem in evaluating ICOT's performance claims relative to currently existing computers: ICOT does not seem to go to much effort to release the data to back up the declared performance of its computers. The few pages of data that were released at the 1992 conference are wholly inadequate. There is no demonstration of 100 million LIPS computational performance, for example. In this 1992 conference report, most of the attention is given to comparing ICOT machines to *other* ICOT machines: demonstrating, for example, how much faster the newest ICOT machine, PIM, is than an older ICOT machine, Multi-PSI, or that PIM machines with more processors are faster than PIM machines with fewer processors.[56] A Stanford University computer scientist whose research is on advanced parallel-processing techniques points out that focusing on comparing its newer machines to its older machines plays to ICOT's advantage:

This is the same thing advocates of LISP [a popular artificial intelligence language] did with LISP machines. They used to compare them to previous generations of LISP machines and say, "Look how much faster we are now." Then people came along and said, "Let's compare this to general-purpose workstations." And we discovered that it was not necessarily any faster to run LISP on these specialized machines. It serves [ICOT's] purpose to not make it easy to compare performance with general-purpose machines.[57]

Moreover, the performance benchmark programs that ICOT used in the performance evaluation it did publish are troubling. They are applications so narrow and programs so small that it is far from clear that they are meaningful in the more general world of computing. Indeed, only *one* software program was used to test and report the performance of a parallel PIM machine, the crowning hardware achievement of the *decade-long* Fifth Generation consortium. The performance test was a *puzzle* program, where the computer sorts out the proper arrangement of puzzle pieces in a 40-space or 60-space box.[58] Without denying that the Fifth Generation computer's ability to solve a box puzzle may have implications for useful, real-world problems, it is also undeniable that a box puzzle is *not* a useful, real-world problem. Performance benchmarks for ICOT's Fifth Generation computers must be established with substantial, significant software programs.

ICOT's performance data thus bypass *the fundamental performance issue,* the question that most of the 1992 conference attendees (and indeed the computer industry at large) were really interested in: What is the relative performance of ICOT's computers compared to what's already out there, running *real* programs? Are they fast? Or are they slow? The numbers given do not even begin to answer that question.

In this apparent hesitance to disclose complete performance information about its computers, we see once again the severe structural contradictions that ICOT faced. On the one hand, the Fifth Generation consortium was genuinely committed to a free international exchange of information, a precedent-setting, fundamentally important revolution in attitude and approach for a MITI consortium. This was MITI interacting with the outside world, not just plotting the triumph of Japanese industry. On the other hand, ICOT faced tremendous pressures to *succeed*, pressures that had been magnified by the swollen claims and expectations of the 1981 announcement conference.

These two fundamental drives—free information exchange and the quest for success—came to contradict each other when changes in the 1980's began to erode the technological and market premises of the Fifth Generation program. ICOT *wanted* to be open, it strained to be open, but only to the extent that the free flow of information to and from ICOT did not compromise its image as a successful R&D operation. To admit publicly that things had gone wrong—to declare the software a success but the hardware a failure, for example—was impermissible within a basic operating environment that refused to tolerate failure, even in an enterprise that was supposed to push out the frontiers of technology and thus implicitly bore huge risks.

These pressures to succeed appear to have been behind ICOT's aggressive performance claims in a context of scant performance data, performance claims that do not seem to be credible to those who are familiar with the PIM computers. The *Nikkei AI* investigators compared PIM's performance unfavorably to existing RISC machines,[59] and most of the Fifth Generation corporate research managers whom I interviewed felt that the PIM machines clearly fell short of existing commercial technology. As one manager puts it:

PIM is not much to speak of [*taishita koto wa nai*]. . . . Of course, there's really no way to compare PIM with current machines being sold, since the ICOT software won't run on them. But if you did put the software on these other [non-ICOT] machines, there is no question that it would run faster. That's why when they say this is the fastest machine in the world, it's because there is no other machine in the world that runs the software.[60]

This was in July 1992, shortly after ICOT's final international conference. Fortunately, as noted earlier, it now appears that there will be an opportunity to run ICOT software on general-purpose hardware. Although the official MITI-sponsored Fifth Generation project came to a close in FY 1992, ICOT was granted a two-year funding extension from the Japan Information Development Center (JIPDEC), a public/private association associated with MITI. The aim of the extension is to allow ICOT to "port" (transfer) its software from ICOT's own specialized computers to general-purpose UNIX workstations and DOS-based, IBM-compatible PCs.

This is clearly the only hope for ICOT's Fifth Generation software to have any future use in the worldwide computer science community, so the decision to port the software to UNIX and DOS computers is probably a wise one, especially from the perspective of trying to preserve a legacy for the Fifth Generation consortium. However, in making ICOT software available on a broader range of computers, it will undoubtedly become strikingly clear that ICOT's specialized PIM computers do not have the price/performance to justify the heavy opportunity costs of pouring large amounts of technical talent and funding into developing a dizzying array of special-purpose ICOT computers. Although the companies lost that fight with ICOT management during the first ten years of the Fifth Generation consortium, in the end they have been proved right.

In sum, Fifth Generation trod its specialized path when the rest of the computing world had long since discovered that interchangeable, standard hardware and software offered far more choices and cost-effective solutions for computer users. This is the most devastating charge against Fifth Generation: the lost opportunities embodied in its special-purpose approach to computing. In the end it produced specialized machines that no one wanted to use. Had Fifth Generation from the outset articulated a vision of futuristic computing research based upon *openness*, a vision that effectively made use of commercially available hardware and software, its history might have been quite different.

The TRON Consortium

The TRON consortium's attempt to install BTRON as Japan's standard educational personal computer is the most obvious example of failure among all the consortia studied here. BTRON failed to win the Japanese government's stamp of approval, and in the aftermath of the Japanese government's decision to abandon BTRON as a standard in the summer of 1989, all of the major Japanese manufacturers in the TRON consortium ended their BTRON PC efforts. It was clear that they had been interested in making BTRON machines only as long as the Japanese government guaranteed BTRON a monopoly in the Japanese educational computer market.

Even Matsushita, Japan's consumer electronics giant, decided that BTRON had no hope of ever winning market share in personal computers. Matsushita had been the major backer of BTRON, seeing in it an opportunity to break into the computer market as a major player, and had written the system software used for every BTRON prototype computer. Although a member of the Matsushita group, Matsushita Communication Industrial, did use BTRON software as the basis for a high-end word processor introduced in April 1990, the machine did not sell well. Matsushita never fielded a BTRON PC.

This was deeply disappointing to the architect of TRON, Ken Sakamura, who as he watched all of the other manufacturers fold their BTRON tents in the summer of 1989, clung to his hope that Matsushita, Japan's largest electronics maker, would introduce a BTRON machine and ignite the market for BTRON PCs. For in this game of global computer poker, Sakamura declared, Matsushita was "almighty."[61] But almighty Matsushita thought otherwise, eventually declaring that it was abandoning BTRON, with the excuse that it feared that introducing a BTRON PC would ignite trade tensions and hurt sales of its Panasonic, National, and Technics products overseas. This was classic *tatemae*, a face-saving way out for Matsushita, which did not want to embarrass Sakamura and itself by stating publicly that it saw no future for BTRON PCs.

BTRON's problem was not that it was not good. BTRON was good. Or at least it could have been, had it been given sufficient support by an interested party with deep pockets. But those deep pockets could not be found, because the major Japanese firms recognized that new computers that are merely "good" are not that interesting. To overcome the tremendous advantage of NEC's DOS-based machines, existing software and a user base that numbered in the millions, BTRON had to be not just good, but spectacularly good, so good that those millions of NEC users would be willing to junk their existing computers and software for the sake of BTRON. And BTRON was just not that compelling. Besides, if they wanted a user-friendly PC, they could buy an Apple Macintosh, which had been on the market for five years by 1989 and had also accumulated a substantial software base and user community. Eventually, a tiny Tokyo company called Personal Media introduced a BTRON laptop computer, but not only was the company small and lacking any strength in its distribution and sales channels, there was hardly any software for the machine, and sales never went anywhere. BTRON has a market share in the Japanese PC industry that rounds off to zero. Sakamura's vision of openness and pervasiveness for the world computer market, for the world computer society, could not bear fruit in BTRON. With the death of the BTRON educational PC, Sakamura had to turn to other avenues to spread the gospel of TRON. He continued to push his varied TRON projects—CTRON, ITRON, MTRON, the TRON chip, TRON House, TRON Building, TRON City, TRON Car (he seemed to have an endless list of things that he could TRON)—but the freshness, the excitement, the fervor of the days of BTRON were gone.

SEVEN

Structural Change, 1975–1985, and the Breakdown of Japanese High-Tech Industrial Policy

> Japan has come to be considered an "economic power" by the other countries of the world. Thus, if we consider the direction in which our industries should proceed, it becomes clear that we no longer need chase the more developed countries, but instead should begin to set goals of leadership and creativity in research and development and to pioneer the promotion of such a project throughout the world.
>
> > Tōru Moto-oka et al., "Challenge for Knowledge Information Processing Systems" (October 1981)

> One of the problems being a pioneer is you always make mistakes and I never, never want to be a pioneer. It's always best to come second when you can look at the mistakes the pioneers made.
>
> > Seymour Cray, founder of Cray Research, the world's number one supercomputer company

Why was it that MITI could achieve success in the VLSI consortium, but was consistently hampered in its efforts in Supercomputer, Fifth Generation, and TRON? The argument here is that a common variable explains this erosion in MITI policy success. Japan's emergence as a technological and economic giant in the 1980's destroyed MITI's ability to carry out an effective industrial policy.[1]

Figure 5 diagrams the causal argument. Japan's economic transition drove changes in the size and content of MITI high-tech consortia, which eroded their effectiveness. This transition can be described in a number of different ways, but for the purposes of the argument here, three aspects are most important: (1) the increased size and competitiveness of Japanese firms; (2) Japan's movement to the technology frontier; and (3) the positive shift in Japan's trade balance and its overseas market share in key high-tech and industrial products.

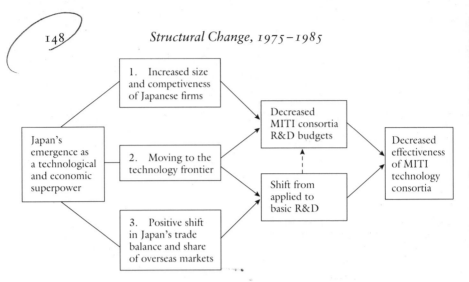

5. Explaining Shifts in MITI High-Tech Consortia: Key Variables and Causal Diagram

These three aspects of Japan's new technological and economic situation crippled MITI's industrial policy.[2] *First*, increasingly confident Japanese firms cast off their dependence on MITI and refused to contribute funds to its consortia. Moreover, MITI's technology budgets shrank drastically in size in comparison to the surging technology investments of Japan's robust electronics firms. *Second*, MITI discovered that pushing out on the technology frontier was much more difficult than "catch-up" policies that targeted existing technologies that had been perfected by the United States. *Third*, trade pressures exacerbated by Japan's huge trade surpluses and its inroads into high-value-added, high-tech markets overseas increasingly constrained MITI's policy options.

The rest of this chapter builds the case for this argument. It begins by briefly describing Japan's ascendance economically and technologically and then examines the specific linkages between this economic ascent and declining policy effectiveness.

Be forewarned that the style of argument assumes that the reader has already gone through Chapters 3–6, since this chapter draws liberally on evidence and conclusions presented there.

Japan's Emergence as a Technological and Economic Giant

In 1975, when MITI and NTT were grappling over the appropriate structure for the VLSI consortium, Japan faced very different economic circumstances from those that prevailed in the early 1980's, when Fifth Generation, Supercomputer, and TRON were launched. The Japanese were the hardest hit of all the major advanced industrialized economies by the OPEC oil shocks—inflation hit 18 percent, the GNP dropped for the first time since the end of World War II, and Japan's current account, reflecting its overall balance of payments with other countries, plummeted from a surplus of $7 billion in 1972 to deficits in 1973, 1974, and 1975, with a deficit of $5 billion in 1974 in the trough of the oil shock recession. Japan's economy seemed to be on the ropes; with its heavy dependence on imported oil, Japan seemed unlikely to continue to outperform the other advanced industrialized economies in this new age of expensive energy.

But it did. Japan managed a rapid shift away from energy-intensive, heavy industries toward higher-value-added, more knowledge-intensive industries in the mid 1970's. After riding out the second oil shock created by the Iranian revolution of 1979, it proceeded to churn out massive and ever-growing trade surpluses with the world, while at the same time seizing huge portions of technology- and manufacturing-intensive industries such as semiconductors, automobiles, and sophisticated consumer electronics and office equipment. Foreign governments, in particular the European Community and the United States, clamored for trade restraints against the onslaught of Japanese imports. Japan had come of age. It was without question the most feared economic competitor in the world.

The ascent of Japan and the relative decline of the United States were symbolized most graphically in the second Reagan administration when U.S. borrowing to cover the so-called twin deficits, trade and budget, combined to push the United States into net national debt. The United States became the largest debtor nation in the world, and riding the wave of its trade surpluses, Japan became the largest creditor.

It is clear from reviewing the postwar statistics of the Japanese economy that this outcome has been the result of a steady and at times spectacular economic advance, despite occasional setbacks such as the twin oil shocks. Over the decades after World War II, Japan achieved growth rates that far outpaced those of its industrialized competitors, not only the United States, but also European countries that were rebuilding from the war and achieved high growth themselves. Indeed, it is only in retrospect that we can even call Japan an "industrialized competitor" of the United States, because for the first several decades of the postwar era, it hardly seemed a competitive threat in industrial goods.

TABLE 13

Japanese Economic Growth and Its Increasing Technological Content

Years	Average GNP growth rate	Labor contribution	Capital contribution	Technological advancement contribution	Relative contribution of technological advancement
1967–73	9.73%	0.27%	4.55%	4.9%	50.4%
1974–79	3.69%	0.04%	0.75%	2.91%	78.9%
1980–84	4.26%	0.2%	0.88%	3.19%	74.9%

SOURCE: Wakasugi 1986: 2.

Table 13 details Japan's outstanding economic growth rates and the increasingly technology-driven content of that growth. Notice that even after the oil shocks, when it was supposed to have hit its "mature" phase and growth was expected to stagnate, the Japanese economy, although it slowed down, continued to outpace its industrial competitors.

By the early 1980's, the relative advance of Japan, both economically and technologically, became increasingly visible in several important structural dimensions, such as the transition from intermingled small current account surpluses and deficits that distinguished the Japanese economy in the 1970's to the massive, permanent surpluses that emerged in the 1980's. A transition had occurred: Japan had moved from being a nation playing "catch-up," a technological and economic follower, to being a leading, technology-driven economy on a par with the United States.

It is hard to pinpoint the exact year of this transition, because it was not that kind of transition. There are transitions that are instant: you are unmarried, you are married. And there are transitions that are more of a process, transitions that develop over time: you are young, you are old; you are a developing economy, you are a developed economy. Japan's techno-economic transition was more the latter, a process, a series of events and circumstances that accumulated over several years in the late 1970's and early 1980's to indicate Japan's new status. As a result, it was strikingly clear in, say, 1985 that the Japanese economy had moved into a new stage of development as a leading advanced industrialized economy, with new burdens and new responsibilities, that Japan was no longer economically where it had been in 1975. The statistical data that follow focus on documenting that fundamental changes occurred in Japan in a rapid and tightly compressed way between 1975 and 1985, the key period in the country's transition to economic and technological superpower status. The rest of this chapter is devoted to describing the nature of this transition as it relates to the declining significance of Japanese industrial policy.

Key Factor #1: The Increased Size and Competitiveness of Japanese Firms

Riding the wave of domestic and export growth, by the early 1980's, Japan's largest computer and electronics companies were no longer the nervous firms that had feared the onslaught of market liberalization and IBM. In the late 1970's post-liberalization period, they had met the enemy and emerged stronger than ever. As shown in Figure 6, Japanese manufacturers' share in their domestic computer market actually increased, rather than decreased, after liberalization.

This growth in domestic market share was in tandem with phenomenal growth in exports and production of computer-related equipment. As can be seen in Table 14, from 1971 to 1985, the production of the Japanese computer industry increased tenfold and its exports *140-fold*. In contrast, imports increased only fourfold. Japan had had a trade deficit in computer-related equipment all through the 1970's. In 1971, Japanese computer-related *imports* were nine times exports, but by

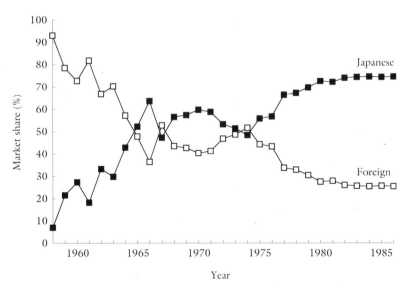

6. Japanese Computer Companies' Increasing Market Share in Japan's Domestic Market, 1958–1986. (Data from Anchordoguy 1989: 34–35)

TABLE 14

Surging Growth in the 1970's and 1980's:
Japanese Production, Imports, and Exports of Computers
and Related Equipment

(unit: ¥10 billion)

Category	1971	1975	1980	1985	1989
Production	34.6	54.1	129.2	337.9	565.9
Imports	9.3	13.0	21.4	35.8	56.9
Exports	0.98	3.2	16.7	138.3	240.0

SOURCE: JIPDEC 1991: 45.

TABLE 15

The Abrupt End of Corporate Funding Contributions
to MITI High-Tech Consortia

MITI consortium	Start year (fiscal)	Corporate share of consortium funding
Fontac	1962	50%
VHSCS	1966	50%
PIPS	1971	0%
New series	1972	50%
VLSI	1976	60%
Next generation computer	1979	53%
Optoelectronics	1979	15%
Supercomputer	1981	0%
Future electron devices	1981	0%
Fifth generation	1982	0%
Real world computing	1992	0%

1985, this trade situation had been dramatically reversed: *exports* were four times imports.

How this growth fed into corporate revenue can be seen in Figure 7, which shows the 1975–85 *real* (inflation-adjusted) revenue/budget growth of MITI and the five major Japanese computer and electronics firms that had participated in the VLSI consortium. Even when adjusted for inflation, these firms were four to seven times larger in 1985 than they had been in 1975. In the same time period, MITI too had a growing budget, but MITI funding could not keep pace with the explosive growth of these Japanese firms.

The growth in corporate size and competitiveness made industrial policy more difficult for MITI. The companies became less reliant on MITI and more independent. They had gone to MITI in 1975 for help with VLSI technology, actively seeking a joint government/business partnership to ward off the competitive threat from U.S. firms, especially IBM. But in the early 1980's when MITI naturally assumed that the firms would participate in follow-on projects to VLSI, as spelled out in Chapter 5, they did not want to participate. Ultimately, they agreed to do so only extremely reluctantly under MITI pressure and on the condition that they would contribute no funds to the consortia.

This cutoff of corporate contributions can be seen clearly in Table 15, which shows the percentage of various consortium budgets that were borne by the companies. Up until the 1980's, MITI and the firms had almost always shared the funding of MITI consortia.[3] In the 1980's, however, corporate funding contributions to MITI consortia budgets went to zero, as if they had fallen off of a cliff. And they have stayed at zero through the most recent major MITI consortium, Real World Computing, launched in 1992.

Two factors lay behind the companies' cutoff of funds. First, they no longer saw their foremost competitive threats as external to Japan. When they were still weak relative to U.S. companies in the 1960's and

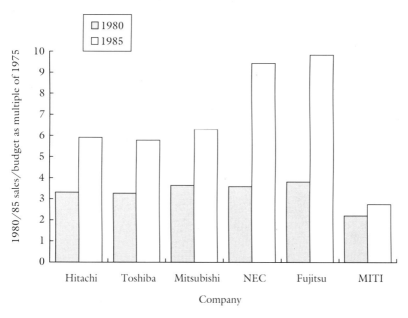

7. The Early 1980's Transition: Company Revenue Growth Far Outstrips MITI Budget Growth. (Corporate data from Toyo Keizai, Japan Company Handbook, various years; MITI data from Historical Statistics of Japan)

1970's, they enthusiastically sought government protection and subsidies. However, by the 1980's, as the Japanese firms rolled back U.S. firms in both Japan and the United States, it became increasingly clear to them that their major competitors were in fact one another. To join together to fight off a common enemy such as IBM in the 1960's and 1970's was one thing—to join together in the 1980's to jointly develop technologies that they would then use to compete primarily against one another was quite different. As we saw in Chapter 5, it was not anything the companies were interested in.

The second factor driving this abrupt end to corporate funding was the switch from applied to basic R&D as a focus for MITI consortia. The reasons for this shift are described in greater detail below, but I should note here that it eroded corporate interest in MITI consortia by decreasing the companies' expected payoffs. While the VLSI consortium directly funded corporate R&D work on immediate, commercially relevant technologies, later consortia largely did not. As a result of this MITI policy shift to basic R&D, the companies felt that Fifth Generation and parts of Supercomputer were pursuing fanciful, futurist technologies that had little hope of finding commercial relevance.

Disagreements between MITI and the companies over the appropri-

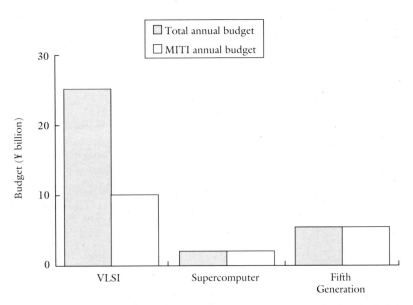

8. The Shrinking Size of MITI Technology Consortia. (VLSI budget includes NTT)

TABLE 16

R&D Spending as a Proportion of Revenues in the Japanese
Communications, Electrical, and Electronics Industries, 1965–1992

Year	Pct.	Year	Pct.	Year	Pct.
1965	2.44	1980	3.94	1987	5.78
1970	3.48	1981	4.21	1988	5.66
1975	4.17	1982	4.72	1989	6.10
1976	3.80	1983	4.85	1990	6.12
1977	3.71	1984	4.60	1991	6.63
1978	3.89	1985	5.25	1992	6.42
1979	3.91	1986	5.63		

SOURCE: Statistics Bureau, *Report on the Survey of Research and Development*, Sōkatsu-hyō (general tables) "Time series in intramural expenditure on R&D as percentage of sales by industry (Companies)—Disbursement," various years.

ate research agenda were most stark in Fifth Generation. As described in Chapter 5, the companies in the architecture group were strongly committed to their proposal for networked, personal, intelligent computers. Presumably, their money would have followed had MITI adopted it. But when MITI rejected it in favor of something more futuristic, the companies refused to contribute the half of the consortium funding that MITI expected.

The end to corporate contributions had an extremely negative effect on MITI consortia as a vehicle for industrial policy. Figure 8 shows how total funding in *absolute* terms fell dramatically from VLSI to Fifth Generation and Supercomputer. Notice that combined MITI funding on an annual basis for Fifth Generation and Supercomputer, which took place over roughly the same period, was little different from that of VLSI.

The problem, however, was that the corporate funding (and to a lesser extent NTT funding) has disappeared, so that the overall size of the 1980's consortia was much, much smaller. With shrunken consortia budgets, MITI was not nearly in as good a position to fund major work to push key technologies forward. It simply did not have the resources.

Even worse for MITI, its consortia budgets did not fall just in *absolute* terms: they fell even more precipitously in *relative* terms. As Japanese firms got larger and larger, they could afford to spend increasingly large sums on R&D and new equipment. The proportion of sales revenues devoted to R&D in the overall Japanese electronics industry increased roughly 60 percent from 1975 to 1992 (Table 16).

Increased R&D and investment activity changed even more dramatically when the focus is narrowed to the VLSI consortium's area, semiconductors. In the six years from 1978 to 1984, capital investment as a proportion of semiconductor sales increased from 12 percent to 28 percent (Table 17).

With companies' revenue bases exploding and the proportion of revenue devoted to R&D also surging, Japanese corporate R&D budgets and capital investment for new equipment increased exponentially through the 1970's and 1980's. From 1965 onward, Japanese corporate R&D spending roughly doubled every five years, with a particular surge from 1980 to 1985, which was followed by a slowdown in growth as Japanese firms consolidated their R&D spending positions (Table 18).

Corporate capital investment in new equipment to exploit this R&D and new technologies was also skyrocketing. Total capital investment by the five major firms in MITI's VLSI consortium increased over

TABLE 17

Japanese Semiconductor Industry Capital Investment as a Percentage of Total Revenues, Mid- and Post-VLSI Consortium

Year	Total capital investment/sales	Year	Total capital investment/sales
1978	12%	1982	19%
1979	15%	1983	24%
1980	18%	1984	28%
1981	18%		

SOURCE: *Nihon handōtai nenkan* (Japan Semiconductor Yearbook) 1985: 159.

TABLE 18

R&D Expenditures of Japanese Electronics, Communications, and Computer Industries, 1965–1992

Year	¥ billion	Year	¥ billion	Year	¥ billion
1965	31	1980	536	1987	1498
1970	130	1981	664	1988	1710
1975	234	1982	791	1989	1942
1976	285	1983	959	1990	2150
1977	272	1984	1096	1991	2372
1978	314	1985	1322	1992	2253
1979	383	1986	1360		

SOURCE: Statistics Bureau, *Report on the Survey of Research and Development*, Sōkatsu-hyō (general tables), "Time series in composition of intramural expenditure on R&D by industry (Companies)—Disbursement," various years.

TABLE 19

Total Corporate Capital Investment of VLSI Consortium
Companies, Pre- and Post-VLSI Consortium

(unit ¥ billion)

Company	1975	1985	1990
Hitachi	17	204	263
Toshiba	19	190	197
Mitsubishi	16	112	134
Fujitsu	20	202	185
NEC	17	210	270

SOURCE: 1975 data from *Nihon keizai shimbun*, Oct. 4, 1976; 1985 and 1990 data from Tōyō Keizai, *Kaisha shikihō* 1986 & 1991.
   NOTE: Consistency between these two data series has been confirmed in overlapping years.

TABLE 20

Corporate Semiconductor Capital Investment of VLSI Consortium
Companies, 1975–1991

(unit ¥ billion)

Year	NEC	Hitachi	Toshiba	Fujitsu	Mitsubishi
1975	3.5	1.5	3.0	0.9	4.0
1978	14	10	6	12	6
1979	22	15	10	16	8
1980	30	23	13	27	10
1981	40	34	20	33	13
1982	48	42	32	43	23
1983	67	81	97	64	36
1984	140	130	148	131	70
1985	100	90	90	54	58
1986	40	30	68	22	18
1987	40	40	70	40	16
1988	70	70	90	65	45
1989	90	95	95	88	72
1990	105	110	125	90	88
1991	100	80	100	96	90

SOURCE: 1975 figures are from *Nihon keizai shimbun*, Oct. 4, 1976. 1978–91 figures are from *Nihon handōtai nenkan* (Japan Semiconductor Yearbook), various years.
   NOTE: Consistency between these two data series has been confirmed via a third dataset in overlapping years.

twelvefold between 1975 and 1985 (Table 19, and their capital spending in semiconductors, the technology target of the VLSI consortium, increased by over a factor of thirty-five (Table 20).

   The problem for MITI, however, was that its budget to fund consortia was not at all increasingly exponentially—at best, it was increasing

TABLE 21

MITI Consortia's Declining Share of Total Japanese R&D Activity

Year	Total Japanese electronics, computer, and communications R&D (¥ billion)	MITI consortia budgets (¥ billion)	MITI consortia as % of total
1965	31	0.03	0.1%
1970	130	2.3	1.8%
1971	132	1.3	1.0%
1972	165	10.4	6.3%
1973	195	35.5	18.2%
1974	238	39.3	16.5%
1975	234	29.2	12.5%
1976	285	29.9	10.5%
1977	272	17.3	6.3%
1978	314	20.1	6.4%
1979	383	13.9	3.6%
1980	536	9.0	0.2%
1981	664	2.5	0.4%
1982	791	3.3	0.4%
1983	959	7.6	0.8%
1984	1,096	10.0	0.9%
1985	1,322	10.5	0.8%

SOURCE: Wakasugi 1990: 216–17.

TABLE 22

R&D and Capital Investment in the Middle of the Fifth Generation Consortium: The Five Companies in both VLSI and Fifth Generation

(¥ billion)

Company	1985 R&D spending	1985 Capital investment
Hitachi	250	204
Toshiba	165	190
Mitsubishi	106	112
Fujitsu	145	202
NEC	230	210

SOURCE: Tōyō Keizai 1986.

a few percentage points a year. So company R&D budgets came to far outstrip the funds that MITI could scrape together. Table 21 shows the trend in corporate R&D funding in the microelectronics and communications sector in contrast to MITI electronics/computer consortium budgets, and Figure 9 displays the relative weight of MITI funding

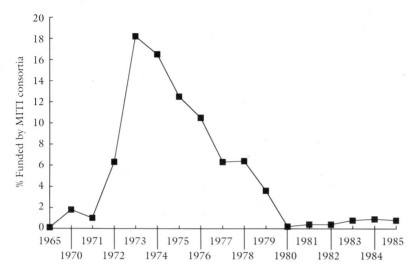

9. MITI Consortia's Declining Share of Total Japanese R&D Activity. (Data from Wakasugi 1991: 216–17)

graphically. As one can see, MITI supplied through its consortia as much as 18 percent of total R&D funding during the early 1970's; by 1980, this had plunged to 0.2 percent, and it remained below 1 percent throughout the first half of the decade.

The implications for the MITI consortia studied here are obvious. The VLSI consortium's activities comprised almost three-quarters of semiconductor industry R&D and 37 percent of both R&D and capital investment at the peak in 1977 (Table 9). This was of *considerable* importance to the participating companies. In contrast, the less than ¥1 billion (on average) that Fifth Generation, the major MITI consortium of the 1980's, directed each year to the major participating firms paled in comparison. ¥1 billion is not an inconsequential sum, but in the context of almost nine hundred times that amount in annual corporate R&D spending by the five major participating firms, plus equivalent spending on capital investment (Table 22), it is clear that MITI's contribution was little more than a drop in the bucket for them.

The bottom line was that by the 1980's, the combination of (1) relative shrinkage of MITI consortium funding and surging corporate R&D and equipment spending and (2) the refusal of companies to kick in funds for MITI consortia dramatically reduced the scale and scope of MITI's activities. MITI could not hope for successes like those it had helped achieve in the 1970's.

Key Factor #2: Moving to the Technology Frontier

This massive increase in corporate R&D funding and new equipment spending was driven not just by increasing corporate size, but also by Japan's shift to the technology frontier, the second factor that decreased the effectiveness of MITI's high-tech consortia. As Japanese firms caught up with U.S. firms technologically, they were no longer in a position to borrow, license, or re-engineer the fruits of U.S. firms' R&D. Instead, they were forced to increase their R&D spending in order to create their own new technology.

Aspects of Japan's technological "catch-up" can be seen in a variety of areas. In addition to the increasing commitment of the companies to research and development, there were also changes in (1) overall Japanese national R&D spending (the flip side of this increased corporate commitment); (2) Japanese firms' patent holdings; and (3) Japanese

TABLE 23

Japan in Technological Transition: Cross-National R&D Spending as a Percentage of GNP

Year	United States	Japan	West Germany	France
Cross-national R&D spending				
1920	2.57	1.8	n/a	1.59
1925	2.2	1.95	2.3	1.72
1980	2.29	2.03	2.48	1.77
1985	2.83	2.73	2.75	2.27
1992	2.64	2.96	2.64	2.44
Cross-national ranking				
1975	2	3	1	4
1992	2 (tie)	1	(2 tie)	4
Increase, 1970–92	6%	61%	n/a	53%

SOURCE: Science and Technology Agency (STA) 1994: 4.

TABLE 24

The Increasing Japanese Dominance of Patent Grants in Japan

Percent	1970	1975	1980	1985	1992
Japanese	69.3	79.2	82.5	84.5	85.8
Foreign	30.7	20.8	17.5	15.5	14.2

SOURCE: Science and Technology Agency (STA) 1994: 79.

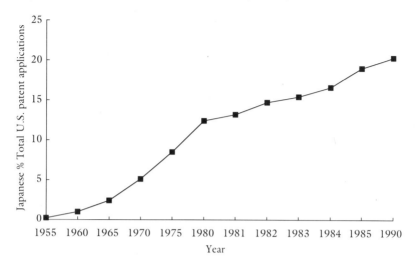

10. The Increasing Japanese Share of U.S. Patent Applications. (Data from Science and Technology Agency (STA), Indicators of Science and Technology, various years)

payments to license foreign technology. Spending on research and development is one measure of a nation's efforts to develop new technologies. Japan devoted a substantially lower proportion of its GNP to R&D than the United States for the first forty years of the postwar period. By the end of the 1980's, however, it had moved past the United States and Germany to the number one position in the world. This Japanese R&D spending as a percentage of GNP increased 61 percent from 1970 to 1992, compared to 6 percent in the United States.

A nation's patent holdings are another measure of its technology capability. Here again Japan advanced rapidly in the 1970's and early 1980's, but only kept even in its gains after 1985. In Japan from 1970 to 1985, the proportion of Japanese patents granted to foreigners dropped by half, as Japanese companies increasingly seized the initiative in new technology areas.

The surge in Japanese patents was not just a domestic phenomenon. Figure 10 shows how the share of Japanese patent applications in the United States more than tripled from 1970 to 1985. This surge in applications was matched by U.S. patent awards, which increased nearly 50 percent for Japan in just five years, from 11.6 percent of all U.S. patents in 1980 to 17.8 percent in 1985.[4] By 1987, the three top recipients of U.S. patents were Japanese firms: Canon, Hitachi, and Toshiba.

TABLE 25

Japan's Increasing Technological Independence:
The Shrinking Technology-Licensing Trade
Deficit in the 1970's and 1980's

Year	Bank of Japan data	Management and coordination agency data
1971	12%	20%
1975	23%	39%
1980	26%	67%
1985	30%	80%
1992	45%	91%

SOURCE: Science and Technology Agency (STA) 1994: 88–89.

Finally, the closing balance-of-payments gap in Japanese technology licensing and royalty payments to foreign companies indicate that by the 1980's, Japan was increasingly a net producer, rather than a consumer, of new technology. As a rapidly growing economy, its technology balance of payments (licensing revenues minus licensing payments) is a *lagging* indicator of technological advancement, both because the new technologies it develops can take several years for licensing revenues to build up and because old technologies it licensed continue to demand payments, although they gradually diminish as the technologies grow out-of-date.

Japan's technology balance of payments improved significantly through the 1970's and 1980's. Table 25 shows data from the Bank of Japan and Japan's Management and Coordination Agency that track Japan's technology position.

Unfortunately, the two data sets are wildly different in their projection of the Japanese technology balance, with the Bank of Japan concluding that Japan still had a large deficit as the 1990's began, while the Management and Coordination Agency determined that Japan had finally moved into balance after several decades of large deficits. That these hugely differing data sets continue to be produced year after year by the two government organizations, with no compromise or common standard of measurement agreed upon, is yet another strange instance of Japanese bureaucracies failing to achieve common ground. Be that as it may, what is in total agreement in both data sets is that Japan's overall position continuously and rapidly improved through the 1970's and 1980's. The trend is clear: Japan is increasingly extracting revenue from its technology activities. This can also be seen in the Management

TABLE 26

Japan's Increasing Technological Independence:
Corporate Overseas Licensing Payments as a
Percentage of Internal Corporate Spending
on R&D, 1975–1992

Year	Pct.	Year	Pct.
1975	10%	1985	6%
1980	11%	1992	6%

SOURCE: Science and Technology Agency (STA), *Indicators of Science & Technology*, 1972, 1977, 1982, 1987, 1994: table 7-1-3, "Technology Trade by Industry, Payments."

and Coordination Agency's data on the U.S.–Japan bilateral technology position, which shows Japanese licensing *revenues from* the United States increasing over 500 percent, from ¥22 billion to ¥112 billion, in 1981–92, while *payments to* the United States only increased 90 percent (¥154 billion to ¥292 billion) in the same period.[5]

The increasing prominence of Japanese domestic R&D efforts in comparison to the licensing of foreign technology is also quite evident. In 1965, overseas licensing payments were still one-quarter of Japanese company R&D expenditures; as Table 26 shows, by 1975, this had fallen to under half of that, and it fell half again in the 1980's to 6 percent of company R&D in 1992, 6.4 percent in electronic machinery industries.

In sum, the decrease the relative size and significance of MITI consortia budgets in the face of massive increases in Japanese corporate R&D and capital equipment spending was not just a product of increased company size alone. It went hand in hand with dramatic advances in Japan's technology position, which called upon Japanese companies to do more original (and expensive) R&D, rather than borrow technology from abroad.

For Japan moving to the technology frontier meant an increasing need for its own R&D efforts and a greater focus on more basic research to create new technologies and new knowledge. In response to this need, as we have seen above, the companies substantially increased their R&D activity. MITI, in turn, explicitly shifted the focus of its high-tech ventures from applied to basic R&D in the 1980's. Since this shift to basic research was also a response to foreign pressure and criticism of MITI's "unfair" industrial policies, its influence on the effectiveness of the consortia will be discussed in the following section.

*Key Factor #3: The Positive Shift in the Japanese Trade Balance
and Overseas Market Share*

The worsening of trade tensions between Japan and its trading partners in the late 1970's and early 1980's marked the end of an era for
MITI. No longer would its aggressive promotion of Japanese industry
be tolerated.

It was the heightened intensity, not the existence, of trade pressures
on Japan that was new in the 1980's, for foreign criticism of Japanese
trade practices did not start then. The United States, which as Japan's
largest export market and the guarantor of Japan's national security
was crucial among Japan's trading partners, had been voicing complaints about Japanese trade practices since the 1960's; indeed, the
Japanese liberalization of the semiconductor and computer markets in
1975–76 was in response to U.S. demands. Ironically, this liberalization was a major factor in the Japanese government's decision to launch
the VLSI consortium, which was to serve as a funding vehicle to help
the Japanese firms cope with the rigors of liberalized competition. And
it was the VLSI consortium that proved to be a turning point on U.S.
attitudes toward MITI technology consortia.

Through the 1960's and 1970's, the United States restricted its objections to Japanese industrial policy to MITI's policies of market closure—its elaborate web of tariffs, quotas, and regulatory approvals designed to keep foreigners out unless Japan absolutely needed the
technology, and then to make sure the foreign firm was squeezed hard
so that Japan could get the technology at minimum cost. But by the mid
1970's, the U.S. trade position had eroded significantly, turning into a
permanent deficit in 1976 (Table 27). These deficits soared in the first
Reagan administration when the United States roared out of its deep
recession and sucked in imports on an unprecedented scale.

In diagnosing what was wrong with the U.S. balance of payments, it
was clear to U.S. policy makers that Japan was a major offender. The
United States had run a merchandise trade deficit with Japan, offset
by surpluses in services and royalty payments, since the early 1960's.
However, the Japanese merchandise trade surplus with the United
States took off in the mid 1970's, doubling about every two years
through the mid 1980's until it flattened out at $40–50 billion an-
nually. What was particularly galling from a U.S. perspective was that
these massive Japanese trade surpluses appeared to have been built up
largely on the basis of a soaring merchandise trade surplus with the

TABLE 27

Overall and Bilateral U.S. and Japanese Trade Balances,
1970–1992

Year	Overall U.S. merchandise trade balance ($ billion)	U.S. merchandise trade balance with Japan ($ billion)	Overall Japanese current account balance ($ billion)
1970	3	−1	2
1975	9	−2	−1
1976	−8	−5	4
1977	−29	−8	11
1978	−31	−12	17
1979	−28	−9	−9
1980	−24	−10	−11
1981	−27	−16	5
1982	−32	−17	7
1983	−58	−19	21
1984	−108	−34	35
1985	−132	−46	49
1990	−109	−41	73
1992	−84	−49	118

SOURCE: *Statistical Abstract of the United States; Historical Statistics of Japan; Nihon Kaihatsu Ginkō Tōkei Yōran* (Japan Development Bank Statistical Handbook).

United States. Japan's overall trade surpluses seemed to track its trade surpluses with the United States.

Even more worrisome for the United States, the trade situation in key sectors was mirroring this overall trend. Even high-technology sectors such as electronics were slipping into deficit. Chiefly because of huge imbalances with Japan, and to a lesser extent with the Asian NIES, the U.S. trade balance in solid-state electronics (largely integrated circuits) slipped into the red for the first time ever in 1978, a situation that has remained unchanged to this day. The U.S. overall electronics position followed, falling into deficit in 1983.[6]

In the face of this eroding trade position, the United States put increasing pressure on Japan to make changes to reduce its yawning trade surpluses. When the Japanese government finally acceded to U.S. demands to liberalize the computer and semiconductor markets in the mid 1970's, U.S. attention turned to the next area of MITI activity: its policies of subsidy and support for Japanese firms, largely carried out through its high-tech consortia.

Beginning in 1977, Japanese manufacturers, led by NEC, started to carve out a major share of the U.S. market for 16-kilobit DRAMs, a product on the leading edge of integrated-circuit technology. Although most U.S. producers stopped short of accusing the Japanese of dumping, U.S. firms were convinced that Japanese government support in the form of the VLSI consortium was largely responsible for the Japanese inroads. "Our industry is now competing with 'Japan Inc.,' " declared Will Corrigan, the president of Fairchild, one of the major U.S. semiconductor producers. "It's better to address the problem now than wait until it gets too big."[7]

U.S. industry leaders predicted in doomsday tones (correctly as it turned out in the case of DRAMs) that Japanese inroads into U.S. semiconductor markets were only the beginning, that without U.S. government intervention, the United States might witness a repeat of the Japanese crushing of the U.S. color television industry. "The people in the television industry waited too long," Floyd Kvamme of National Semiconductor Corporation argued. "The [Japanese] program we are reacting to is in its infancy, but now is the time to point out the importance of maintaining a viable semiconductor industry in this country."[8] Kvamme suggested that a boycott of Japanese-made components was one possible solution to the problem.

The same year, eight U.S. major semiconductor producers banded together to form the Semiconductor Industry Association (SIA) and lobby the U.S. government to deal with the Japanese threat.[9] And in June representatives from the U.S. semiconductor industry met with Robert Strauss, the head of President Jimmy Carter's Office of the U.S. Trade Representative (USTR), to complain about the "huge Japanese offensive" and the "secrecy" of the VLSI consortium.[10] "The Japanese themselves downplay their program while refusing to disclose details of its progress," said *Business Week*, echoing the charge.[11]

This was clearly the case. Yasuo Tarui, the director of the VLSI consortium joint lab, had consistently refused invitations to talk publicly about the consortium's research activities. Consortium participants insisted that there was nothing much to talk about: an NEC executive insisted that they were having "a very difficult problem" in trying to get all the companies to cooperate. "This is why there is nothing yet for the VLSI lab to report."[12]

But this response had absolutely no credibility with the Americans. In the first place, they did not believe that there were problems of cooperation. They saw the Japanese government and companies as a well oiled and highly coordinated economic machine: Japan, Inc. In the second place, given Japanese makers' rapid advance into the U.S. DRAM market, they did not believe that there was nothing to report. They were convinced that the Japanese were hiding their technology. Otherwise, why be so secretive about it?

In Japan, the charge of secrecy hit home. The VLSI consortium had to go public or risk U.S. trade retaliation. In November 1977, Tarui traveled to a major electronics conference in Washington D.C., where he gave a keynote speech on the research activities and progress of the VLSI consortium. Tarui's talk seemed to quell U.S. fears. Many of the U.S. listeners wondered what all the fuss was about, because the VLSI joint lab did not seem to be ahead of its U.S. counterparts. In fact, some thought just the opposite: that the Japanese were behind.[13]

Nonetheless, in the U.S. DRAM market, Japanese manufacturers continued to gain ground: by 1979, three of the top five suppliers of 16k DRAMs to the U.S. market were Japanese. IBM, the world's largest DRAM purchaser, was buying only from Japanese producers in 1979; no U.S. firms' products had yet passed its certification process.

Rapidly losing market share in DRAMs, U.S. semiconductor producers were increasingly desperate. In tones substantially more strident than in 1977, they called the VLSI consortium an illegal "cartel" and accused the Japanese semiconductor industry of "unfair" competition based upon closed markets and government subsidy.[14] They appealed to Congress and U.S. Trade Representative Strauss to end this Japanese attack on U.S. markets, and called for an investigation of Japanese dumping by the U.S. International Trade Commission (ITC). The ITC held hearings in the end of May 1979, where representatives of U.S. semiconductor firms accused the Japanese of selling to the United States at half the market price in Japan.[15]

The industry also found a sympathetic ear in Representative Charles Vanik (D-Ohio), the chairman of the powerful Subcommittee on Trade of the House Ways and Means Committee, who hit the floor of the House in January 1979 and blamed Japanese protectionism for the U.S.–Japan trade imbalance. He called for high "compensating" duties on Japanese computers and semiconductors.[16] Vanik pulled no punches in describing his approach:

Free trade per se, with no restraints, has a very small constituency in Congress. I think we're pretty close to setting an import surcharge. We ought to just say: When the U.S. deficit gets to a certain point, the surcharge goes on, and let the other countries worry about how to get it in balance. That's the only way, frankly, of dealing with the Japanese.[17]

The center of the semiconductor trade storm was always the VLSI consortium, and with the consortium scheduled to end in 1980, U.S. industry had a specific demand: it wanted *all* of VLSI consortium patents opened up to licensing by foreign firms. As the chairman of Texas Instruments told an audience of U.S. and Japanese business leaders in Tokyo in January 1980: if the patents were not released, "the VLSI Project will inevitably have to be considered a major non-tariff trade barrier."[18]

MITI had already agreed in March 1978 to open up for licensing VLSI consortium patents that did not involve Japanese government employees, and NTT had followed suit. IBM in particular had expressed deep dissatisfaction that it could not cross-license the patents; since VLSI had been typified as an "anti-IBM" effort, IBM was naturally keenly interested in acquiring the technology and neutralizing any Japanese gains.[19]

MITI was confident that releasing the patents to outsiders would quiet criticism of VLSI as a secret cartel, but it discovered in the following eighteen months how misplaced that confidence was. A particular point of unhappiness for U.S. firms was that the 1978 patent release did not include government and joint government/company patents. Although numbering only around 30 patents, these included such key technologies as NTT's 256k DRAM design and the consortium's equipment and methods to produce a 1-megabit DRAM device.[20] They were the additional patents the U.S. industry was demanding.

In January 1980, with U.S.–Japan trade tensions worsening as Japanese small car imports poured into the United States, and with an eye to the November U.S. presidential elections, MITI took the final step and agreed to allow licensing of all patents from the VLSI consortium to any interested party. NTT joined MITI in this decision. The practical effect of this was to turn over at no cost all of the VLSI patents to the major U.S. semiconductor firms, including IBM and Texas Instruments, since they had cross-licensing agreements with Japanese firms that allowed them to use the Japanese firms' patents.

There was rich irony in this. The VLSI consortium had come full circle. It had started out as an attempt to fight off IBM and other U.S. firms. It had ended by giving away its technology to the same U.S. firms. No other action can describe so succinctly how much the policy environment had changed. In 1975, MITI was trying to do everything it could to protect and promote the Japanese semiconductor and computer industries. But by 1980, the same Japanese firms were rolling back U.S. companies from the Japanese home market and advancing into U.S. markets.

With the U.S. industry continuing to denounce MITI's aid to Japanese semiconductor producers, MITI was in full-scale public retreat from its 1975 goals and was trying to placate an angry America that threatened trade retaliation against unfair MITI policies. Times had changed, and MITI knew it. As the *Nihon keizai (Nikkei)* newspaper pointed out, "MITI's decision to openly license the patents of the VLSI association reflects its strong consideration of how the current situation differs from the time of the association's establishment."[21]

Amid these trade tensions, the difference in approach between the Supercomputer and Fifth Generation consortia suggests that the period 1981–82 was another key crossover point for MITI. Launched in 1981, the Supercomputer consortium had major elements, such as the main vector supercomputer effort by the Big Three firms, that targeted existing technologies, just as VLSI had. Supercomputers went on to become one of the hottest high-tech trade issues between the United States and Japan during the 1980's, with the United States putting heavy pressure on the Japanese government to reform its procurement policies and level the playing field. U.S. officials continually pointed out that Cray's world market share was over twice what it held in Japan, arguing that this indicated market closure.

MITI's response to this is instructive about the sometimes inertial character of its decision making. It did not end the Supercomputer consortium, clearly the most direct way to ward off criticism that it was subsidizing Japanese supercomputer makers. Instead, it forced the Supercomputer effort underground. Whereas Fifth Generation's openness and "international" character were proclaimed with great fanfare during the 1980's, with heavily publicized, heavily attended international conferences to announce its activities in 1981 (the year before its launching), 1984, 1988, and 1992, there were no conferences for the Supercomputer consortium. It toiled in quiet obscurity, an embarrassing relic for MITI of an era when its driving motive was to propel Japanese industry past America's.

In the 1980's, amid deep tensions between the United States and Japan, the Supercomputer consortium was not the face MITI wanted to present to the world. Fifth Generation was in fact that face. As indicated by one of the epigraphs to this chapter, Fifth Generation policy makers were keenly aware that Japan's international position had changed, and that a new strategy and new focus for MITI high-tech consortia was called for. The Fifth Generation consortium would therefore "fulfill our duty as an economic power expected to assume international responsibility by investing in the development of this leading field."[22] Fifth Generation did futuristic, basic research, not the Supercomputer consortium's more applied research. It had open conferences and invited foreign participation (although foreign participation in actual research was negligible), while the Supercomputer consortium did not. With Fifth Generation as its turning point, MITI's new watchwords for its cooperative technology consortia had become (1) basic research; (2) openness; and (3) international contribution.[23]

Responding to New Realities: MITI's Shift to Basic Research

Ironically, this shift in policy away from applied, current technology-oriented R&D to basic, future technology-oriented R&D had *three* negative implications for the effectiveness of MITI's policies: (1) it decreased the return from MITI-funded R&D; (2) it brought MITI into increasing conflict with the Ministry of Education; and (3) it lengthened the timespans of MITI consortia.

Result #1: Decreased Returns from MITI R&D

Funding concentrated "catch-up" targeting of known technologies was much easier than having to push out along an uncertain technology frontier. With catch-up efforts, MITI knew where to spend its money, because it was following a technology trail that had already been blazed by U.S. firms. It could focus all of its money on the particular targeted technology. But once MITI switched to funding future technologies, things became much more complicated. It was no longer clear where and how to spend the money, since future technologies by definition did not exist yet and it was very hard at times to figure out which technologies would prove to be important and which would not.

The implications of this uncertainty for MITI R&D funding patterns were enormous. What had been the right strategy during the catch-up era now became precisely the wrong strategy. Whereas concentrated funding of a single technology area was highly effective during catch-up, since the money was being spent on existing, proven technologies, these same concentrated bets would prove to be highly *dysfunctional* as part of a futuristic R&D strategy entailing basic research. Diversification, not concentration, was the appropriate strategy—MITI had to spread its bets to cover a number of competing technology alternatives or risk betting on the wrong horse and plunging its money into a technological dead-end.

The decreased payoffs inherent to this new basic, futuristic R&D strategy can be clearly seen in the three MITI-led high-tech consortia examined here. The VLSI consortium's CDL/NTIS group labs epitomized the old catch-up strategy. MITI subsidized the companies' existing product-development efforts. Given the short time horizon, the companies did not have to guess about what technologies would succeed a number of years down the road: they simply funded R&D to solve current problems.

In contrast, the VLSI joint lab, Supercomputer, and Fifth Generation had the much harder task of conducting more speculative R&D. The VLSI joint lab's futuristic focus was not motivated primarily by technological necessity: there was plenty of work that could be done (and was done at the group labs) on existing technologies. However, joint-lab research targeted "basic" and "common" problems with a longer time horizon in order to get the companies to participate. They were totally unwilling to do any work at the joint lab on current, competitive technologies.

In choosing basic R&D topics, the joint lab gave primary attention to e-beam direct-write methods, an advanced integrated-circuit production method that was believed to be necessary to achieve VLSI levels of density and compactness. Half of the labs and over half of the funding in the joint lab went to developing this e-beam direct-write equipment, and when the joint lab ended its activities in 1980, the successful creation of this equipment was declared its major achievement.[24]

Unfortunately, as the reader may recall from Chapter 6, the equipment turned out to be unusable. The VLSI consortium (along with many in the industry worldwide) had prematurely predicted the demise of existing optical methods. It had been believed that the e-beam approach would be necessary for the 64-kilobit generation of DRAMs, but optical approaches soon proved able to handle it. Then it became 256 kilobits that would be the end of optics. Wrong again. Today, almost twenty years after the start of the VLSI consortium, whose major research at the joint lab was predicated on the obsolescence of optical methods of integrated-circuit production, we are *still* using the optical approach. We have gone through the 16-kilobit, 64-kilobit, 256-kilobit, 1-megabit, 4-megabit, and 16-megabit generations, and it appears that at least the next two generations of DRAMs, 64-megabit and even 256-megabit, packing 256 million units, or "bits," of information, will also be using these tried and true optical methods.

So the joint lab's main R&D effort, which tried to project ahead and design a successor to the optical technology, turned out to be misguided: it assumed a future that never came. Although some of the e-beam technology was later applied by the companies to the production of photographic masks, key components in the optical process, direct-write e-beam equipment has never been used for the mass production of integrated circuits. It was an R&D investment that went astray.

In the succeeding two MITI consortia, Supercomputer and Fifth Generation, the same problems occurred, as basic research bets on future technologies failed to pay off. In Supercomputer this was the case with the three device technologies, Josephson junctions, HEMT, and gallium arsenide, all of which were expected by MITI to supplant existing silicon technologies and all of which encountered difficulties of reliability or cost/performance when compared to silicon. During the time of the Supercomputer consortium, silicon advanced much further in terms of its performance characteristics than MITI had ever imagined it would. The data-flow supercomputer that was built by ETL in the Supercomputer consortium was another example of a technology bet that did not pay off, as it became clear by the end of the 1980's that data-flow approaches had certain inherent problems, and that other architectures were much more promising.

Similarly, in Fifth Generation, MITI poured several hundred million dollars into "knowledge processing"–based computing in a highly focused bet that this largely unknown and untried technology would become the main engine of computing in the 1990's. The 1990's are far from over, but it is nonetheless quite clear that MITI's expectations have been confounded. There is no indication that the Fifth Generation's knowledge-processing approaches will enter the mainstream anytime soon. Current computing is dominated by the same numeric (as opposed to logic-based) approaches that MITI had predicted the extinction of, and will continue to be so for the foreseeable future. In Fifth Generation, MITI tried to read the far-off future and sponsor a basic research project that would leapfrog the United States and get Japan there first. Once again, however, that particular future never arrived.

In short, when MITI shifted focus from catch-up to speculative R&D, from applied to basic research, it discovered that success was much more elusive than before. It made a number of technology bets, some of them quite expensive, which turned out to be wrong. Time and time again, MITI ran into the problem once expressed by a French novelist, "The future is not what it used to be."

However, it is important to acknowledge that when technology bets turn out to be unsuccessful, it does not *necessarily* mean that they should not have been made. Sometimes reasonable bets do not pay off. The more fundamental point is that there are inherent difficulties in predicting future technology trajectories in industries as dynamic and ever-changing as computers and electronics. In 1980, for example, who would have guessed that the PC would be the dominant computing engine in the world in 1990? PCs were little more than toys for hobbyists;

the IBM PC and the Apple Macintosh did not even exist. Having to switch from catch-up to frontier-leading R&D in this kind of dynamic technology and market environment decisively eroded the efficiency and effectiveness of MITI's R&D funding.

An additional aspect of this shift to basic research and consequent reduction of expected payoffs from R&D has already been touched upon above: when MITI decided it wanted to fund futuristic technologies, the companies lost interest. They were not optimistic about the promise of the speculative technologies that MITI was hawking in Supercomputer and Fifth Generation. As described earlier, they resisted joining the two consortia and did so only under duress and on the condition that they would not have to contribute any funding. The result was to shrink the size and significance of MITI consortia. Without the corporate funding contributions that had made up 60 percent of the VLSI consortium budget, MITI could not keep pace with the increasing costs of leading-edge R&D.

Result #2: Increased MITI Conflict with the Ministry
of Education, Science, and Culture

The *second* negative effect of the shift to a basic, futuristic research orientation was that it increased MITI's need for cooperation from the Ministry of Education (MOE), cooperation that was not forthcoming. Companies were ideal vehicles for doing applied research on technologies matched to current market needs, and MITI funding for this kind of research matched the companies' own incentives very well: create products that sell.

In the case of basic R&D, however, the companies were no longer such ideal partners. This was for two reasons. The first, more general reason might be described as a universal predilection of companies to be cautious about basic R&D spending. There is an extensive economics literature that attempts to explain why companies may hesitate to do basic R&D. Its main points are that (1) basic research is by nature highly speculative, with no guarantee of a payoff; and (2) basic research is difficult to render proprietary, so that even if a company makes a breakthrough, its competitors may be able to copy the results.

Japanese corporate behavior is consistent with the predictions of this literature. When MITI switched its focus from subsidizing applied work on current technologies to subsidizing basic, futuristic research, the companies lost interest. They did not contribute funds to Supercomputer and Fifth Generation, nor to more futuristic consortia not studied here (PIPS, Future Electron Devices, Real World Computing).

The second and more fundamental reason that the shift to basic research eroded the basis for the MITI/company R&D partnership is that it introduced a whole new problem: agreeing on what technologies would be important in the future. In VLSI, most of the funds had gone to work on existing, or "imminent," technologies, so there was not an issue in terms of deciding which technologies to fund. But in Supercomputer and Fifth Generation, MITI and the companies repeatedly clashed over R&D priorities. In Supercomputer, the firms thought the market was too small and that the device technologies had only limited chances of paying off. They did not believe that supercomputers were the most appropriate area to use R&D funds and personnel.

Likewise in Fifth Generation, MITI and the companies could not agree on the research agenda. The firms attacked the proposal MITI eventually endorsed. The companies argued that it was unrealistic, overly ambitious, and too divorced from existing technologies. In the shift to basic research, a new area of conflict thus opened up between MITI and the companies, and a struggle over research priorities ensued. The net result was that the companies substantially reduced their level of commitment to the new MITI consortia. Given that they disagreed with MITI's plans, it is unsurprising that they contributed no money, cut back on the research personnel they assigned to them, and continued to fight with MITI over research priorities during the course of the consortia.

For MITI there was clearly a more appropriate place to do basic research: universities. Companies may not be in the basic-research business, but universities are. Indeed, in the competition for tenure, for prestige, for distinctions such as Nobel prizes and admission to scientific academies, contributions by scientists to the global stock of basic knowledge are perhaps the single most important factor. Consequently, universities were a much more natural venue for MITI's basic research. The companies themselves knew this: they criticized Fifth Generation, the fullest embodiment of this new MITI basic-research approach, as being too "academic." The companies knew what they did, and it was not Fifth Generation research.

That Fifth Generation was a research effort of, by, and for academics could clearly be seen in the published proceedings of the various conferences it sponsored. The conference committees are populated by researchers from government and from universities and other research institutions. Research papers from company researchers are also very much in the minority; most of the papers were from academia or other research institute settings (including ICOT, the Fifth Generation research institute). At the 1992 ICOT conference, for example, of the 93 individuals on conference committees, only 14 were from industry (with an additional 8 from NTT, which started Fifth Generation as a public corporation and was privatized in midstream). Of the 90 outside papers presented, only 24 were from industry, and the bulk of these came from "academic-like" settings, such as companies' main basic-research labs.[25]

The problem, however, was that the universities were the Ministry of Education's turf, not MITI's. In the pre-launch Fifth Generation deliberations, MITI asked the MOE for permission for university participation in the Fifth Generation consortium, and it refused. It was thus the reluctant companies, not eager academics, that MITI had to call upon to push Fifth Generation forward.

Problems MITI has in its relationship with the Ministry of Education also were evident in the TRON consortium's BTRON debacle. Given that TRON targeted software and microprocessor markets dominated by U.S. firms, in the 1980's era of trade tensions, MITI was unable to fund and control the TRON consortium directly. The level of its interest in TRON—as indicated by its squeezing of NEC to participate in BTRON, its sponsorship of the TRON Association's application to become a semi-public foundation (*shadan hōjin*), and its assigning of personnel to monitor the effort privately—suggests that in a different era, MITI would have tried to pull TRON in under its control, funding a TRON consortium whose targeted technologies were highly applied and aimed at unseating dominant U.S. companies, much like VLSI.

However, this was impossible given trade tensions with the United States. As a result, MITI tried to work with the Ministry of Education to create a protected market in education to allow TRON to develop. But as described in Chapter 3, it could not get the MOE to support its industrial policy priorities. The end of the "target applied technologies" option for MITI in the 1980's thus created a degree of dependence on the MOE in TRON. The two ministries' inability to cooperate hindered MITI.

Result #3: MITI Consortia Grow in Duration and Become
Vulnerable to Technological Obsolescence

The *third* negative effect of the move to basic research was the lengthening timespan of MITI consortia. Table 28 shows how the average timespans of MITI consortia doubled in the 1980's.

MITI officials explain this increased duration of consortia as a re-

TABLE 28

*MITI Computer Consortia Timespans and Their Doubling
in the 1980's and 1990's*

Start year	Time-span		Start year	Time-span	
1962	2		1981	8	
1966	6		1981	9	Post-1980
1971	9	Pre-1980	1982	11[a]	avg. length
1972	4	avg. length	1992	10[b]	10 years
1976	4	5 years			
1979	6				
1979	4				

[a]The Fifth Generation consortium was originally scheduled to run ten years and end in early 1992. It was extended another year as a MITI consortium and then an additional two years as a non-MITI "Follow-on Project," under the auspices of the Japan Information Processing Development Center (JIPDEC), a public/private organization linked to MITI. The follow-on project is scheduled to shut down in March 1995. Total length including the two non-MITI extension years is thirteen years.
[b]Planned

sponse to the new basic research focus: basic research, after all, takes more time to bring to fruition, because it starts at a less advanced stage of development.[26] Since it is very important for MITI to show concrete "success" at the end of its consortia, a move to basic research has motivated MITI to extend consortia time frames.

Note that this is in contrast to common practice in the United States. Funding agencies in the United States such as NSF and ARPA (formerly DARPA), for example, fund basic research that is typically in the 1–4 year time frame. If the research is successful, the researchers may well receive funding again at the end of this period, but if not, the funding ends. The basic rule is to keep funding cycles short, so as to not prolong R&D that is off track.

The advantage of these short funding cycles can be seen in the problems that crop up in MITI's longer projects. Ten-year R&D consortia can result in funding projects long after technological and market conditions have made the initial R&D funding choices obsolete. This happened in both the Supercomputer and Fifth Generation consortia, despite MITI's attempt to limit this possibility by dividing the consortia schedules into distinct periods, at the end of which progress would be reviewed and any necessary changes in R&D priorities and funding would be made. It is clear, however, that these reviews did not alter the initial priorities of the consortia. As a result, research was being done at the end of the consortia's lives based upon decisions made ten years earlier.

The consortia researchers themselves knew that MITI's long time frames were problematic. Over and over in interviews, researchers indicated that they felt the consortia would have had a greater chance for success if their lifespans had been cut down to, say, three years, or at most five years. As one Supercomputer researcher put it: "Ten years ago, in a single stroke—bam—we decided the research agenda for the next ten years. . . . It's fine if you predict accurately, but it's just very hard to know what technology is going to look like ten years ahead."[27]

In Supercomputer, this funding and priority inertia exhibited itself both on the device side and on the systems side. It was clear in the mid 1980's that advances in silicon technology threatened the usability of the three non-silicon device technologies being developed. Moreover, IBM's decision to abandon Josephson junctions in 1983 could have been used as an opportunity to redirect resources to other areas. But MITI would not allow the companies to withdraw from JJ research; it was confident that they could succeed where IBM had failed by using different chemical compounds to make JJ devices. Unfortunately for MITI, it proved to be wrong, and IBM proved to be right. Josephson junctions failed to fulfill their promise. Furthermore, on the systems side, by 1987–88, it was clear that the major vector supercomputer's performance would not match that of supercomputers in the real world. But the company researchers once again were not allowed to abandon their dubious task.

Likewise, in Fifth Generation it was clear by the mid 1980's that MITI had made a number of assumptions that were being wiped out by advances in market technologies. Fifth Generation was too much oriented toward large systems, which were being killed off by faster and cheaper microprocessor-based systems. It was also too specialized; UNIX and open systems were the wave of the future. Yet, Fifth Generation persisted along its original course, with hardly a nod to the realities of the marketplace.

Thus, in the presence of these rigid R&D priorities, longer time frames driven by the switch to basic research proved to be quite unhealthy. It meant that technical priorities that were out of date would continue to run their course over a longer period of time. It also invited substantial frustration on the part of the companies, which were much more in tune with changing market needs and were appalled by the consortia's R&D inflexibility. But they proved unable to overcome the entrenched interests in favor of carrying on with the original R&D plans.

Good-Bye to the Good Old Days: Structural Change and the Degradation of MITI-Led Cooperation

Up to this point, this chapter has described how Japan's emergence as a technological and economic superpower complicated MITI's task. In so doing, we have focused on how this change decreased the effectiveness of MITI high-tech consortia, without giving special attention to the role of cooperation, conflict, and competition in these consortia. While I have linked changes in the level of cooperation—for example, the effect of companies' refusal to contribute funds to new MITI consortia—to changes in policy effectiveness, this has been presented in a context of explaining decreased policy effectiveness, not the role of cooperation per se.

In the interest of clarity, then, what follows will summarize and make explicit the linkages between structural change and the relative presence or absence of cooperation in these high-tech consortia. This will be brief, since it primarily repositions earlier analysis in order to focus the spotlight on the cooperation dynamic. Despite being somewhat repetitious, however, I believe it is worth spending some time here to illuminate these linkages. Cooperation or the lack thereof is an important variable. It serves as an intervening factor (variable) that is both influenced by structural change and itself affects the possibility for successful consortia outcomes.

It is important to understand that "cooperation" here is meant to be a neutral term. Admittedly, it is difficult to think about cooperation in a neutral way, because the word itself in both English and Japanese (*kyōchō*) is imbued with positive meaning. When we want to talk about "bad cooperation," we typically switch to other words, such as "collusion." Nonetheless, in many contexts, particularly economic ones, it is absence of cooperation—for example, in the form of competition—that is desirable.

Japan's techno-economic transition has clearly affected levels of cooperation in technology consortia. The most important change has occurred in the relationship between MITI and companies. With the increasing size and competitiveness of Japanese firms, they have felt less dependent upon MITI and less willing to accept MITI marching orders when they believe their own interests lie elsewhere. This has been paired with corporate resistance to the new R&D priorities MITI has tried to implement as part of its new focus on basic research.

As a consequence, MITI/company cooperation has decreased dramatically. The most dramatic evidence of this change in corporate attitude was the sudden abandonment of corporate contributions to MITI high-tech consortia. This has had a very serious, very negative effect on MITI policies. As capital requirements for leading-edge R&D have increased, MITI has been unable to muster the funds to pursue projects of size and significance without making huge bets on very focused technology areas and running the risk of total failure should the particular technology choice not succeed. In a broader sense, it has also meant a lack of corporate commitment to MITI high-tech consortia, since corporate money is not at stake.

This had obvious implications for the degree of company effort and resources that went into the newer consortia. Researchers from both the Supercomputer and Fifth Generation consortia reported difficulty in getting other parts of their companies to help them when they needed manufacturing assistance or other help.

A less subtle effect was erosion of the relative power of the companies within the consortia. Since they were not contributing any money, it appears that MITI felt freer to ignore their input. Although more research is warranted, the available evidence does suggest that corporate financing contributions brought with them corporate influence over consortia decisions.

In VLSI, where the companies contributed most of the funds, the consortium showed flexibility in responding to company initiatives. Originally, there were no plans for the VLSI consortium to fund work on new optics equipment, such as a stepper, since it was believed that optics was out of gas and all advanced integrated-circuit manufacturing would soon have to move to direct-write e-beam methods. When a Toshiba executive called this conventional wisdom into question, arguing (correctly it turned out) that optical equipment would remain the manufacturing method of choice for at least the next few generations of memory chips, consortium management allowed the companies to allocate some funds to work on optical equipment. Why could this change in course occur in VLSI but not in Supercomputer and Fifth Generation? One explanation is that since 60 percent of the total VLSI consortium funding was coming from the companies, their hand was strengthened in internal negotiations.

In contrast, in Supercomputer and Fifth Generation, where the consortia were 100 percent MITI-funded, the companies had no such leverage and were rebuffed repeatedly. This damaged the two consortia's research efforts. Without effective channels for input from the companies, which were more sensitive than MITI to current market conditions, these two consortia were more likely to lose touch with changes in market technologies. They lacked the disciplining effects of market responsiveness and internal dissent, a dissent that had the power to change R&D directions based upon the leverage provided to the companies by their financial contributions.

The second effect of structural change was that it brought MITI and the Ministry of Education into increasing conflict. This was because MITI's new focus on basic research increasingly pushed it into the other bureaucracy's sphere of activity, and the two bureaucracies clashed. MITI sought access to university research labs as partners in Fifth Generation's basic research, and was blocked. In TRON, where MITI was trying to avoid overt intervention that might inflame trade tensions with the United States, it sought MOE assent to the creation of a new computer standard in the schools based upon BTRON. The MOE, however, did not share MITI's commitment to this industrial-policy goal and pushed for a computer standard that incorporated the old MS-DOS-based standard, which was precisely what MITI was trying to supplant.

In short, the new policy environment that MITI faced in the 1980's brought with it an erosion in cooperation and compliance from the major companies it had historically sought out as allies. It also created more significant conflicts with the Ministry of Education than had existed before. In the old era, MITI could make its industrial policy without consultation, but TRON and Fifth Generation put it squarely on the MOE's turf, and disagreements soon followed. In both cases, the lack of cooperation from companies and from the MOE compromised MITI's policies and decreased their effectiveness.

This is not to conclude, however, that the key issue for effective industrial policy is "cooperation" broadly defined. Indeed, the most successful example of a joint technology consortium discussed in this book, the VLSI consortium, is hardly a story of harmonious cooperation. MITI squabbled with NTT over the consortium's organization, and ultimately a largely redundant, dualistic structure emerged, in which MITI and NTT groups competed under the cover of joint operations. VLSI was not just the scene of bureaucratic conflict: the companies also refused to work together on key technologies. It is clear that it was a competitive dynamic, not a cooperative one, that mobilized MITI action on VLSI and drove company efforts. The presence of NTT and the consequent overlapping of jurisdictions between MITI and NTT, moreover, turned out to be extremely healthy in stimulating positive competition to accelerate their respective VLSI efforts.

Moreover, the key lessons of failures in cooperation in these consortia are not that better, more cooperative institutions need to be designed. Rather, they are that attempting to pound competitive firms or bureaucracies into cooperative arrangements risks failure. In the ill-fated attempt by Fujitsu, Hitachi, and NEC to design an advanced vector supercomputer together, it was probably unrealistic from the beginning to assume that these three fierce competitors could work together on such sensitive technologies. The vector supercomputer debacle suggests that MITI would have been better off trying to leverage existing competitive dynamics, rather than to bend or break them.

The changing fortunes of MITI in the new era of reduced consortia budgets, futuristic research, and increasing cleavages between the companies and MITI were aptly summed up by a former Japanese prime minister in a story he told one of the VLSI consortium research managers.[28] The prime minister described MITI and the companies as a driver and horse team. Up through the 1970's, MITI had been the driver, guiding the company horses through difficult competitive terrain. MITI was clearly in command and the companies depended upon its leadership. By the 1980's, however, the power relationship had reversed. The companies had grown tremendously in size and capability. Through their overseas expansion, they had acquired broad-based information networks that had come to surpass MITI's. It was now the horses, swift and muscular, who set the direction and pulled along the driver. The day of centralized government leadership had passed. It was the age of companies.

EIGHT

Lessons from the Japanese Experience

The reason Japan strikes fear in the hearts of foreign producers, even in areas of high technology, is the alleged effectiveness of government targeting.

But is industrial policy the main reason for Japan's competitiveness? Can it be given credit for Japan's economic achievements? What about the successes of the non-targeted industries, such as precision equipment and consumer electronics? And why is so little mention made of the problems encountered in such targeted sectors as space, large jet aircraft, and petrochemicals? The successes of non-targeted industries and the problems in certain targeted sectors suggest that the reasons for Japan's spectacular track record go well beyond the realm of industrial policy—into broad areas of the political economy as a whole.

Daniel Okimoto, *Between MITI and the Market*

The main arguments of this book have been *threefold*, centering on the contention that there has been a breakdown in MITI's postwar industrial policy regime. *First*, beneath the veneer of cooperation in Japanese high-tech consortia, the evidence indicates that there are tremendous levels of conflict and competition that severely compromise the consortia's cooperative goals. *Second*, there has been a striking decrease in the effectiveness of 1980's consortia in comparison to what was possible in the VLSI consortium in the mid and late 1970's. *Finally*, the analysis brings together these two threads of conflict/competition and declining policy success by arguing that Japan's emergence as a leading high-technology economy on a par with the United States in the 1980's drove a decrease in both levels of cooperation, especially between MITI and Japan's major firms, and in MITI's policy success. Let us examine each of these threads in turn.

Cooperation in the consortia examined is highly limited, largely because competing companies and competing bureaucracies successfully resist efforts to force cooperation. Thus, the explicit, elaborate structural apparatus to promote cooperation in the high-tech consortia that have created Japan's international reputation for successful cooperation between government and industry in the field of technology is often nothing but a public show: seemingly cooperative institutions and divisions of labor in R&D mask an underlying reality of fierce corporate and bureaucratic competition.

It is important to be clear, however, that the argument here is *not* that *no* cooperation occurs within these high-tech consortia. Cooperation between competitors is the consortia's raison d'être. They are designed specifically to foster it, so a *total* lack of any common sharing of activities or results would be hard to imagine. Nonetheless, with the exception of shared intellectual property rights, some of the consortia actually do come close to a total lack of *significant* cooperation between key participants, suggesting how hard it can be to design into institutions outcomes that are inconsistent with the goals of the participants.

The increasing tensions between the companies and MITI in the 1980's also have important implications in the evaluation of MITI policy success. Specifically, since the late 1970's, the major Japanese electronics companies have shown a decisive *lack* of interest in participation in joint consortia. If "cooperative" technology consortia successfully overcome market failures in R&D and thus provide important competitive benefits to participating companies, the companies' recent lack of desire to participate is puzzling. This corporate lack of interest would seem to provide prima facie evidence that consortia in their recent forms have not been important vehicles for improving corporate competitiveness.

This is, in fact, what we find in this book. I argue that as Japan entered the 1980's, its growing economic and technological power constituted a structural transition in its position in the global economy. Japan had moved from being a follower, both technologically and economically, to being a world-class competitor in a broad array in high technologies.

This new techno-economic situation seriously eroded MITI's ability to run an effective industrial policy. Increasingly, large Japanese firms cast off their dependence on MITI and refused to contribute funds to MITI consortia. MITI's technology budgets shrank drastically in size in comparison to the surging technology investments of Japan's robust electronics firms. MITI discovered that pushing out on the technology frontier was substantially more difficult than "catch-up" policies that targeted existing technologies perfected by the United States. And trade pressures exacerbated by Japan's huge trade surpluses and key inroads into high-value-added and high-technology markets overseas increasingly constrained MITI's policy options.

The result was that MITI's two major technology efforts in the 1980's, Supercomputer and Fifth Generation, were hamstrung by small budgets, company resistance, and a focus on highly speculative, futuristic technologies in an attempt to create original Japanese technologies and avoid the trade frictions caused by MITI's previous focus on targeting current technology areas dominated by the United States. In turn, MITI was hamstrung in its policies toward the third major consortium in the 1980's, TRON. Trade tensions kept it from playing a more active role, and it was forced to depend upon the Ministry of Education in setting standards for the BTRON personal computer. MITI and the MOE found that their interests did not match. In the 1980's, MITI faced dramatically different structural conditions, and its vaunted industrial policies went astray.

Policy and Competitive Implications

There are a number of lessons that we can draw from this story of hobbled cooperation and crippled policies. Most fundamentally, the evidence presented here underscores the limits of industrial policy. In MITI's 1980's failures, there are dire warnings for would-be industrial policy makers everywhere. Nonetheless, we have to recognize that political incentives make it inevitable that governments will try their hands at various forms of industrial policy. In such cases, Japan's experience reaffirms the importance of government policies that promote *competition*, not cooperation, between private sector actors. In Japan the promise of intercompany cooperation within government consortia has proven to be false. In the single case of success examined here, the VLSI consortium, it was vigorous competition between corporate foes (in plain violation of the cooperative intent of the consortium) that drove technological innovation forward.

Before moving to a more detailed discussion of these policy and competitive implications, let me take a moment to emphasize the analytical limits of this book. Much as I might hope that this book captures the timeless, universal essence of industrial policy, the reality is that we need to be clear about what has been studied here and what has not, what we can generalize to and what we cannot. Certain aspects of the Japanese experience do not map easily onto other nations.[1] The most important of these that worked to MITI's *disadvantage* is Japan's continuing massive trade surpluses and accompanying trade tensions, which have severely restricted MITI's ability to formulate any policies that directly promote the competitiveness of Japanese industry. A country that does not face these pressures to reduce trade surpluses would clearly have more freedom in designing its industrial policies. On the other hand, it is also the case that many of MITI's *advantages*, such as its insulation from interest groups in forming high-tech policies, are not readily found elsewhere and would render bureaucracies in other countries even less likely than MITI to achieve policy success.[2]

Second, since this is an analysis of industrial policy with respect to high technology, it may not address policies for more static and mature industries or industries in decline. Declining industries have different dynamics, such as the presence of deeply rooted interest groups with strong historical ties to political actors, or certain regions, and the absence of high tech's dynamic of rapid technological change.[3]

Third, since this is an analysis of the time period in which Japan made the transition to being a leading advanced industrialized economy, certain lessons clearly do not apply to countries that are still in their developing stages economically, that are still capable of pursuing "catch-up" policies with some greater hope of effectiveness.

In sum, the policy and competitive implications that flow out of this book apply most strongly to industrial policies for high technology in advanced industrialized countries. Bearing this in mind, let us now turn to an examination of some of these policy and competitive implications.

The Limits of Industrial Policy

Most centrally, the experience of Japan and MITI gives us reason to be extremely cautious about government-led industrial policies for high technology. MITI, after all, has substantial advantages over most national bureaucracies. In addition to its proven track record in working with domestic industries to promote competitive advantage, it is highly insulated in its high-tech policies from domestic political pressures and special interests that might distort policy profiles away from the pursuit of efficiency to the pursuit of pork. In the four technology consortia studied here, the role of Japanese domestic politics was almost nonexistent. There is only one instance where domestic politics played a significant role and changed the nature of MITI policy: in the decision to allow Mitsubishi Electric into the VLSI consortium. Even this was hardly an act of pork-barrel politics. Mitsubishi was clearly an important semiconductor manufacturer and was the most active among the participating VLSI companies in pursuing cooperative R&D relationships. Although not MITI's original intent, letting Mitsubishi in was a small compromise, the exception that proves the rule of MITI's tremendous policy autonomy.

MITI is truly amazing in its ability to move ahead with policies without having to bend decisions to political demands. Contrast the continuing placement of its consortia headquarters in the Tokyo area with the drawn-out political struggle over what state or what region gets government technology projects in the United States. The battle over the superconducting supercollider, for example, was brutal, with Texas, heavily weighted in the political leadership of Congress and then President George Bush's adopted home state, eventually taking the prize. MITI consortia are not local prizes auctioned off to the highest bidder.

Moreover, MITI can draw from the highest elite of Japanese society—its personnel, mostly educated at elite national universities such as the University of Tokyo, are clearly among the finest minds in the country. MITI is an awesome brain trust, and its officials work legendary long hours on behalf of its policies. The joke goes that MITI's Japanese name, Tsūshō sangyō shō, is more aptly rendered as Tsūjō zangyō shō, the "Ministry of Always Overtime." MITI is also a career agency; officials stay with it until they retire, creating an institutional continuity, history, and esprit de corps that contribute to stable policies and weigh against capriciousness. MITI personnel will be there a decade later to reap the rewards or feel the failure of its policies.

It was this finely tuned industrial-policy machine that ran aground in the 1980's. Since MITI so clearly brought substantial experience and advantages to the industrial-policy-making table, policy makers elsewhere would be well advised to take note of MITI's experience in the 1980's and consider whether their bureaucracies, their governments, and their political system have any hope of doing any better—or might possibly do much worse.

Fortunately, MITI's high-tech consortia in the 1980's were small enough in size and scope that even when they went astray, they did not drain too much money from taxpayers' pockets or consume too much valuable engineering and scientific talent. However, one can easily imagine much grander government initiatives, such as the ill-fated supersonic transport, with much bigger purses and thousands of workers, that exact a much heavier cost. We live in an age of limits—policy makers need to be aware of significant costs in terms of lost opportunities when money and men and women are squandered on fruitless endeavors. In the undertaking of government industrial policy, policy makers would be well advised to consider the Hippocratic injunction first of all to do no harm.

This is not to rule out government initiatives to promote national competitiveness. Government can and should be responsible for laying the groundwork for economic growth through sound economic policies. But if MITI's recent experience suggests the potential pitfalls of sector-specific approaches like high-tech industrial policy, then governments should look first to more general economic policies that make less of a demand on bureaucratic vision. It is frequently unclear whether technology A or technology B will ultimately prove to be successful, or whether sector A or sector B is the best bet, but it is quite clear that certain economic fundamentals remain eternal: all things held equal, more savings are better than less, a highly educated workforce is better than a less educated one, budgets that are in or near balance are better than ones that are grossly out of whack.

Prudent policy makers are thus well advised to make economic policies that preserve the fundamental economic bases for national competitiveness, growth, and wealth their first priority. Much as targeted, sector-specific industrial policies have both a resonance with targeted industries and a certain broader political appeal, it is so obvious that it almost seems too simplistic to point out that if there has been a fundamental problem with current U.S. government economic policies in the past decade, it has nothing to do with industrial policy or a lack thereof. Despite continuing deep economic strengths, such as America's unparalleled venture capital and university infrastructure and a system of fierce, open industrial competition that allows new, aggressive competitors opportunities to innovate and prosper, we also face serious economic challenges. We are a nation that undersaves and underinvests, with a yawning trade gap and a government budget deficit that chews up private saving; with a major health-care crisis, in terms of cost and coverage, making it both an issue of social policy and national competitiveness; with an educational system that fails to educate a significant portion of our future leadership and our future workforce to the level necessary to preserve America's economic strength.

It is these broad areas, these truly fundamental issues, that should continue to be the highest priorities of U.S. economic policy. Better education. More savings. Lowered deficits. Reining in rampant health-care inflation. These, not industrial policy, are the fundamental economic issues facing America's policy makers.

The argument for giving first priority to sound general economic policies, rather than to sector-specific ones, is reinforced by the problems MITI has had in trying to target future technologies. With Japan on the leading edge of technology in the 1980's and MITI trying to push along this new technology frontier, the major Japanese companies objected vehemently to its choices in supercomputer and Fifth Generation technologies. Yet MITI continued to push these projects forward and pressured the companies to participate.

To ask why MITI did so raises questions about the ability of governments to choose wisely among competing technology alternatives. As noted above, MITI, after all, is highly insulated from political pressures in its high-tech policy decision making. It did not face special interest lobbying, pressure from Congress, and the pork-barrel demands that have bedeviled large U.S. science projects. Nonetheless, MITI opted for supercomputers and Fifth Generation "thinking machines" for eminently political reasons, although these were more in the nature of bureaucratic self-promotion than of special-interest politics. One cannot avoid concluding that the compelling reason for MITI's interest in Supercomputer and Fifth Generation was that they were "big science."

By big science, I mean that in choosing to do supercomputers and artificial intelligence, exotic, unproven, bleeding-edge technologies, MITI had an opportunity to produce THE FASTEST COMPUTER IN THE WORLD or THE FIRST [fill in blank] EVER, a series of firsts and bests, a number of which it actually racked up over the course of its consortia. This was heady stuff. It was bound to create a big splash and bring MITI big attention and big budgets.

The problem is, however, that no matter how exciting and wonderful it may be to be the fastest or the first, in computers in the 1980's, the major applications and market, the major areas for growth, the major sources of competitive advantage—all things industrial policy makers are supposed to think about—were not supercomputers and artificial intelligence. Moreover, they never will be supercomputers, by definition a rare and exotic area, and for the past several decades, they have shown no signs of being artificial intelligence. The Japanese firms realized this—which is why they resisted the Supercomputer consortium and fought the agenda of the Fifth Generation consortium, two efforts at being first and fast.

While MITI was sponsoring these headline-grabbing consortia to produce revolutionary new computers, in the 1980's a whole new kind of computer, a whole new computer *industry* was born: personal computers based upon microprocessors and standardized software. And in its birth it destroyed the old regime of mainframes and minicomputers.

When software is included, worldwide sales for personal computers were approaching $100 billion a year a decade after IBM launched the PC onto its path of glory. This is where MITI's industrial policy makers should have put their priorities—in these little computers, slow and uninspiring perhaps when compared to supercomputers or "thinking machines," but the heart of the computer industry nonetheless, whose growth rates and ability to transform the economic landscape were matched by none. Yet MITI did not.

Thus, if even an industrial policy agency like MITI, elite, motivated, and highly insulated from pork-barrel pressures, seems systematically to go after high-profile, gold-plated projects, it is highly likely that industrial policy bureaucracies elsewhere will face the same tendencies and the same outcomes. It is the need to satisfy *customers*, demanding, cost-conscious customers, and the constant fear of the *competition* that drive commercial projects toward the real and the realistic. Lacking the discipline provided by both customers and competition, government efforts are far freer to pursue technological pipedreams. And it is the taxpayer who pays the piper.

While governments may be better served by caution, rather than activism, in promoting new industries, realistically it is inevitable that such government intervention does occur. Competition in high-tech sectors has too much resonance in terms of national security, national employment, national competitiveness, and national prestige for politicians and bureaucrats to want to leave outcomes to purely market forces. There are also institutional structures that have built up over time, such as the huge U.S. government lab system, that create the basis for continuing government activities in technology.

If government high-tech policies are inevitable, then what are some of the specific lessons this study has to offer? The question is important, because all technology policies are *not* created equal. There are both policies that are clearly more damaging than others and policies that have more hope of success.

In brief, the Japanese experience over the past two decades suggests that governments should emphasize: (1) the promotion of competition over the promotion of cooperation; (2) shared funding and decision making with the private sector; (3) pluralism and diversity in funding profiles, rather than concentrated technology bets; and (4) short-term (maximum 3–4 year) funding cycles rather than long-term ones.

Listening to the Market: Promoting Competition, Not Cooperation

Many observers of Japanese high-tech consortia have suggested that MITI's joint research projects represent an important new role for government-sponsored joint R&D to overcome redundancy and create economies of scale and scope in research,[4] but I find little support for this "neo-cooperativist" argument. In the first place, the description of cooperative behavior in Japanese technology consortia is factually inaccurate. As is described in considerable detail in this book, Japanese high-tech consortia are more aptly characterized as structures of conflict, of competition, or, in the better cases, of uneasy coexistence, than as cooperative structures. Moreover, despite explicit attempts to build cooperation into the structure of these technology consortia, typically at the behest of the Ministry of Finance (MOF) and politicians, competing bureaucracies and corporations find behind-the-scenes ways to undercut these cooperative structures.

Because of the competitive undercurrents that work against cooperation, it is the more easily policed and enforceable forms of cooperation that are the most likely to survive. For example, the single most prevalent form of *genuine* cooperation that spans the MITI high-tech consortia is the agreement to hold all patents jointly within the consortium. Nothing else even comes close: researchers who are intended to work together do not, companies that are supposed to observe R&D divisions of labor do not. Why is patent sharing largely successful? The patent-sharing rule is quite clear and straightforward. It is also inexpensive to enforce because it is easy to track companies' patent activities. Nonetheless, at least one analyst has argued that in the Supercomputer consortium, even this form of cooperation broke down, inasmuch as MITI allowed firms to submit consortium R&D results as private patents in order to give the firms more of an incentive to do R&D.[5]

A more fundamental attack on the neo-cooperativist argument is that not only does it have the basic factual story wrong, but the presumption of the benefits of cooperation seems to be misplaced. It is quite clear that it is not a cooperation dynamic, but a *competitive* one, that plays the major role in driving R&D by the consortia forward.[6] What we see in Japan is companies and bureaucracies working on overlapping, not distinct, research areas, firms and bureaucracies that are distrustful of one another and are each trying to best the others. For example, in the case of VLSI, the most successful of the consortia studied here, most of the funding went to independent company VLSI efforts in separate company labs, not to the much ballyhooed VLSI joint lab.

Even the patent-sharing rule described above, although quite clearly an example of cooperation between firms (when it is obeyed), is in a sense really a device to promote competition. Patents, after all, grant intellectual monopolies that prevent other firms from exploiting patented technologies. A patent-sharing rule effectively tears down barriers to entry based upon intellectual property rights. It broadly distributes access to technologies; all firms can make use of the shared patents in their market competition.

The Japanese experience in high-tech industrial policy would thus seem to advise a shift away from the 1980's-born focus on the government's role in creating or allowing *new* forms of company-to-company cooperation and back to a consideration of how governments can reinforce that *old* form of economic behavior, competition.

Listening to the Market: The Importance of Public/Private Checks and Balances

If the first lesson in industrial policy calls for harnessing the forces of market competition, the second policy lesson reinforces this market orientation by calling for shared policy and operational responsibility between the public and private sectors. To put this lesson in its boldest terms, if the choice is made to push specific technology areas, governments should *always* split organizational control and financing with the private sector.

The effects of the increasingly unilateral nature of MITI decision making in the 1980's underscores the dangers of making industrial policy without corporate inputs. It was a heavy blow for MITI when *all* of the major Japanese companies lost interest in its consortia in the 1980's, refusing to contribute funds and treating their participation as a regrettable, albeit unavoidable, duty. MITI thereby lost the sensitivity to market competition and market needs that the companies could have brought to the table, and its 1980's consortia went off track, seeking speculative technologies that ultimately did not come to fruition. If this 1980's MITI experience is instructive, 100 percent government funding is an open invitation to squander money on projects of little commercial relevance and will undoubtedly lead to more techno-pork than significant technological innovation in countries where policy making is prey to interest-group penetration.

In stressing the advantages of market-driven competition, rather than intercompany cooperation, and of involving companies in reaching decisions about industrial policy, so that bureaucrats do not make policy in a vacuum, I should make it clear that I place no blind faith in the market. Just like government bureaucracies, markets can be dysfunctional. They can be oligopolistic and monopolistic, with prices too high and innovation too low. And companies can express all of the human frailties of the men and women who run them. Companies can be lazy; they can pay fat salaries to executives while underinvesting in the future. They can build shoddy products and refuse to fix them. They can collude with other companies.

Yet, if there is a faith here, it is that *competitive* markets and companies in competitive markets show these defects to a much lesser degree; that the competitive market dynamic helps keep prices lower and incentives to innovate higher, and is more responsive to the needs of efficiency, quality, and service than government or uncompetitive markets. The logical corollary is that when government comes to tread in the industrial-policy area, it should do everything it can to preserve these healthy dynamics. It should be a forceful advocate for competition and use cross-consultation with the private sector as a tool to avoid policies that distort competitive markets.

At the same time, in cases where government funds are being used, corporate input should be checked and balanced by corporate financial contributions. There is no faster way to turn Uncle Sam into Uncle Sugar than to tell companies that the government bank is open and they can make withdrawals for free. Companies are in the business of making money—they accept it when offered. Asking companies to bring money to the table when they seek government technology support is an effective policy rule to make sure that the private sector does not abuse government funding and squander resources on no-win projects.

Flexible Diversity: Spreading Technology Bets

In acknowledging that technological uncertainty is ever-present and technology flows are diverse, it is critical that funding diversify risk by pursuing multiple solutions to technology problems. There is a tendency to view simultaneous pursuit of competing solutions as "waste," particularly in times of budget shortage, but the risks of failure from single-focus, targeted efforts are too great. In the Japanese consortia studied here, there were numerous instances of technologies that seemed, not merely promising, but *absolutely certain* to dominate future markets, such as the VLSI consortium's electron-beam technology and Supercomputer's non-silicon devices, but that failed to overcome critical technical hurdles to fulfill their promise.

"The best way to predict the future is to invent it," the computer scientist Alan Kay has said, and MITI clearly had some such maxim in mind in choosing ambitiously to stretch the horizons of known technology in its consortia over the past two decades. But the best way to invent the future is to make sure all of the major technology possibilities are covered. No government funding agency should ever bet the future on one technology.

And perhaps I should add: no government should have just *one* funding agency funding a particular technology area. Competition among government agencies in *funding* seems to be distinctly more functional than competition between government agencies in the area of *regulation*. The positive effects of the competition between MITI and NTT in propelling MITI's VLSI efforts forward and between MITI and the Science and Technology Agency (STA) in supercomputers are quite a contrast to the frustrations and roadblocks the Ministry of Education inflicted on MITI when it sought to integrate schools and universities into its industrial policy making. Clearly, when bureaucracies are primarily oriented toward regulatory compliance and control of private actors, and their jurisdictions overlap, this can create jurisdictional disputes and regulatory uncertainty that retard private-sector activity.

Funding agencies are not primarily regulatory, however, but are designed to be *responsive*: they are allocated funds to solve a certain problem. In these cases, overlapping jurisdiction creates the basis for competition, and this "bureaucratic competition" can have some of the disciplining effects of free-market competition, creating action where passivity once reigned. MITI, for example, moved to action on VLSI in the face of NTT's efforts; likewise, it took on supercomputers in order to head off an effort by STA.

Flexible Diversity: Keeping Funding on a Short Leash

In line with diversifying funding channels and allocations, short funding cycles allow for quicker withdrawal from technology projects that head off track or technologies that no longer appear viable. In funding long projects, MITI has taken the view that long funding cycles create a more certain investment environment, which encourages investment in leading-edge technologies. There is perhaps some truth to this (although one suspects that a more compelling reason is that the planning, funding, and consensus-building process for MITI's major consortia typically takes several years, so MITI needs a long running time for its consortia to justify these sunk planning costs). However, the vicious downside to these long funding cycles, seen over and over again in MITI's long-term technology consortia, is that they also encourage ventures that continue inertially along their predetermined paths, blissfully ignoring changes in the external technology environment.

More effective funding can be seen in U.S. funding agencies, such as the Department of Defense's ARPA (Advanced Research Projects

Agency), the National Science Foundation (NSF), and the Department of Commerce's Advanced Technology Program (ATP), whose funding cycles are typically limited to a few years. ATP, in fact, statutorily limits funding of a particular technology project to either three or five years, along with mandating cost-sharing between ATP and the recipient organization/company. These operating rules help ward off the trap of continuing funding because of accumulated bureaucratic or political interests, along with creating a strong incentive to finish the project on time, with no extensions.

Given MITI's troubles since the early 1980's in spite of the considerable strengths it brought to industrial policy, it is hard to be optimistic about government-led industrial policy. Governments and businesses would be better advised to turn their attention to the more fundamental bases of national competitiveness: skills, savings, investment, and the maintenance of vigorous competitive markets. Nonetheless, the stark political reality is that governments will inevitably make industrial policies. It is my hope, however, that observing the guidelines offered here may help make those policies more fruitful.

Thinking Clearly About U.S. High-Tech Consortia

Up to this point, I have deliberately avoided reference to the U.S. cooperative consortia that have sprung up in response to the Japanese ventures analyzed in this book. This has been primarily because the U.S. efforts are sufficiently complex that I would prefer to withhold comment pending more complete research.

However, events have overtaken that caution. In May 1994, the Clinton administration announced bold plans to provide up to $1 billion to the U.S. LCD display industry, indicating a continuing U.S. policy commitment to "cooperative" consortia as a way of bolstering U.S. high-tech competitiveness. The administration's announced policies include support for the U.S. Display Consortium, formed by thirteen U.S. firms in 1993 and already receiving $200 million annually from the U.S. Department of Defense, and for efforts to promote joint manufacturing and subsidies for domestic production of LCDs. In this context, my decision not to address U.S. consortia and related policies in light of Japan's actual consortia experiences seems increasingly ill-advised. U.S. policy makers continue to embrace the mislearned "cooperative" lessons of Japan's consortia—lessons I argue should be largely discredited.

To turn briefly, then, to these U.S. consortia, let me raise a few issues relative to the two major U.S. consortia launched in the 1980's, MCC and Sematech. Neither is viewed with much regard in Japan, where electronics executives speak unguardedly of "the failure of MCC and Sematech."[7] MCC, a computer/microelectronics consortium created in response to Japan's Fifth Generation effort, has had the longer and more troubled history. It has rotated through a series of top managers and business strategies and has found it impossible to sustain itself financially without U.S. government contracts. Although the original intent was for MCC to be entirely financed by the private sector, by the early 1990's, according to one inside report, at least half of its roughly $50 million/year funding was coming from the Department of Defense, and, as one former MCC official put it, "from non-namable three-letter agencies . . . both of them."[8]

Much like Fifth Generation, which MCC consciously mimicked, MCC has had trouble producing technologies justifying its earlier hopes and goals, and one wonders how long or in what capacity it will continue. Again, as with Fifth Generation and Supercomputer, the problem has not been that MCC is not creating world-class technology, but that the technology has often proved little relevant to market needs. "The companies had no problems with MCC's high risk projects, but problems of commercializability. Even if MCC did incredible technology, without a sense of what companies could do with it, they couldn't readily apply it."[9]

A major problem with MCC has been that what with tensions and coordination problems among the participating companies, the economies of scale expected from this "Japanese-like" cooperative consortium have never materialized. One analyst has described MCC as doomed by a "major American shortcoming—a weakness of intercompany cooperation."[10] Of course, the present analysis of Japan's consortia reveals that this "major *American* shortcoming" is in fact an *international* one—that consortia elsewhere also appear to be unwieldy vehicles for fostering high-tech competitiveness.

Sematech, a semiconductor research consortium launched in 1987 to rescue the battered U.S. semiconductor industry is several times larger than MCC and more widely touted. Throughout the early and mid 1980's, the U.S. semiconductor industry continued to lose market share to the Japanese in both semiconductors and semiconductor production equipment. Sematech was founded by fourteen U.S. semiconductor manufacturers, each of which contributes funding to its research activities. Through ARPA (formerly DARPA), the Department of Defense's Advanced Research Projects Agency, the federal government has contributed on the order of $100 million in annual funding, about half of Sematech's budget. In sum, Sematech has spent well over $1 billion since its launching.

The public case for Sematech's success has been quite simple. Since Sematech's launching, the United States's share of worldwide semiconductor markets, which hit its trough in 1988, has rebounded, with the United States taking the lead back from the Japanese in 1993. Sematech and industry officials are quick to point to Sematech as a key factor in the U.S. semiconductor industry's rebound. Other observers (such as Angel 1994) point to the rebound in market share, not in semiconductors themselves, but in semiconductor production equipment, as an indicator of Sematech's success, and note that Sematech is reported to have improved communication and cooperation within the semiconductor industry, particularly between semiconductor producers and equipment suppliers.[11]

These claims demand careful scrutiny. While I do not rule out the possibility that Sematech may have been successful, it is also clear that the evidence to demonstrate this claim has not been adequately put forth. It appears that the Sematech case is substantially more complicated than the simple success story offered by its backers.

In addressing the potential indicators of Sematech's success, firstly the linkage between the rebound in the United States's worldwide semiconductor market share and Sematech activities appears tenuous at best. That market share increase has been driven primarily by improved sales by the big three U.S. merchant semiconductor producers, Intel, Motorola, and Texas Instruments, particularly Intel, which on the basis of its overwhelming dominance of the world PC microprocessor market soared to a number one ranking in world semiconductor sales. All three companies deserve kudos for intelligent execution of shrewd business strategies in the late 1980's. To try to link their recent market success in semiconductors, and thus the U.S. rise in semiconductor market share, to Sematech just does not make sense.

Moreover, while no one would deny that Sematech's activities *coincided* with a rebound in the U.S. semiconductor industry, MITI's Supercomputer consortium is a compelling example of how government funding of a technology area and industry's success in that area in the marketplace can be totally unrelated. As described earlier, when MITI was funding the Supercomputer consortium during the 1980's, the major Japanese supercomputer firms, all participants in the MITI consortium, were seizing market share in the worldwide supercomputer market. This would seem to be prima facie evidence for the success of MITI's funding. Yet, as a close investigation of the Supercomputer consortium documents, there was *no* relationship between these two phenomena: the MITI consortium's R&D was unrelated to the firms' market-oriented supercomputer activities, and a case might even be made that the MITI consortium drained scarce technical talent away from the more market-relevant supercomputer efforts of the Japanese firms.

In terms of the next potential indicator of Sematech success, the potential positive effects of Sematech on market share in semiconductor equipment, this, too, faces the same problem of causation as the above claim about semiconductor market share. Surging sales in the early 1990's by such top U.S. equipment manufacturers as Applied Materials, KLA Instruments, and Lam Research are difficult to ascribe to Sematech without evidence explicitly linking Sematech activities to these sales, evidence more sophisticated than mere self-reports from Sematech members. As the U.S. General Accounting Office, which reviewed Sematech for Congress in 1992, put it: "How much of this change [in semiconductor equipment market share] is attributable to Sematech's efforts, however, is not clear."[12]

More critically, if one looks at the external research contracts that Sematech let out through 1992, the single largest area of research expenditure was in the area of advanced lithography equipment, Sematech's bold bid to try to break the hold of Nikon and Canon, the leading suppliers in this area. Indeed, the $108 million Sematech dedicated to this effort was over twice the amount of money spent on the next-largest project (Multilevel metals, $53 million) and four times that spent on the third-largest project (CIM/Manufacturing systems, $25.4 million).[13] The concentration of technical and financial resources in this single area was much like the Japanese VLSI consortium's focus on e-beam lithography—both were expensive bets, and neither yielded the expected payoffs. Despite improvements in U.S. advanced lithography equipment (so-called "steppers"), one could hardly have expected Nikon and Canon to abandon their own efforts to advance this critical technology, so Sematech chased a moving target and failed to make a dent in U.S. market share in this area.

Finally, there can be little question that Sematech does deserve credit for improving communication channels among semiconductor makers and equipment suppliers. But it is here that we get into the difficult issue of opportunity costs. Without denying this particular success, for example, one needs to consider whether Sematech's $1 billion could have been spent in more effective ways. On the issue of communication, one U.S. scientist who has participated in Sematech argues: "Sematech works as a forum for the exchange of ideas—it is a meeting ground and consensus can be formed. . . . But the money is not well spent. If the goal is to be a social club for these people to get together, it's a pretty expensive way to do it." [14]

In short, the crucial, and, I would argue, unanswered, question with regard to Sematech is not merely, "Did any positive results emerge?" but rather, "Was what emerged worth the money, technical talent, and management and policy-maker resources poured into it?" Would $1 billion have been better spent on university research that might spin off into new business enterprises, for example, or in launching multiple, smaller projects with less coordination overhead and less likelihood of political or institutional inertia prolonging their existence. It is worth noting in this regard that government subsidy of Sematech was originally scheduled to last just five years and has been prolonged beyond that by Congress against the explicit desires of DARPA (now ARPA), Sematech's funding agency. DARPA wanted to end Sematech funding in 1992 and roll those Sematech funds into other microelectronics projects, but has been compelled by Congress to continue subsidies, with no end in sight.

In conclusion, it would appear that the experiences of the two major U.S. consortia in electronics since the 1980's have yet to offer positive evidence endorsing consortia as an effective policy instrument to promote high-tech competitiveness. Moreover, the two consortia's continuing existence ought to raise warning flags about how difficult it can be to end large projects once a large revenue stream from the U.S. government is in place.

Thinking Clearly About Japan: Rolling Back the Revisionists

In producing policies that work, we also would be well served by a clearer vision of Japan, now next to the United States clearly the world's dominant economy, and apparently a model to governments worldwide for promoting high technology and economic growth. One line of thinking, frequently referred to as "revisionism," has become increasingly important, offering both a vision of Japan and a set of policy prescriptions to guarantee foreign access to Japanese domestic markets. "Revisionist" thinkers such as Chalmers Johnson, Clyde Prestowitz, James Fallows, Karel van Wolferen, and Laura D'Andrea Tyson, it is said, have "been successful in changing the world's perception of Japan." [15] The "revisionist Japan" they describe is, among other things, a Japan of solidarity and insularity, of bureaucratic control and predatory targeting of overseas markets. I argue, however, that both as a guide to reality and a basis for policy, such "revisionism" is deeply flawed.

The central tenet of "revisionism" is an emphasis on Japanese *difference*, the argument that the workings of capitalism and political economies that we accept as normal and legitimate elsewhere do not apply to Japan. According to the revisionists, the Japanese political economy has features such as clubby government/business and *keiretsu* relations, high and durable nontariff trade barriers, and aggressive targeting of important industries of the future.

These features are said to be *internationally "distinctive."* Tyson refers to the "distinctive features of Japanese capitalism," which include "cooperative business-government relations,"[16] while van Wolferen condemns the Japanese "free-market" fiction and "the mingling of the private and public domains in Japan," concluding that "the workings of the System inevitably negate effects that would be normal anywhere else in the industrialized world."[17] And Fallows adds: "The problem is the one-sidedness of Japan's ambitions. By continuing to launch new industrial assaults rather than simply buying better, cheaper products from abroad, Japan suggests that it does not accept the basic reciprocal logic of world trade. If more than a handful of countries behaved this way, there couldn't be any international trade."[18] The point of view is summed up by a vice president of the U.S. Chamber of Commerce in Tokyo, who explained to *Business Week* that "it doesn't matter how good you are, how hard-working, how much you look at the long term, or how much you spend on R&D. A Japanese decision to buy your product is *not going to be based on the market principles we're familiar with* [emphasis added]."[19]

Why single out "revisionism," even briefly, in a book on Japanese high-tech industrial policy? Simply put, because the "revisionists" are important. They have been called "the intellectual opinion makers of the 1990s,"[20] and their beliefs are a source of U.S. policy toward Japan today. Their argument, its vision and definition of the Japanese political economy, is so sweeping that it is impossible to avoid in an assessment of Japanese high-tech industrial policies—too much analytic space overlaps. "Revisionist" thinkers have, moreover, brought their policy prescriptions into this book's analytical domain. As noted in the 1989 *Business Week* article that helped popularize the perspective: "Revisionists talk about a new industrial policy in America in which the government would encourage research and development cooperation and set up agencies to direct international trade and industry."[21]

As evidenced in this book, I believe that this "revisionist" policy prescription is highly problematic. An industrial policy akin to what the Japanese have practiced in recent high-tech consortia is an invitation to a party to which we do not want to go. More fundamentally, the underlying analytical assumptions of "revisionism," indeed the name itself, are troubling. "Revisionism" suggests that there is something new here, that these are rebels boldly challenging the conventional wisdom on Japan.

This strains historical fact. As new, cutting-edge thinkers, the "revisionists" are more sheep in wolves' clothing. The view that emphasizes Japan's "different" political economy has in fact been well entrenched in Western thinking (and Western business grievances) for decades. For example, James Abegglen's articulation of the concept of "Japan Inc." and the publication of Eugene Kaplan's *Japan: The Government-Business Relationship*, which emphasized tight business/bureaucratic linkages in the Japanese political economy, date back over *two decades*.

Thus, the "revisionists" offer what amounts to an *old orthodoxy*, not a new revision, of Japanese difference and closedness, but in a *new package*, an articulation that draws resonance both from the assertion that there is something new there and from the establishment of a common front among the various individuals who hold these views. In ideological unity, there is power. One person's ideas are merely a "point of view." Multiple persons become a "school of thought."

What is truly new about "revisionism" appears to be not the ideas themselves but the audience for the ideas. With the United States facing a yawning trade gap with Japan, U.S. policy makers and business decision makers are increasingly receptive to the idea that Japanese "difference" is behind American difficulties. This, I would speculate, is why there has been no pitched public battle, pro and con, no heated debate about the merits of the argument. The "revisionists" appear to have made major inroads in the area of public policy because their argument is both familiar and enticing. Of course, there is a business-cycle effect here: when the U.S. economy gunned out of recession in 1993 while Japan continued to wallow in its longest recession in postwar history, the "revisionists" receded in prominence in tandem with the apparent decline in the Japanese competitive threat.

Let me now turn to some specific flaws with "revisionism." Three are central:

1. *An overemphasis on (a) the positive effects of state intervention in markets and (b) the advantages of market closure.* As is strikingly apparent in the quotations from Johnson, Tyson, and van Wolferen

that open Chapter 1, Japanese industrial policy and the substitution of a reputedly tight government/business relationship for open-market principles are seen by "revisionists" to place Japanese industry at an international competitive advantage. Heavy bureaucratic intervention, trade barriers, business collusion, and so on, which unquestionably have dysfunctional aspects and impose competitive costs, seem to have no negative hold on this "revisionist Japan." As I argue at length in this book, however, the reality is that there *are* costs and there *are* dramatic failures in Japanese industrial policy, and these costs and failures appear to have increased substantially since Japan became an advanced industrialized economy.

The problems created by government interference in free markets and the subsequent rigidities and lack of responsiveness to market demands are not unique to Japan either: they encumber other countries, such as Korea, that have sought to follow Japan's example of Johnson's "stated-guided market system." As one analyst of the Korean economy puts it: "Korea's No. 1 problem is the bureaucracy. If you talk to some Korean businessmen, it's like they have a bowling ball strapped to their legs."[22] This is perhaps an argument that only an American would dare to make, but in this sense Japan has had a substantial advantage over Korea: its huge market has made it much more of a target than Korea for extremely heavy, decades-long U.S. pressure to liberalize and deregulate. America, in the form of *gaiatsu* (foreign pressure), has become an essential Fourth Estate in the Japanese political economy, helping to break down the encumbering and stultifying restrictions on free competition created by bureaucratic regulatory control.

In short, a case can be made that American *gaiatsu* applied for America's benefit in opening Japanese markets to U.S. goods and services has in the long run benefited Japan as much, if not more. This is certainly the case in terms of the net welfare gains for the Japanese nation as a whole, both static and dynamic, from opening up markets to competition-driven efficiencies. It is also likely, I would hypothesize, that American *gaiatsu*-driven market opening has helped Japanese industry itself by creating conditions of competition that drive firms to more efficient behavior and force them to look to overseas markets. "Revisionists" suggest that closed Japanese markets allow Japanese firms to use domestic profits to fund overseas export drives. I do not deny that such cross-subsidy is possible. But as is suggested by the cases of the Japanese semiconductor industry in the early 1970's and the personal computer industry in the 1980's (there being substantial market entry barriers to foreign/new firms in both cases), there is another underappreciated, countervailing dynamic in closed Japanese domestic markets: rather than fueling export drives, the protection of closed domestic markets can sap Japanese firms of the incentive to seek overseas markets.

The major Japanese semiconductor firms did not set up their first overseas sales offices until 1975–76, when the end of tariff and quota protection for the domestic market made it clear that they had to export to generate the economies of scale to survive competitively against the big U.S. firms. Similarly in PCs in the 1980's, the fat oligopolistic profits of NEC, Toshiba, and Fujitsu (particularly and overwhelming NEC's) turned these electronics giants inward as they fought for a greater share of the hugely profitable, outrageously overpriced, under-competitive Japanese PC market. Personal computers never became the major Japanese export product they were expected to be, and U.S. and Taiwanese PC firms powered ahead of Japan in world markets.

2. *An overemphasis on bureaucratic power.* As Johnson puts it in his book on MITI's industrial policy, "Japan's is a system of bureaucratic rule." One of the main thrusts of this book has been to document that this notion of the Japanese political economy, certainly in the case of MITI's industrial policy, is now grossly overstated and out of date. While the Ministry of Post and Telecommunications and the Ministry of Finance, among others, cling to their regulatory fiefdoms, MITI has lost substantial power and faces a serious battle to maintain its policy leverage and prestige.

Ironically, some of the "revisionist" policy prescriptions, such as establishing sector-specific market-share targets for Japan, would in fact strengthen the very actors—the government ministries who would enforce the targets on the Japanese companies—whose power the "revisionists" bemoan as a barrier to market-based capitalism. If the U.S. government is serious about eliminating any market-intruding power of the various Japanese bureaucracies, a power that in high-tech sectors is clearly on the wane, the last thing we should set as a policy goal is to rescue these bureaucracies by giving them a newly enhanced tool, such as the monitoring of market share and production quotas, with which to manipulate Japanese companies.

3. *An underrecognition of pluralism in the Japanese political economy.* Van Wolferen is the most extreme here, calling Japan a collusive "System" with a capital S to emphasize the dominant, unified force at work. Put bluntly, this notion of sweeping, transcendental unity in the Japanese political economy has no basis in fact. As can be seen in Japanese high-tech policy, companies fight, bureaucracies fight, bureaucra-

cies and companies fight, and policies fail or get killed off because of internecine and external power struggles. To deny the existence of this pluralism is to deny the United States opportunities in its trade policies, where Japanese barriers to free-market competition remain, to seek allies within Japan for desirable policy changes. In sum, a fundamental problem with "revisionism" is that for a theory that purports to describe what "Japan is really like," it does an exceedingly poor job of describing what Japan is really like.

What Is to Be Done? Policy Prescriptions for MITI and Japan

As documented at length in this book, MITI has not fared well with high-tech consortia in recent times, especially because of structural changes that picked up speed in the early 1980's. How should MITI respond to these changes?

A critical issue is whether or not MITI should continue its pursuit of high-visibility high-tech consortia such as those investigated in this book and its ongoing Real World Computing. It is hard to recommend such a course. Much of this story has already been told in Chapter 7, but to sum up here, structural changes in the late 1970's and early 1980's eroded much of the structural basis for MITI's success in these policies. MITI went from offering compellingly large financial inducements to comparatively weak Japanese electronics firms in the 1970's to offering relatively small incentives to extremely strong Japanese firms in the 1980's. The power balance had swung away from MITI and toward the companies, which no longer heeded MITI's call.

There are fundamental problems with the policy instruments chosen as well. As instruments of MITI policy, consortia have too many disadvantages and are too clumsy a vehicle for furthering focused policy ends. In bringing together an array of companies with diverse interests, inevitably including competitors, MITI has to devote too many of its human resources and too much of its prestige simply to preventing the extremely strong centrifugal forces from tearing the consortia apart.

Moreover, in addition to committing its prestige and human resources to them, MITI also finds itself overselling its consortia plans. Budgets are tight, and funding leading-edge technological development calls for large budgets that themselves require major public sales efforts, as well as persuading conservative Ministry of Finance bureaucrats to authorize funds. The result is a self-defeating cycle of overselling in order to secure political, public, and MOF budgetary support, followed by a need to downplay expectations once budgets are secured and/or overplay the results achieved. The process inevitably invites cynicism about MITI's evenhandedness and the process of lurching from overselling of results—at first, expected results at the beginning of consortia, and finally actual results at the end of consortia—erodes the sense of balance and integrity that MITI has commanded over the years.

If not the continuation of traditional MITI policies, what road, then, should MITI embark upon? The question deserves serious consideration, for MITI's continuing functioning as an important ministry hinges on the answer. Put bluntly, MITI is in trouble—it has policy jurisdiction, but it has lost power and prestige. It no longer has the tools to command industry as it used to, and its reputation has suffered. Indeed, in an *Asahi shimbun* survey of upper-level bureaucrats of all of the Japanese ministries in spring 1994, MITI was the *only* major ministry named over twenty times in response to the question: "What ministry do you believe it would be fine to eliminate?" MITI's total of twenty-three thumbs-downs compared to one for the Ministry of Posts and Telegraphs, two apiece for the Ministry of Finance and the Ministry of Construction, four for the Ministry of Transportation, seven for the Ministry of Education, ten for the Ministry of Labor, and fifteen for the grossly protectionist Ministry of Agriculture, which had the second-highest score.[23]

MITI's decline has not gone unnoticed within the ministry itself. Most of MITI understands that it must seek a new path, and there is considerable commitment to deregulation and reform within the ministry. It may come as something of a shock to veteran Japan hands, but the MITI of the 1960's and 1970's, which was largely oriented toward promotion of domestic industry at the expense of foreign competition (the "anti-openness MITI"), has made a radical about-face. "Pro-openness" is the order of the day, and most sections of MITI are explicitly committed to rectifying Japan's large positive trade imbalance and promoting competition in the Japanese market. As a subcommittee of MITI's Industrial Structure Council emphasized in February 1994, "in all fields, fundamental deregulation of government regulation, reform of existing systems, and the rectifying of existing private sector business practices should be undertaken with the aim to correct domestic to international price disparities, create new industries, encourage new vitality and improve international access to the Japanese markets."[24]

This is not mere lip service to reform. Along with (naturally) the Ministry of Foreign Affairs, MITI is clearly the most internationalist of Japan's major ministries and is the most committed to domestic deregulation. The reasons for this are simple and compelling. MITI's *own* interests increasingly (and some would say ironically) align with the forces advocating deregulation of the Japanese bureaucracy. What has made MITI's industrial policy task more difficult in the 1980's and 1990's is that despite an immense pool of bureaucratic talent and deep ties with Japanese industry, it finds itself hampered in putting these strengths to use, as other Japanese ministries have often played a negative, blocking role toward new MITI policy initiatives. Some of these conflicts have been described in this book, such as MITI's struggle with the Ministry of Education over access to Japan's universities as leading-edge research sites.

They also include other areas, however, such as MITI's desire to play a more active role in telecommunications and new media (conflict with the Ministry of Post and Telecommunications) or in the financing of new businesses and provision of venture capital (conflict with the Ministry of Finance). Everywhere it turns, MITI seems to confront other major ministries with regulatory jurisdiction and powers over new policy areas. With MITI having been largely stripped of its own major regulatory powers by the early 1980's, it too requires a level playing field, the knocking down of bureaucratic regulations and barriers that prevent MITI from charting new policy paths.

This is why, for example, one can read in MITI's public reports fierce criticism of the state of Japan's financial system, where among other things "market functions are underdeveloped," "principles of competition do not fully apply," and "Japanese corporations are forced to resort to inefficient modes of procurement of industrial financing."[25] The critique rings true, as does MITI's call for the internationalization of the yen and deregulation and restructuring of the financial system to increase competition and the variety of financial services and products available. The problem, however, is that MITI has no power to do these things. This is the mighty Ministry of Finance's bailiwick, and MITI needs the MOF to take action before financial markets are more opened up and MITI can pursue policies that take advantage of new opportunities and risk capital to promote new industries and new enterprises.[26]

MITI does try to dodge the regulatory net of other ministries and continues to be creative about seeking new problem areas in which to exercise leadership. A classic example of this is MITI's proposal to introduce daylight savings time (called "summer time" in Japanese) to allow Japanese summer evenings to stay lighter for recreation longer and mornings to be cooler. Anyone who has ever spent summer months in Japan, where it seems to be light at 4:30 A.M., already hot by the morning commute, and dark at 7:30 P.M., can instinctively sense the promise of MITI's proposal. What may not be so obvious is that "time" policy was an obvious candidate for a MITI initiative, simply because no other ministry could claim jurisdiction over the setting of Japan's clocks. Thus, unlike with other areas of dense ministerial regulation and control, MITI could freely move in. MITI has proceeded to make a compelling economic case for daylight savings time in Japan, generating econometric data to demonstrate that its introduction will both stimulate Japan's domestic economy and reduce energy consumption.[27]

Nonetheless, the search for holes in other ministries' policy nets can only take MITI so far. For continued power, MITI needs change. That change should come in three areas. First, MITI needs to seek a more expansive vision of its policy role and agenda. Japan has profound structural problems that need to be resolved. The term *kokusaika* (internationalization) has had considerable currency in Japan since the mid 1980's to describe the need for Japan to open up to the outside world, economically, culturally, and politically. However, if one had to make a judgment call, Japan's fundamental economic problems are not international, but domestic. Not *kokusaika*, but rather *kokunaika* (literally "country-inner-ization") is critical—the creation of a vibrant domestic economy and society and the solving of deeply rooted structural problems. These domestic problems include the continuing gross imbalance between Japan's high cost of living and costs in other major industrialized countries, its overcrowded major city centers, and Japan's rapidly aging population and startlingly low birthrate. With about 1.5 children being born to the average Japanese woman over her lifetime, Japan's birthrate is well below the population replacement rate.

MITI last went through an organizational overhaul in the early 1970's, two decades ago, and perhaps it is time for another one that would articulate a new vision of Japanese prosperity and refocus policy away from traditional industrial concerns and toward grappling with more fundamental issues such as Japan's quality of life and aging population structure that have not just economic but profound social dimensions as well.

Secondly, in pursuing this new course, MITI must push aggressively for Japan's domestic deregulation. Deregulation is absolutely crucial both for MITI and for Japan. It will not only buttress MITI's ability to make policy in new areas but will also contribute to *kokunaika*. One major reason articulated for the wide discrepancies between Japanese prices and overseas prices is government regulation and barriers to competition that drive up Japanese prices.

The third new emphasis for MITI should be in its industrial policies: a swing away from large companies and toward smaller companies. MITI has traditionally oriented itself (outside of its dedicated small-business arm) toward large companies, inviting only a few big companies, for example, to join the high-tech consortia described in this book. This needs to end, for several reasons. The first is that from a purely operations perspective, MITI is much better suited to dealing with smaller companies. Big companies need MITI less financially. Big companies also have better information networks. MITI's analytic expertise, information resources, and vast human network will have much more powerful positive effects when directed toward smaller firms that may lack these advantages.

Reorientation toward smaller companies would also directly enable MITI to address a major weakness in the Japanese economy—the shortfall of venture capital and the lack of a robust small-business sector, particularly in high technology, that can spur innovation and seize leading-edge markets. Japan continues to be pummeled at the leading-edge of high technology by venture-capital-financed U.S. startups that seize market initiatives and stake out intellectual property rights by inventing new products and processes for new markets.

Moreover, creating an economic climate in Japan that is more "small-company friendly" would help resolve Japan's most pressing international economic issue: its yawning trade surplus and the continuing trade friction arising from charges that the Japanese economic system is biased against new entrants. In short, Japan's small-company problem is in many ways a concomitant of the problem of foreign access—strengthening anti-trust law and breaking down oligopolistic business practices would allow both small domestic companies and foreign companies to increase their market opportunities substantially.

This book has looked at Japanese industrial policies on high technology over the past two decades. From the mid 1970's on, Japan was dramatically transformed from a follower, technologically and economically speaking, into a leader. Japanese companies moved to center stage, and MITI retreated. And as companies and bureaucracies struggled over government policy, the public face of placid cooperation was diligently maintained, obscuring an underlying reality of harsh internal and external competition. It is this fierce and winnowing competition, not cooperation, that is the central dynamic in Japan's modern industrial policy and, indeed, in much of Japanese society.

Reference Matter

Notes

Chapter One

1. James Fallows (1989a, 1989b) and Clyde Prestowitz (1988) round out the group of those considered major "revisionists." The final chapter of this book includes a brief critical assessment of such "revisionism."

2. Despite important challenges (e.g., Komiya, Okuno, and Suzumura [1988], Patrick et al. [1986], Saxonhouse [1979], Yamamura [1982, 1986], and Okimoto [1989]), the cooperative-functional thesis continues to dominate, not merely the revisionist approach, but also the academic literature on MITI industrial policy and particularly MITI high-tech consortia. In the literature on Japanese high-tech consortia, the analytical focus of this book, Wakasugi 1986 and 1990, Anchordoguy 1989 and 1991, Fransman 1991, Sigurdson 1986, and Sakakibara 1983 typify this cooperative-functional school. In terms of *cooperation*, they posit a substantial degree of collaboration between the Japanese government and business in the carrying out of Japanese industrial policy. Indeed, the relationship is seen to be well ordered and well entrenched—a "Japanese Technology-Creating System" (Fransman 1991: 1). Or as Frank Upham (1987: 167) puts it, in a broader work that explores the relationship between the legal system and pressures for structural reform, Japanese companies and MITI "exist in a state of cooperative interdependence."

This literature on high-tech consortia also sees MITI's industrial policy as quite *functional*, to the extent that it can serve as a model for other countries on how to shape government/business relations in an advanced economy. One of the primary reasons for this success is perceived to be the cooperation described above: MITI-guided interfirm cooperation avoids the "potentially wasteful aspects of competition" (Anchordoguy 1989: 8); "market processes do not tend to generate an appropriate amount of research cooperation," Martin Fransman argues (1991: 6). Moreover, close government/business consultation is seen as disciplining the state to produce policies that conform well to basic market forces.

3. Gerald Jiro Hane's (1992) excellent doctoral dissertation stands apart from the above-described cooperative-functional literature in finding competitive dynamics to be more fundamental than cooperative ones in the operations of superconductor and engineering-ceramics consortia.

This analysis differs from Hane's on two counts. First, by focusing more closely on the negotiations leading up to the consortia, I have uncovered more conflict in MITI policy making than Hane does. In the Supercomputer and Fifth Generation consortia most of the conflict between MITI and the participating companies took place during pre-consortia negotiations—for example, as the two sides struggled over the consortium's organization and agenda. Second, whereas Hane tends to emphasize *technical* success or breakthroughs arising from R&D, I emphasize *market* or *product* success. Applying a stronger opportunity-cost criterion to R&D, I argue that technical success may be inadequate to justify R&D activity if it is not linked to marketable products. Technical talent and R&D funds are too limited to consume on displays of purely technical brilliance. As Jerry Sanders, the CEO of Advanced Micro Devices, Inc., a major U.S. semiconductor producer, has put it, "What's the point of being the technological leader if you're not making money?" (*Forbes*, Nov. 26, 1979).

4. The evidence in this book of Japan's major electronics companies increasingly resisting and/or ignoring MITI's wishes in high-tech consortia thus flies in the face of Chalmers Johnson's claim: "There have been occasions when industries or enterprises revolted against what the government told them to do— incidents that are among the most sensational in postwar politics—but they did not, and do not, happen often enough to be routine" (1982:10). In fact, as is documented in Chapter 4, conflict between MITI and the companies *is* routine, at least in the electronics sector.

5. For a view emphasizing the role of conflict in Japanese industrial development, see David Friedman's depiction of it as "the consequence of myriad political struggles" (1988:26).

6. Yamamura 1982 warns against overlooking the costs of an "addiction to guidance and cartels" (104). This theme emerges also in Yamamura 1986.

7. "The information industry can be considered the most successful of MITI's high technology undertakings" (Imai 1986:164).

8. Americans "are usually smugly devoted to their 'theories' that bureaucrats could not possibly 'pick winners' or otherwise help an economy to prosper. They have stuck to such theories through 25 years of trade deficits and in the face of overwhelming evidence to the contrary throughout East Asia" (Johnson 1994:22). "We must adopt our own industrial policy. Japan and the other high-growth economies of East Asia have demonstrated that the state can be a critically important contributor to the success of market economies" (Johnson 1993:25–26).

9. NTT's work on VLSI began in 1975, and the MITI VLSI joint lab was shut down in 1979 (at the end of fiscal year 1979—in calendar-year terms, the beginning of 1980). See Chapter 3 on the interaction between MITI and NTT over VLSI.

10. I would note here that in pointing out that international trade tensions made an official MITI-led TRON consortium impossible, I am not suggesting that in the absence of those trade tensions, TRON would inevitably have emerged as a MITI consortium. It is far from clear that TRON's founder, Ken Sakamura, or the major TRON participating companies would have invited or sanctioned MITI's playing a more direct role.

11. In addition to participants, I interviewed a few nonparticipants who

were either experts in the technology area involved or had tracked the activities of the consortia (e.g., other academics, securities analysts, and journalists).

12. Given the sometimes highly charged nature of the material (for example, Japanese R&D managers or MITI officials expressing frustration or bitterness about some of the things that had gone wrong), going off the record was inevitable. An on-the-record interview would either not have occurred or would have reflected only an official, party-line view of events.

In the chapters that follow, I have kept the promise of interview confidentiality. None of the names from these off-the-record interviews appear, and as far as possible the names of the companies themselves have not been given either. In lieu of these names, interviews are cited by the date of the interview (I usually scheduled multiple interviews on a single day) and by an assigned code that represents both the company and the division. These codes are consistent throughout the book—for example, when I quote comments by managers identified as being from company A in chapters 2 and 4, they are from the same company. This is admittedly somewhat cryptic, but it meets the interviews' condition of strict confidentiality.

Chapter Two

1. The figure that 85 percent of the VLSI funding went to the companies' "group labs" comes from Ken-ichi Imai (1986: 143), a Japanese economist who has done important work on industrial organization, network theory, and high technology. I have not been able to generate a figure this precise in my analysis of VLSI consortium documents and media reports and in my participant interviews, but all of the evidence nonetheless points in the same direction: that the overwhelming majority of the VLSI consortium budget was spent outside of the joint lab. Whether it was 70 percent or 80 percent or 90 percent would depend upon the particular accounting practices employed. I am thus highly confident that Imai's figure accurately reflects the allocation of funds.

2. To give an example of how "information is not readily available," in July 1992, I met with a senior NTT manager who, upon hearing of my need for more written materials from the NTT VLSI program, said that he was probably the only one who had kept most of the documents from the effort, and emptied his cabinet of a two-foot-high stack of materials. But after stacking them up high on the table that separated us, the manager pointed out that these 1970's documents were marked "For internal company use only," so he regretfully would not be able to make them available to me.

3. Senior academic, University A, author interview, July 21, 1992. This perspective continues to have a strong hold in the Japanese scientific community. It was echoed in 1992, for example, by a group of twenty leading Japanese scientists (Arima et al.: 1992), primarily university professors, who in conjunction with the Fujitsu Research Institute (Fujitsu sōgō kenkyūsho) called for an increased Japanese commitment to supercomputing in their joint volume *Adovansudo kompyūtingu: 21 seiki no kagaku gijutsu kiban* (Advanced Computing: The Twenty-first Century's Science and Technology Foundation).

4. Gartner Group 1991: 207.

5. Senior academic, University A, author interview, Nov. 17, 1992.

6. The exceptions to these separate lab activities were (1) when Fujitsu, Hi-

tachi, and NEC sent their researchers to MITI's ETL to learn Josephson junction technologies in 1983–85, and (2) the final integration of the company-built computer systems in 1989.

7. See the discussion of von Neumann's role in articulating the concept of a digital computer in Hennessey and Patterson 1990: 24–25.

8. Ken Sakamura, author interview, University of Tokyo, Nov. 11, 1992.

9. Ibid.

10. See, e.g., Sakamura 1987 and 1989. The title of Sakamura 1989 gives the flavor of the ambitious language Sakamura is prone to in describing the project: *Dennō mirai ron: TRON no seiki* (The Future of the Electronic Brain: The Century of TRON).

11. Sakamura 1987 suggests additional priorities of TRON, including the stimulation of Japan's own technology base and ease of use (4–32).

12. TRON Association 1991: 5.

13. Sakamura 1987 gives an overview of the design philosophy and parameters of ITRON, BTRON, CTRON, MTRON, and the TRON chip. Sakamura 1989 provides a more thorough discussion of TRON application projects, such as TRON City.

14. Sakamura 1987 devotes a chapter to explaining the advantages of the new TRON keyboard (160–78).

Chapter Three

1. Vogel 1985: 164

2. Quoted in *Asahi shimbun*, Oct. 5, 1981.

3. Fransman 1991: 104.

4. MITI official, Section D, author interview, May 12, 1993.

5. MOE official, Section A, author interview, Nov 20, 1992.

6. Ferguson and Morris 1993: 33–34.

7. Ibid.: 35, 89.

8. Senior academic, University B, author interview, July 17, 1992.

9. Ibid.

10. Ibid.

11. *Nikkei sangyō shimbun*, Jan. 31, 1975, cited in *Kompyūtopia*, Aug. 1975.

12. NTT R&D manager, author interview, July 27, 1992.

13. Ibid.

14. Ibid.

15. *Nihon keizai shimbun*, Mar. 30, 1978.

16. *Asahi shimbun*, Apr. 7, 1977.

17. Technically, the MITI VLSI consortium did not close down operations until 1990, some fifteen years after it started. However, the joint lab facilities that were used by the consortium were shut down and returned to NEC at the end of FY 1979. In the 1980's, the VLSI Association, the official name of the consortium, continued to exist to supervise the handling of intellectual property rights, repayment of the MITI subsidies, and some additional private company research that was nominally carried out under the auspices of the consortium, but actually was just independent company research. Most observers thus treat FY 1979 as the end of the VLSI consortium. Similarly, NTT contin-

ued VLSI research after its two three-year programs ended in 1981; however, this analysis deals only with NTT efforts that coexisted with the MITI-led consortium.

18. NTT R&D manager, author interview, July 27, 1992.

19. Ibid.

20. Fransman 1990: 150; MITI official, Section C, author interview, Nov. 11, 1992.

21. *Asahi shimbun*, Aug. 2, 1978.

22. ETL scientist, Section B, author interview, Nov. 16, 1992.

23. *Asahi shimbun*, July 2, 1980.

24. Hane 1992: 310.

25. *Nikkei sangyō shimbun*, July 20, 1984.

26. *Nihon keizai shimbun*, June 19, 1980.

27. *Nihon keizai shimbun*, Dec. 17, 1980. The ETL announcement did not mention NTT by name; rather, it pointed specifically to the GaAs technology NTT had used.

28. *Asahi shimbun*, Nov. 11, 1982.

29. Uemae 1985: 129–32.

30. Computer science journalist, author interview, Nov. 10, 1992.

31. Company A research manager, Section A, author interview, July 23, 1992.

32. Kazuhiro Fuchi, ICOT, author interview, July 24, 1992.

33. "A Lull in the Fifth," *Datamation*, Sept. 15, 1985.

34. Ibid.

35. U.S. Embassy report cited in Kahaner 1991.

36. Feigenbaum, McCorduck, and Nii 1988: 200.

37. ETL scientist, from notes of interview conducted by Stanford University colleague, June 1992.

38. Since AIST is considered a "technical" operation, in fact, the top spot at AIST is always reserved for a *gikan*.

39. Uemae 1985: 73.

Chapter Four

1. MITI official, Section B, author interview, July 27, 1992.

2. Ibid.

3. Ibid.

4. Quoted in Fransman 1991: 63.

5. Senior VLSI joint lab manager, author interview, Nov. 18, 1992.

6. Masato Nebashi, the managing director of the VLSI consortium, puts the number of researchers in each lab from the lead company as on average around 60 percent. The numbers were probably higher for the microfabrication labs and lower for the other labs. Chō LSI gijutsu kenkyū kumiai 1990: 82.

7. Quoted in ibid.: 83.

8. Senior VLSI joint lab manager, author interview, Nov. 18, 1992.

9. Hane 1992: 297.

10. ETL scientist, Section B, author interview, Nov. 16, 1992.

11. Ibid.

12. Ibid.

13. Senior academic, University A, author interview, July 21, 1992.
14. U.S. Office of Technology Assessment 1991: 267.
15. ETL scientist, Section A, author interview, Nov. 16, 1992.
16. Company C researcher, Section B, author interview, July 22, 1992.
17. Quoted in Fransman 1991: 152.
18. ETL scientist, Section A, author interview, Nov. 16, 1992.
19. Company C researcher, Section B, author interview, July 22, 1992.
20. ETL scientist, Section A, author interview, Nov. 16, 1992.
21. Company C researcher, Section B, author interview, July 22, 1992.
22. Quoted in Fransman 1991: 151.
23. ETL scientist, Section A, author interview, Nov. 16, 1992.
24. Company D researcher, Section B, author interview, Nov. 18, 1992.
25. ETL scientist, Section A, author interview, Nov. 16, 1992.
26. Company D researcher, Section B, author interview, Nov. 18, 1992.
27. Ibid.
28. Company A researcher, Section B, author interview, July 28, 1992.
29. Company D researcher, Section B, author interview, Nov. 18, 1992.
30. ETL scientist, Section A, author interview, Nov. 16, 1992.
31. Ibid.
32. The $100 million dollar estimate is from Gartner Group 1991: 35.
33. ETL scientist, Section A, author interview, Nov. 16, 1992.
34. Ibid.
35. Uemae 1985: 34.
36. Uemae 1985: 48.
37. Fuchi wrote extensively in the early 1980's about Fifth Generation computing and "knowledge processing" (the term he preferred to "artificial intelligence"). See Fuchi 1983 and Fuchi and Akagi 1984.
38. The "systematization" committee is also referred to as the "systemalization" committee in the 1992 Fifth Generation international conference proceedings.
39. Uemae 1985: 105–6.
40. Kazuhiro Fuchi, ICOT, author interview, July 24, 1992.
41. Quoted in Uemae 1985: 113.
42. Ibid.: 110.
43. Ibid.: 111.
44. Ibid.: 104.
45. Ibid.: 114.
46. Kazuhiro Fuchi, ICOT, author interview, July 24, 1992.
47. ETL scientist, Section A, author interview, Nov. 16, 1992.
48. Uemae 1985: 135.
49. *Asahi shimbun*, Oct. 5, 1981.
50. Feigenbaum and McCorduck 1983: 109.
51. Kazuhiro Fuchi, ICOT, author interview, July 24, 1992.
52. Company B research manager, Section A, author interview, July 16, 1992.
53. Quoted in "A Lull in the Fifth," *Datamation*, Sept. 15, 1985.
54. *Nikkei sangyō shimbun*, July 28, 1992.
55. Ibid.

56. Ibid.

57. Company B research manager, Section A, author interview, July 16, 1992.

58. Company D research manager, Section A, author interview, July 23, 1992.

59. Ibid.

60. Kazuhiro Fuchi, ICOT, author interview, July 24, 1992.

61. See, e.g., Fransman 1991: 53–55. Anchordoguy 1989 offers a more balanced view, more in keeping with Japanese notions (122–24).

62. Company A research manager, Section A, author interview, July 23, 1992.

63. As noted in Table 1, after the official end of the Fifth Generation project in FY 1992 [on a calendar basis, March 1993], ICOT continued on a smaller, non-MITI project for yet another two years in order to try to disseminate the Fifth Generation project's results. It is expected to shut down finally in March 1995.

64. RISC was first conceptualized and implemented by an IBM scientist, John Cocke, "one of the great figures in the recent history of computing technology" (Ferguson and Morris 1993: 38). Unfortunately, IBM allowed the technology to languish, and smaller competitors stole a march on it in the booming 1980's RISC workstation market. See Ferguson and Morris 1993 for a detailed and highly readable account of RISC's fateful odyssey within IBM (37–50).

65. Kazuhiro Fuchi, ICOT, author interview, July 24, 1992.

66. Company B research manager, Section A, author interview, July 16, 1992.

67. Company A research manager, Section A, author interview, July 23, 1992.

68. Yagi 1992: 11. I would note, however, that the final two elements of Tsutomu Yagi's new paradigm—UNIX workstations and RISC microprocessors—are substantially less certain than the trends to downsizing and open architectures. UNIX, for example, faces tough competition from other new operating systems, such as Microsoft's Windows NT.

In turn, while it is true that RISC microprocessors have permanently reworked approaches to microprocessor design and no new major microprocessors have been introduced since the mid 1980's that are non-RISC, Intel continues to dominate the world microprocessor market with its non-RISC (but in certain ways increasingly "RISC-like") x86 microprocessor architecture. Intel and Intel-compatible x86 chips continue to be at the heart of most personal computers (i.e., so-called "IBM-compatible" PCs) shipped in the world. IBM, Apple, and Motorola's jointly developed PowerPC microprocessor, which began shipping in quantity in early 1994, is the RISC design that poses the most significant, immediate threat to Intel's non-RISC microprocessor near-monopoly. The game is thus far from won (if it ever will be) for UNIX and RISC challengers to computing's status quo.

69. Senior academic, University A, author interview, July 21, 1992.

70. Company B research manager, Section A, author interview, July 16, 1992.

71. Kahaner 1992.

72. Stanford University computer scientist, Laboratory A, author interview, Sept. 23, 1992.

73. Company A research manager, Section A, author interview, July 23, 1992.

74. Kazuhiro Fuchi, ICOT, author interview, July 24, 1992.

75. *Nikkei Weekly,* June 13, 1992.

76. MITI official, Section A, author interview, July 17, 1992.

77. Company B research manager, Section A, author interview, July 16, 1992.

78. NEC manager, author interview, Nov. 9, 1992.

Chapter Five

1. It is important to point out, however, that although minimal, intercompany research cooperation was not nonexistent. In fact, intercompany R&D cooperation in the form of (1) joint R&D and (2) information exchange, helped along by the perception of giant IBM as a common threat, was higher in the VLSI consortium than in any of the other three major consortia examined here. The primary forms cooperation took were information exchange and patent sharing. Patent sharing was the easiest. All patents were the common property of the VLSI Association and the members, no matter which company had done the research. This patent rule was clear, readily policed, and required only the most passive of intercompany cooperation, so it worked well.

In terms of information exchange, there were common technical meetings and seminars and research memoranda. Here again, though, most of the information flow from the joint lab to the group labs took place *within,* not between, companies. Joint lab researchers would "return home" (*satogaeri*) and report on the activities of the joint lab to their home companies. As documented later in this chapter, joint R&D was far less prevalent than these muted forms of information exchange: actual intercompany joint R&D was limited to the small joint lab, and even there it was highly constrained.

2. *Nihon keizai shimbun,* Oct. 4, 1976.

3. Ibid.

4. Quoted in Fransman 1991: 67.

5. *Nihon keizai shimbun,* Jan. 19, 1981; also Chō LSI gijutsu kenkyū kumiai 1990: 82

6. Quoted in Chō LSI gijutsu kenkyū kumiai 1990: 82.

7. Sakakibara 1983: 24.

8. Quoted in Sakakibara 1983: 23.

9. Quoted in Fransman 1991: 67.

10. In discussing the VLSI consortium, Tarui 1984 asserts that 16 percent of all joint lab patents were interorganization patents, but the data that Fransman (1991) provides produce a figure of 15 percent. The two figures are so close as to be essentially interchangeable, and since Fransman provides a patent-by-patent breakdown of the joint patent data, I use the Fransman data here.

11. Fransman 1991: 36.

12. Ibid.: 53.

13. I should point out that Yasuo Tarui objects to this characterization of cooperation at the joint lab. "You cannot use 15% / 100% for the measure of cooperation," he says, because the "nature of patent[s] [is] originality," which Tarui argues springs from individuals. Thus at the joint lab, he notes, 59 percent of the patents came from individual researchers, which "had no connection with cooperation with anybody." Tarui points out that if one excludes all of these individual patents and uses only joint patents as a baseline, 39 percent of all joint patents were between researchers from different organizations, a proportion he calls "substantial" (personal correspondence to author, Aug. 19, 1993).

I concur that Tarui's starting point, that *R&D is fundamentally not joint or cooperative*, is a defensible and sensible position. However, assuming minimal joint activity and ruling out individual patents from the scope of investigation, as Tarui advocates, flies in the face of MITI's official description of the joint lab as "Cooperative Laboratories," a characterization widely accepted in the literature (see Chapter 6, n. 1, below). The question being asked here is therefore, did the VLSI consortium genuinely produce high levels of joint/cooperative R&D? In finding that most research was done independently outside of the joint lab and that joint research was minimal, *even at the joint R&D lab*, contributing to only 15 percent of total patents, my answer is no. The cooperative reputation of the VLSI consortium is misplaced.

14. The argument of the NEC manager quoted in Anchordoguy 1989 (177) that the VLSI companies got a return *500 percent* greater on their e-beam R&D because they participated in the joint lab is thus quite difficult to defend. In the first place, the "five times greater" figure seems to have been pulled out of thin air. It probably refers to the fact that there were five companies at the joint lab and hypothesizes a one-to-one correspondence between the number of companies and the return on R&D. However, the analysis here shows that interaction between the companies was so minimal that this kind of return would have been impossible, even leaving out the additional coordination costs imposed by the joint lab. Marie Anchordoguy was the contractor who originally wrote the analyses of Japanese industrial policy included in the U.S. Office of Technology Assessment 1991. For her original report, see Anchordoguy 1991, which repeats the claim of a 500 percent gain in returns to R&D.

15. "There were always arguments and more competition than cooperation overall," Doane 1984 concludes (162–63).

16. For an excellent history of Toshiba's technological development and business strategy in the semiconductor area from the 1950's to the present, see Nakagawa 1989, chs. 7–9 of which cover the VLSI consortium period.

17. Doane 1984: 165.

18. Quoted in Fransman 1991: 81.

19. Company A researcher, Section C, author interview, Mar. 3, 1992.

20. Company A researcher, Section C, author interview, Nov. 2, 1992.

21. This lack of joint patents is confirmed by a corporate participant. Company E researcher, Section B, author interview, Sept. 23, 1993.

22. Fransman 1991: 168.

23. ETL scientist, Section B, author interview, Nov. 16, 1992.

24. We should be careful to note that these ambiguous usages do not appear to be the personal predilections of the reports' authors. Given that this "name-

less" style spans a wide variety of texts written by various consortium participants, it appears that the authors are conforming to some sort of MITI policy,
explicit or implicit.

25. Fransman 1991: 244–45.

26. This can be seen, e.g., in reports in *Nihon keizai shimbun*, Sept. 30,
1981, and *Asahi shimbun*, Apr. 2, 1982.

27. Company C researcher, Section B, author interview, July 22, 1992.

28. ETL scientist, Section A, author interview, Nov. 16, 1992.

29. Company C researcher, Section B, author interview, July 22, 1992.

30. Ibid.

31. Fransman 1991: 168.

32. Hane 1992: 322.

33. ETL scientist, Section A, author interview, Nov. 16, 1992.

34. This is confirmed in interviews with two of the consortium participants
and with ETL scientists.

35. Company A researcher, Section B, author interview, July 28, 1992.

36. Company C researcher, Section B, author interview, July 22, 1992.

37. Company A researcher, Section B, author interview, July 28, 1992.

38. Ibid.

39. Company C researcher, Section B, author interview, July 22, 1992.

40. ETL scientist, Section A, author interview, Nov. 16, 1992.

41. Fujitsu research manager, Section A, author interview, July 16, 1992.

42. Company D researcher, Section B, author interview, Nov. 18, 1992.

43. Ibid.

44. The term "company men" reflects the reality that the researchers were
all or almost all men.

45. ETL scientist, Section A, author interview, Nov. 16, 1992.

46. Company D researcher, Section B, author interview, Nov. 18, 1992.

47. In doing the initial work separately and then coming together at the end
for final integration, the vector supercomputer effort violated an operating rule
that researchers at MCC, a U.S. consortium that sprang up in response to Fifth
Generation, had come to understand. As a project manager reported to an
MCC investigative team, "When we see problems, it's often because they don't
understand that you don't go build computer programs and build hardware
and someday at the waterfront integrate them" (Curtis et al. 1988: 14).

48. Hitachi researcher, author interview, Nov. 18, 1992.

49. Ibid.

50. Fransman 1991: 228.

51. Company C researcher, Section A, author interview, Nov. 10, 1992.

52. Quoted in Fransman 1991: 215.

53. An MIT professor visiting ICOT found these incompatibilities among
the five PIMs quite surprising, declaring that it results in "serious portability
problems for the software" (Nikhil 1991).

54. Iwashita Shigeaki, executive director of Japan Systems Research Institute, a Tokyo software company, quoted in *Business Week*, Apr. 13, 1981,
p. 123.

55. Company B research manager, Section A, author interview, July 16,
1992.

56. For a Japanese perspective on the impact of RISC microprocessors on
the computer business, see Yagi 1992, esp. pp. 17–24, 140–50.

57. The U.S. RISC makers had an additional advantage over the TRON chip in the performance improvements that RISC microprocessors brought to desktop computing applications. For reasons that are not clear, Sakamura has been extremely derisive of the RISC approach. He has vehemently criticized the new RISC chips, insisting that his more conventional TRON architecture (typically labeled CISC—complex instruction set computer) was far superior. Sakamura even claimed that his TRON chip was not RISC and not CISC, but *SISC*, a *Smart* Instruction Set Computer (1987: 61–82), a statement that was so clearly a public relations gambit that it was hardly likely to win over the microprocessor design community.

58. While the Toshiba and Matsushita instruction counts are identical, it appears that some of the underlying instructions are different, so their respective TRON microprocessors are incompatible.

Chapter Six

1. Sigurdson 1986, Sakakibara 1983, Fransman 1991, and Anchordoguy 1989 all suggest that joint R&D efficiencies in the VLSI consortium were fundamental to its success. Baldwin and Krugman 1988's econometric analysis of posited Japanese market closure in 16K DRAMs in the late 1970's is sometimes mistakenly considered an analysis of the VLSI consortium. The authors clearly separate out market closure effects from the VLSI consortium's subsidy effects, and analyze the former, not the latter. (In doing so, Baldwin and Krugman suggest that if market closure existed, it likely helped the Japanese semiconductor industry, but at a net welfare loss to the Japanese economy, although they are quite open about the fact that their model is highly preliminary and that different interpretations of the data are possible.) It is important to understand that, as I explain in Chapter 2, the VLSI consortium was an explicit response to the end of MITI-regulated market closure in 1975–76.

2. If we were to invoke a term economists use, this broad class of spillovers could also be thought of as akin to externalities. The use of the term "externality" is avoided here, however, given that we are not talking about discrete transactions with clearly defined boundaries where what is internalized and externalized can be readily stated. Moreover, some spillovers, such as the training of engineers, while they are clearly secondary effects of consortia activities, were also consciously among consortia goals and thus not particularly "external."

3. In using multiple indicators to evaluate these four consortia, I follow the economics literature on "project evaluation" and government technology or "innovation" policy, which stresses the need for multiple indicators to increase evaluation reliability. See, e.g., Rothwell 1985 and Gibbons 1988. The literature on project evaluation that focuses on government efforts to stimulate technology innovation tends to be unabashedly self-critical, declaiming the lack of genuine evidence (White 1981) brought to bear in evaluating these government projects. "Finally, having discussed [government technological] innovation policy in some detail, it must be admitted that we know very little about its effectiveness. It is a fact that few innovation policy initiatives have been subjected to objective assessment regarding their efficacy. There is, thus, a pressing need for detailed impact assessment across a wide range of countries," Rothwell and Zegveld 1981 concludes (153).

Noting that much of the literature that purports to evaluate government technology projects and policies is in fact of a *"monitoring* (what happened?)" nature, rather than a more policy-relevant *"evaluative* (did it make a difference?)" approach, Gibbons 1988 calls for further research using the latter approach's more stringent and data-intensive criteria. This book hopes to be an example of such research and to provide a level of detail about major Japanese technology-innovation projects that, at least in a small way, contributes to filling the international "evidential gap" on government technology policies.

4. In emphasizing the role of the group labs, not the joint lab, I part company with both contemporaneous media views of VLSI (see, e.g., *Nihon keizai,* Apr. 7, 1980, which called the joint lab "the central organ" and "the brain" of the consortium) and with retrospective scholarly assessments of VLSI, including Fransman 1991, Sigurdson 1986, Anchordoguy 1989, and Sakakibara 1983, all of which emphasize the joint lab. "The most important point I think is the existence of the cooperative laboratory. The project succeeded in integrating various development capabilities of its member firms, who were competitors in the same market, by providing a 'place' for organized activities," says Sakakibara 1983 (17). Fransman does not even discuss the group labs; his analysis focuses solely on joint-lab activities.

5. The argument here is that the e-beam effort was a *major* failure, not that it was a *total* failure. After the joint lab had shut down in the early 1980's, several of the participating companies, working on their own, managed to salvage some of the e-beam technology by redirecting it to the making of photographic masks used in the optical approach that the joint lab had hoped to supplant.

6. Anchordoguy 1989 points approvingly to the joint lab's e-beam R&D as an example of the VLSI consortium's success, overlooking the disappointing technical failure that occurred in e-beams (177).

7. Sigurdson 1986: 105.

8. Ibid.: 79.

9. Estimate from Company A researcher, Section C, author interview, Nov. 2, 1992.

10. Fransman 1991 and Anchordoguy 1991 similarly declare the Supercomputer consortium a success, but a close examination of the consortium's outputs contradicts this conclusion, as will be seen in the analysis that follows. (For a slightly amended version of Anchordoguy 1991, see U.S. Office of Technology Assessment 1991, for which Anchordoguy wrote the supercomputer analysis.) Hane 1992 assesses only the Josephson junction effort within Supercomputer and is positive about its technical outputs. As explained in Chapter 1, n. 3, my analysis parts company with Hane in emphasizing a more market-based criterion for evaluating success: technical breakthroughs are inadequate to posit the success of *industrial policy* when the technologies are irrelevant to market needs.

11. MITI 1990: 93–94.

12. Hashimoto et al. 1990: 7.

13. Ibid.

14. The Fujitsu team that reported these results did mention that the 10.9 gflops (gigaflops or billion computations/second) result based upon their one-second software program was a "maximum speed," but no other measurement

data in terms of gigaflops are given to supplement this "maximum." The only gflops result reported is the 10.9 gflops number, based upon which it was declared that the vector supercomputer was "achieving the 10 GFLOPS target speed" (Hashimoto et al., 1990: 7).

15. ETL scientist, Section A, author interview, Nov. 16, 1992.

16. Ibid.

17. Company D researcher, Section B, author interview, Nov. 18, 1992.

18. MITI 1990: 94; NEC team: Nishi et al. 1990: 15.

19. ETL scientist, Section B, author interview, Nov. 16, 1992.

20. Company C researcher, Section B, author interview, July 22, 1992.

21. ETL scientist, Section B, author interview, Nov. 16, 1992.

22. Company A researcher, Section B, author interview, July 28, 1992; I do not know what happened to the Oki machine.

23. Kahaner and Kung 1990.

24. Company C researcher, Section B, author interview, July 22, 1992.

25. See, e.g., MITI 1992a, 1992b, and ICOT 1992. A more extensive discussion of Fifth Generation's goals and accomplishments follows.

26. Fransman 1991 is more positive on Fifth Generation's achievements, but arguably both pays insufficient attention to its opportunity costs and overplays its positive spillover effects, both of which are analyzed in sections that follow.

27. Much of this description of the early planning period is drawn from Junichiro Uemae's 1985 book *Jyapanīzu dorīmu* (Japanese Dream), an in-depth, highly celebratory look at the Fifth Generation effort. Uemae's reportage is excellent, providing a level of detail on the early years of the planning and operation of Fifth Generation that is unparalleled.

28. Kurita 1988 offers the most complete account of the various U.S. and European responses to the Japanese Fifth Generation program, including the U.S. Strategic Computing Program and other DARPA and NSF activities, the U.S. MCC (Microelectronics and Computer Technology Corporation), the European Esprit II, and the British, German, and French programs.

29. Moto-oka et al. 1982: 7.

30. Fuchi 1992: 2.

31. This is confirmed in a number of interviews with different Fifth Generation participants.

32. Fuchi 1992: 1.

33. Ibid.

34. ICOT 1983: 396.

35. *Nikkei AI* 1991: 36–37.

36. Doi, Furukawa, and Fuchi 1989: 16.

37. Cf. Moto-oka and Kitsuregawa 1985: 112; Moto-oka and Kitsuregawa 1984 is the Japanese version.

38. Doi, Furukawa, and Fuchi 1989: 16.

39. Ibid.

40. Ken Sakamura's public rhetoric became considerably more subdued when TRON began to encounter problems such as the failure of BTRON to win standardization in the Japanese education market.

41. U.S. scientist, author interview, Mar. 25, 1993.

42. *Nikkei AI* 1991: 20.

43. Quoted in "'Fifth Generation' Falls Short of Goals," *Washington Post,* June 2, 1992.
44. MITI 1992c.
45. Company F research manager, author interview, July 29, 1992.
46. *New York Times,* June 5, 1992.
47. *The Independent* (London), June 8, 1992.
48. "Japan's Research Goes Flat," *The Times* (London), June 12, 1992.
49. "'Fifth Generation' Became Japan's Lost Generation," *New York Times,* June 8, 1992.
50. This included an AI *book* boom, with numerous books emerging to discuss the world-changing effects of artificial intelligence. Pico Tano's (1984) title *Jinkō chinō no shōgeki* (The Shock of Artificial Intelligence) captures the mood of the era well.
51. "'Fifth Generation' Became Japan's Lost Generation," *New York Times,* June 8, 1992.
52. Company F research manager, author interview, July 29, 1992.
53. Uchida 1992: 48. The ICOT manager's discussion in this section is highly hedged, as appropriate to this kind of comparison, calling for porting Fifth Generation (KL1) software to RISC chips so that actual comparisons can be made.
54. See also Kurozumi 1992's comparison of *single-processor* performance of PIM machines to RISC machines and contention that PIM processor performance is closing in on RISC performance (18). Takashi Kurozumi was a top ICOT research manager.
55. Saeki 1992: 20.
56. Taki 1992: 66–70.
57. Stanford University computer scientist A, author interview, Aug. 14, 1993.
58. Taki 1992: 68–70.
59. *Nikkei AI* 1991: 27–28.
60. Company D research manager, Section A, author interview, July 23, 1992.
61. *Nikkei Electronics* (Japanese-language), May 14, 1990, p. 116.

Chapter Seven

1. That changes in Japanese industrial structure and/or stage of economic development can have important implications for the Japanese government/business relationship or government economic policy is quite intuitive and has been pointed out by a number of analysts. See, e.g., Patrick 1986 and Murakami 1986 on Japanese high-tech industrial policy; Saxonhouse 1988 on economic structural change and Japanese economic performance, which applies some useful econometric tools to the problem; Yamamura 1982 on administrative guidance and cartels; Eads and Yamamura 1987 on industrial policy and the broad political-economic context in which it operates; and Noguchi 1982 on fiscal policy.

In noting that these analysts have trod the ground of Japanese structural change before me, I would add that the particular contribution of this chapter is to document and explicitly link changes in the *macro* political and economic

environment to *micro*-level changes in MITI high-tech policy profiles and outputs. Trade tensions, for example, are linked to a lengthening timespan for
MITI high-tech consortia.

2. Eads and Yamamura 1987 suggests that changes in Japan's industrial
policy-making context may well negatively affect future industrial-policy performance. This analysis confirms that reasoning. I focus, however, on a differently configured set of change variables that relate more directly to high-tech
policies. (For example, Eads and Yamamura's "pro-growth consensus" variable is not seen to play a role here.) Eads and Yamamura's specified changes
are: (1) changes in government capabilities; (2) a reduced kit of industrial-
policy tools; and (3) changes in the pro-growth consensus.

3. The single exception is revealing: it was the futuristic PIPS consortium
(1971–80), an earlier highly ambitious MITI effort whose goals of advanced,
quasi-intelligent computer processing were in many ways similar to Fifth Generation's. The firms balked at contributing funds; it was too futuristic for their
taste.

4. Japan, Science and Technology Agency 1991: 90.

5. Japan, Science and Technology Agency, *Indicators of Science and Technology*, 1993; 1994: 96–99.

6. American Electronics Association, *Electronics Market Databook*, various years.

7. Quoted in *Business Week*, July 11, 1977.

8. Ibid.

9. Or as Jerry Sanders, then president of Advanced Micro Devices, Inc., put
it, the SIA's goal was "to make sure the industry's position is presented to the
U.S. government on a lot of issues" (ibid.).

10. *Asahi shimbun*, 1/7/78.

11. *Business Week*, Oct. 24, 1977.

12. Quoted in ibid.

13. *Electronics News*, Nov. 12, 1977.

14. Cartel: *Nihon keizai shimbun*, May 12, 1978; Unfair: *Business Week*,
Dec. 3, 1979.

15. *Nihon keizai shimbun*, June 1, 1979.

16. *Nihon keizai shimbun*, Feb 9, 1979.

17. Quoted in *Forbes*, May 14, 1979.

18. *Nihon keizai shimbun*, Jan. 1, 1980.

19. *Asahi shimbun*, Mar. 17, 1978.

20. *Nihon keizai shimbun*, Feb. 18, 1980.

21. *Nihon keizai shimbun*, May 12, 1978. As an epilogue to the VLSI consortium story, even after the VLSI joint lab shut down in early 1980, the U.S.
Semiconductor Industry Association (SIA) found no satisfaction in market
trends. Japanese firms continued to gain market share. By 1982, the SIA was
again threatening to file a dumping suit against the Japanese firms. The Reagan
administration held off the SIA with promises to remedy the situation, but after
most of the U.S. producers were knocked out of the DRAM market, despite
spending hundreds of millions of dollars in their race against the Japanese, the
SIA filed a dumping suit in 1985. For an excellent review of recent and projected future developments in the Japanese semiconductor and affiliated industries, see Shimura 1992. For sources on Japan's semiconductor industry devel-

opment, see Shimura 1979, 1980, 1981, 1982, 1992; Nakagawa 1981, 1989; Kikuchi 1992; and Aida 1991–92, the four volumes of which are companions to a remarkably popular NHK documentary series in 1991 on the development of the Japanese electronics industry.

22. Moto-oka et al. 1982: 4.

23. A good example of the new MITI policy profile in the semiconductor area is its "atom level" semiconductor project unveiled in December 1992, which proposes to develop technology for 16-gigabit DRAMs, 1,000 times denser than the existing leading-edge product. Unlike VLSI, however, the consortium is explicitly international in character, with MITI expecting over 40 firms from the United States, Europe, and Japan to participate. See *Nihon keizai shimbun*, Dec. 3, 1992.

24. See, e.g., *Asahi shimbun*, Feb. 14 and Mar. 12, 1980.

25. By "outside" papers, I refer here to the 90 papers that make up volume 2 of the conference proceedings. The papers in volume 1 are largely devoted to presentation and discussion of ICOT's own research results.

26. MITI official, Section C, author interview, Nov. 11, 1992. This "basic research = longer time frame" reasoning was reaffirmed by a top ICOT official. Yoshihisa Ogawa, ICOT, author interview, Nov. 19, 1992.

27. Company A researcher, Section B, author interview, July 28, 1992.

28. Company A research manager, Section C, author interview, Mar. 3, 1993.

Chapter Eight

1. Although acknowledging certain difficulties in making cross-national comparisons from Japan to other countries, I do not, however, treat Japan as particularly distinctive in its political economy. It is no more difficult to compare the United States to Japan than the United States to France or any other country. On this, see esp. Saxonhouse 1982 and 1988 on patterns of Japanese trade structure and their relative lack of cross-national distinctiveness.

2. Japanese high-tech industrial policy is thus in stark contrast to Peter Hall's description of economic policy in France and the United Kingdom: "In these nations, for instance, economic problems are also always political problems. Contemporary economic difficulties and the attempts to find solutions to them cannot be analyzed in isolation from associated political dilemmas" (1986: 280–81).

3. See, e.g., Samuel 1987's excellent, theoretically guided historical analysis of the Japanese energy industry, which has been more dominated by static or decline dynamics and has thus generated a more robust relationship between Japanese business and the state. Samuel's description of business/government dealings as framed by "reciprocal consent" is problematic if applied to the MITI high-tech policies described here, however, in which corporate consent to MITI policy initiatives is at best grudging and often nonexistent. Both my findings and Samuel's are conditioned by the reality that "Reciprocal consent" is more likely to operate as a framework of business/government interaction in more technologically and institutionally stable and more state-dependent industries, such as energy, than in high technology.

4. See, e.g., Sigurdson 1986, Sakakibara 1983, Fransman 1991, and Anchordoguy 1989.

5. Hane 1992: 324.

6. Yamamura 1986 adds that MITI-led joint consortia tend to favor large firms and reinforce tendencies to market concentration in Japan, results hardly consistent with the underlying premises and philosophy of U.S. anti-trust law.

7. Company E manager, Section D, author interview, Nov. 9, 1992.

8. Former MCC official, author interview, Dec. 11, 1992.

9. Ibid.

10. Sobel 1986: 241.

11. Angel 1994 offers an assessment of the environment and strategies that led to the U.S. semiconductor industry's rebound.

12. U.S. General Accounting Office 1992: 2. The GAO did not seem to find the claim of Sematech members that they bought more U.S. equipment because of Sematech compelling. After all, Sematech is receiving a $100 million subsidy a year from the U.S. government so one would hardly expect its members to *deny* that Sematech is useful.

13. Ibid.: 30.

14. Company G research scientist, author interview, Dec. 3, 1992.

15. "Why Japan Can Still Say No," *Business Week*, July 5, 1993.

16. Tyson 1992: 58.

17. van Wolferen 1988: 6, 44, 47.

18. Fallows 1989a: 50.

19. "Rethinking Japan," *Business Week*, Aug. 7, 1989, p. 47.

20. Ibid., p. 49.

21. Ibid., p. 46.

22. Quoted in "South Korean Functionaries Thwart Kim: Unless Business Is Set Free, Nation Could Become a Toothless Tiger," *Asian Wall Street Journal*, Mar. 31, 1994, p. 1.

23. *Asahi shimbun*, Apr. 5, 1994. Nobuyoshi Namiki, a former elite MITI official, has joined the fray, continually denouncing MITI as decrepit and arrogant (Namiki 1989, 1994). The tone of things is a far cry from MITI's heyday, when books such as Saburō Shiroyama's *Kanryōtachi no natsu* (The Summer of the Bureaucrats) (1975), written in the year Namiki left MITI, celebrated MITI's power.

24. MITI 1994: 17.

25. Ibid.: 24.

26. Yamaguchi 1987 seems quite premature in declaring the end of MOF's power.

27. *Mainichi shimbun*, Apr. 28, 1994.

Works Cited

Aida, Yutaka. 1991–92. *Denshi rikkoku: Nihon no jijōden* (The Founding of an Electronics Nation: Japan's Own Story). 4 vols. Tokyo: NHK Press.

American Electronics Association. Various years. *Electronics Market Databook.* Palo Alto, Calif.: American Electronics Association.

Anchordoguy, Marie. 1989. *Computers Inc.: Japan's Challenge to IBM.* Cambridge, Mass.: Council on East Asian Studies, Harvard University; distributed by Harvard University Press.

———. 1991. *Japanese Policies for the Supercomputer Industry.* Contractor Report. Washington, D.C.: Office of Technology Assessment.

Angel, David P. 1994. *Restructuring for Innovation: The Remaking of the U.S. Semiconductor Industry.* New York: Guilford Press.

Arima, Akito, Shūzō Murakami, and Yasumasu Kanada. 1992. *Adovansudokompyūtingu: 21 seiki no kagaku gijutsu kiban* (Advanced Computing: The Twenty-first Century's Science and Technology Foundation). Tokyo: Baifūkan.

Baldwin, Richard E., and Krugman, Paul R. 1988. "Market Access and International Competition: A Simulation Study of 16K Random Access Memories." In Robert C. Feenstra, ed., *Empirical Methods for International Trade,* pp. 171–97. Cambridge, Mass.: MIT Press.

Chō LSI gijutsu kenkyū kumiai (VLSI Technology Research Association). 1990. *15 nen no ayumi* (A Fifteen-Year History). Tokyo: VLSI Technology Research Association.

Curtis, Bill, Herb Krasner, and Neil Iscoe. 1988. "A Field Study of the Software Design Process for Large Systems." *MCC Technical Report* STP-233-88, July 18, 1988.

Denshi gijutsu sōgō kenkyūsho (Electrotechnical Laboratory). 1990. *Kagaku gijutsu-yō kōsoku keisan shisutemu no kenkyūkaihatsu: Seika happyōkai ronbunshū I* (Proceedings of the Conference on Achievements of the National R&D Program "High-Speed Computing System for Scientific and Technological Uses," Part I). June 1990.

Denshi jōhō tsūshin gakkai (Institute of Electronics, Information, and Communication Engineers (IEICE)). 1990. *Denshi jōhō tsūshin gakkai gijutsu kenkyū hōkoku* (IEICE Technology Research Report). CPSY90–5–11. Computer system. 6/22/90.

Doane, Donna L. 1984. "Two Essays on Technological Innovation: Innovation and Economic Stagnation, and Interfirm Cooperation for Innovation in Japan." Ph.D. diss., Yale University, Department of Economics.

Doi, Norihisa, Koichi Furukawa, and Kazuhiro Fuchi. 1989. "Overview of Fifth-Generation Computer Systems Project." *Science and Technology in Japan*, Feb. 1989, pp. 14–16.

Eads, George C., and Kozo Yamamura. 1987. "The Future of Industrial Policy." In Kozo Yamamura and Yasukichi Yasuba, eds., *The Political Economy of Japan*, vol. 1: *The Domestic Transformation*, pp. 423–68. Stanford, Calif.: Stanford University Press.

Fair Trade Commission. 1985. *Kenkyū kaihatsu to dokusen kinshi seisaku* (R&D and Anti-Trust Policy). Tokyo: Gyōsei.

Fallows, James M. 1989a. "Containing Japan." *Atlantic Monthly*, May 1989, 40–54.

———. 1989b. *More Like Us: Making America Great Again*. Boston: Houghton Mifflin.

Feigenbaum, Edward A., and Pamela A. McCorduck. 1984. *The Fifth Generation: Artificial Intelligence and Japan's Computer Challenge to the World*. New York: New American Library.

Feigenbaum, Edward, Pamela McCorduck, and H. Penny Nii. 1988. *The Rise of the Expert Company: How Visionary Companies Are Using Artificial Intelligence to Achieve Higher Productivity and Profits*. New York: Times Books.

Ferguson, Charles E., and Charles R. Morris. 1993. *Computer Wars: How the West Can Win in a Post-IBM World*. New York: Times Books.

Fransman, Martin. 1991. *The Market and Beyond: Cooperation and Competition in Information Technology Development in the Japanese System*. New York: Cambridge University Press.

Friedman, David. 1988. *The Misunderstood Miracle: Industrial Development and Political Change in Japan*. Ithaca, N.Y.: Cornell University Press.

Fuchi, Kazuhiro. 1983. *Chisiki kagaku e no shōtai* (An Invitation to the Science of Intelligence). Tokyo: NHK Press.

———. 1992. "Launching the New Era." Keynote speech, International Conference on Fifth Generation Computer Systems 1992. Tokyo: Institute for New Generation Computer Technology (ICOT).

Fuchi, Kazuhiro, and Akio Akagi. 1984. *Dai 5 sedai kompyūta o tsukuru* (Creating the Fifth Generation Computer). Tokyo: NHK Press.

Gartner Group. 1991. *High Performance Computing and Communications: Investment in American Competitiveness*. Prepared for the U.S. Department of Energy and Los Alamos National Laboratory. Mar. 15, 1991.

Gibbons, Michael. 1988. "The Evaluation of Government Policies for Innovation." In J. David Roessner, ed., *Government Innovation Policy: Design, Implementation, Evaluation*, pp. 135–46. London: Macmillan.

Hall, Peter. 1986. *Governing the Economy: The Politics of State Intervention in Britain and France*. Cambridge, U.K.: Polity Press.

Hane, Gerald Jiro. 1992. "Research and Development Consortia in Innovation in Japan: Case Studies in Superconductivity and Engineering Ceramics." Ph.D. diss., Harvard University.

Hashimoto, Shin, Sachio Kamiya, Naoaki Kasuya, Nobuhiko Kuribayashi, and Ryoichi Narita. 1990. "Hierarchical Memory Connected Multi-Processor." In Denshi jōhō tsūshin gakkai (IEICE), *Denshi jōhō tsūshin gakkai gijutsu kenkyū hōkoku* (IEICE Technology Research Report), pp. 1–8. CPSY90–5–11. (Computer system). 6/22/90.

Hennessy, John L., and David A. Patterson. 1990. *Computer Architecture: A Quantitative Approach*. San Mateo, Calif.: Morgan Kaufmann Publishers.

Imai, Ken-ichi. 1986. "Japan's Industrial Policy for High Technology Industry." In Hugh Patrick, ed., *Japan's High Technology Industries: Lessons and Limitations of Industrial Policy*, pp. 137–70. Seattle: University of Washington Press.

Institute for New Generation Computer Technology (ICOT). 1992. *International Conference on Fifth Generation Computer Systems, 1992*. Tokyo: Ohmsha.

———. 1983. *Outline of Research and Development Plans for Fifth Generation Computer Systems*. Apr. 1983. Full text reprinted in "Japan and the Fifth Generation," *Byte*, Nov. 1983, pp. 394–400.

Japan Development Bank. 1994. *Tōkei yōron* (Statistical Handbook). Tokyo: Japan Development Bank.

Japan Information Processing Development Center. 1991. *Informatization White Paper*. Tokyo: JIPDEC.

Japan. Science and Technology Agency. 1990. *Nihon no kagaku gijutsu seisakushi* (The History of Japan's Science and Technology Policy). Tokyo: STA.

———. Various years. *Indicators of Science and Technology*. Tokyo: STA.

Johnson, Chalmers A. 1982. *MITI and the Japanese Miracle: The Growth of Industrial Policy, 1925–1975*. Stanford, Calif.: Stanford University Press.

———. 1993. "The Foundations of Japan's Wealth and Power and Why They Baffle the United States." Paper presented to the Workshop on "Japan as Techno-Economic Superpower: Implications for the United States." Santa Fe, New Mexico: Center for National Security Studies, Los Alamos National Laboratory. Nov. 18–19, 1993.

———. 1994. "Puppets and Puppeteers: Japanese Political Reform." MS.

Kagaku Gijutsu-yō Kōsoku Keisan Shisutemu Gijutsu Kumiai (Scientific Computer Research Association). 1990. *Kagaku gijutsu-yō kōsoku keisan shisutemu no kenkyū kaihatsu: Seika happyōkai ronbunshū II* (Proceedings of the Conference on Achievements of the National R&D Program "High-Speed Computing System for Scientific and Technological Uses," Part II). June 1990.

Kahaner, David. 1991. "ICOT." Occasional report transmitted electronically over the INTERNET. Tokyo: U.S. Office of Naval Research. 5/17/91.

———. 1992. "Japan Supercomputing '92 Conference, 23 April 1992." Occasional report transmitted electronically over the INTERNET. Tokyo: U.S. Office of Naval Research. 4/27/92.

Kahaner, David, and H. T. Kung. 1990. "Aspects of Parallel Computing Research in Japan—Hitachi, Matsushita, and Japan Electronics Show 1990." Occasional report transmitted electronically over the INTERNET. Tokyo: U.S. Office of Naval Research. 11/6/90.

Kikuchi, Makoto. 1992. *Nihon no handōtai 40 nen* (Forty Years of Japanese Semiconductors). Tokyo: Chūō Kōron.

Komiya, Ryutaro, Masahiro Okuno, and Kotaro Suzumura. 1988. *Industrial Policy of Japan*. San Diego: Academic Press.

Kurita, Shōhei. 1988. *90 nendai no kompyūta wōzu* (The Computer Wars of the 1990's). Tokyo: Nikkan Kōgyō Shimbun-sha.

Kurozumi, Takashi. 1992. "Overview of the Ten Years of the FGCS Project." In Institute for New Generation Computer Technology (ICOT), *International Conference on Fifth Generation Computer Systems, 1992*, pp. 9–19. Tokyo: Ohmsha.

MITI. 1990. *Kagaku gijutsu-yō kōsoku keisan shisutemu no kenkyū kaihatsu ni kan suru hyōka hōkoku* (Evaluation Report of the R&D on the "High-Speed Computing System for Scientific and Technological Uses"). Aug. 1990.

———. 1992a. *Dai go sedai konpyūta purojekuto no hyōka oyobi kongo no kadai to tenbō no arikata, chūkan hōkoku* (Evaluation of the Fifth Generation Computer Project, along with Future Tasks and Outlooks, Mid-Term Report). Denshi keisanki kiso gijutsu kaihatsu suishin iinkai (Committee on Promoting Fundamental Technology Development in Computers). 6/18/92.

———. 1992b. "Dai go sedai konpyūta purojekuto no hyōka oyobi kongo no kadai to tenbō no arikata, chūkan hōkoku ni tsuite" (About the Evaluation of the Fifth Generation Computer Project, Along with Future Tasks and Outlook: Midterm Report). Electronics Policy Division. Mimeo. 6/18/92.

———. 1992c. "Kaigai kenkyūsha e no ankēto kekka" (Results of the Survey of Overseas Researchers). Mimeo. 6/18/92.

———. 1994. *The Subcommittee for Long-Range Issues of the Industrial Structure Council: Interim Recommendations*. MITI provisional translation. NR-411 (94–1). Feb. 1994.

Moto-oka, Tōru, et al. 1982. "Challenge for Knowledge Information Processing Systems (Preliminary Report on Fifth Generation Computer Systems)." In Tōru Moto-oka, ed., *Fifth Generation Computer Systems: Proceedings of the International Conference on Fifth Generation Computer Systems*, pp. 3–92. New York: North-Holland, 1982.

Moto-oka, Tōru, and Masaru Kitsuregawa. 1984. *Dai go sedai kompyūta* (The Fifth Generation Computer). Iwanami Shoten.

———. 1985. *The Fifth Generation Computer: The Japanese Challenge*. Trans. F. D. R. Apps. New York: John Wiley.

Murakami, Yasusuke. 1987. "Technology in Transition: Two Perspectives on Industrial Policy." In Hugh Patrick, ed. *Japan's High Technology Industries: Lessons and Limitations of Industrial Policy*, pp. 211–42. Seattle: University of Washington Press.

Nakagawa, Yasuzō. 1981. *Nihon no handōtai kaihatsu* (The Development of Japanese Semiconductors). Tokyo: Diamond.

———. 1989. *Tōshiba no handōtai jigyō senryaku* (Toshiba's Semiconductor Strategy). Tokyo: Diamond.

Namiki, Nobuyoshi. 1989. *Tsūsanshō no shūen* (The End of MITI). Tokyo: Diamond.

———. 1994. *Tsūsanshō no hatan* (The Failure of MITI). Tokyo: Kōdansha.

Nihon handōtai nenkan (Japan Semiconductor Yearbook). Various years. Tokyo: Press Journal.

Nikhil, Rishiyur. 1991. "Parallel Processing Research in Japan, Supplement." Occasional report transmitted electronically over the INTERNET. Tokyo: U.S. Office of Naval Research. 5/30/91.

Nikkei AI. 1991. *Tokushū: Dai go sedai konpyūta keikaku no sōkessan* (Special Report: A Comprehensive Final Evaluation of the Fifth Generation Research Plan). Special issue. Summer 1991.

Nishi, Naoki, Naoya Ohno, Yoshiki Seo, Ryōsei Nakazaki, Akira Jippō, Tsuyoshi Kishino, and Akihiro Dohya. 1990. "One-Level File Store hōshiki o saiyō shita taiyōryō kōsoku kioku sochi" (A Large-Scale Memory Device That Used the One-Level File Store Method). In Denshi jōhō tsūshin gakkai (IEICE), *Denshi jōhō tsūshin gakkai gijutsu kenkyū hōkoku*, pp. 9–16. IEICE Technology Research Report. CPSY90–5–11. (Computer system). 6/22/90.

Noguchi, Yukio. 1982. "The Government-Business Relationship in Japan: The Changing Role of Fiscal Resources." In Kozo Yamamura, editor, *Policy and Trade Issues of the Japanese Economy*, pp. 123–42. Seattle: University of Washington Press.

Okimoto, Daniel I. 1989. *Between MITI and the Market: Japanese Industrial Policy for High Technology.* Stanford, Calif.: Stanford University Press.

Okimoto, Daniel I., Takuo Sugano, and Franklin B. Weinstein, eds. 1984. *Competitive Edge: The Semiconductor Industry in the U.S. and Japan.* Stanford, Calif: Stanford University Press.

Patrick, Hugh. 1986. "Japanese High Technology Industrial Policy in Comparative Context." In Hugh Patrick, ed. *Japan's High Technology Industries: Lessons and Limitations of Industrial Policy*, pp. 3–34. Seattle: University of Washington Press.

Prestowitz, Clyde. 1988. *Trading Places: How We Allowed Japan to Take the Lead.* New York: Basic Books.

Rothwell, R. 1985. "Evaluation of Innovation Policy." In Gerry Sweeney, ed., *Innovation Policies: An International Perspective*, pp. 167–88. New York: St. Martin's Press.

Saeki, Toshinori. 1992. "Dai go sedai konpyūta purojekuto no gaiyō to sono kokusai kōken no arikata" (An Outline of the Fifth Generation Computer Project and Its International Contribution). *Bōeki to sangyō* (Trade and Industry) 10, no. 2: 19–22.

Sakakibara, Kiyonori. 1983. "From Imitation to Innovation: The Very Large Scale Integrated (VLSI) Semiconductor Project in Japan." MIT Sloan School Working Paper. Oct. 1983.

Sakamura, Ken. 1987. *TRON o tsukuru* (The Making of TRON). Tokyo: Kyōritsu Shuppan.

———. 1989. *Dennō mirai ron: TRON no seiki* (The Future of the Electronic Brain: The Century of TRON). Tokyo: Kadokawa Shoten.

Samuels, Richard. 1987. *The Business of the Japanese State: Energy Markets in Comparative and Historical Perspective.* Ithaca, N.Y.: Cornell University Press.

Saxonhouse, Gary. 1982. "Evolving Comparative Advantage and Japan's Imports of Manufactures." In Kozo Yamamura, ed., *Policy and Trade Issues of the Japanese Economy*, pp. 239–70. Seattle: University of Washington Press.

————. 1988. "Comparative Advantage, Structural Adaptation, and Japanese Performance." In Takashi Inoguchi and Daniel I. Okimoto, eds., *The Political Economy of Japan*, vol. 2: *The Changing International Context*, pp. 225–48. Stanford, Calif.: Stanford University Press.

Shimura, Yukio. 1979. *IC sangyō daisensō* (The Great War in the IC Industry). Tokyo: Diamond.

————. 1980. *IC sangyō saizensen* (The Frontlines of the IC Industry). Tokyo: Diamond.

————. 1981. *IC sangyō no himitsu* (Secrets of the IC Industry). Tokyo: Chōbun.

————. 1982. *Elekuturonikusu bijinesu saizensen* (The Frontlines of the Electronics Business). Tokyo: Diamond.

————. 1992. *2000 nen no handōtai sangyō* (The Semiconductor Industry in the Year 2000). Tokyo: Nihon nōritsu kyōkai management center.

Shiroyama, Saburō. 1975. *Kanryōtachi no natsu* (The Summer of the Bureaucrats). Tokyo: Shinchō-sha.

Sigurdson, Jon. 1986. *Industry and State Partnership in Japan: The Very Large Scale Integrated Circuits Project*. Research Policy Institute, University of Lund, Sweden. Discussion Paper no. 168.

Sobel, Robert. 1986. *IBM vs. Japan: The Struggle for the Future*. New York: Stein & Day.

Statistics Bureau. Various years. *Report on the Survey of Research and Development*. Tokyo: Statistics Bureau, Management Coordination Agency.

Taki, Kazuo. 1992. "Parallel Inference Machine PIM." In Institute for New Generation Computer Technology (ICOT), *International Conference on Fifth Generation Computer Systems, 1992*, pp. 50–72. Tokyo: Ohmsha.

Tamura, Koichiro. 1992. "General Remarks on the Achievements of the National R&D Program 'High Speed Computing System for Scientific and Technological Uses." In Raul Mendez, ed., *High Performance Computing: Research and Practice in Japan*, pp. 199–214. New York: John Wiley.

Tano, Pico. 1984. *Jinkō chinō no shōgeki* (The Shock of Artificial Intelligence). Tokyo: Nihon Keizai Shimbun.

Tarui, Yasuo. 1984. *IC no hanashi* (The Story of ICs). Tokyo: NHK Press.

Tōyō Keizai. Various years. *Kaisha shikihō* (Japan Company Handbook). Tokyo: Tōyō Keizai Shimpō-sha.

————. 1982. *IC kakumei: Kage no shuyaku-tachi* (The IC Revolution: The Main Actors in the Shadows). Tokyo: Tōyō keizai shimpō-sha.

TRON Association. 1991. *The TRON Project 1991*. Tokyo: TRON Association.

————. 1992. *An Invitation to T-Open*. Tokyo: TRON Association.

Tyson, Laura D'Andrea. 1992. *Who's Bashing Whom: Trade Conflict in High-Technology Industries*. Washington D.C.: Institute for International Economics. Nov. 1992.

Uchida, Shunichi. 1992. "Summary of the Parallel Inference Machine and its Basic Software." In Institute for New Generation Computer Technology (ICOT), *International Conference on Fifth Generation Computer Systems 1992*, pp. 33–49. Tokyo: Ohmsha.

Uemae, Junichirō. 1985. *Jyapanīzu dorīmu* (Japanese Dream). Tokyo: Kōdansha.

Upham, Frank K. 1987. *Law and Social Change in Postwar Japan.* Cambridge, Mass.: Harvard University Press.

U.S. General Accounting Office. 1992. *Federal Research: SEMATECH's Technological Progress and Proposed R&D Program.* GAO/RCED-92-223BR. Washington D.C.: Government Printing Office. July 1992.

U.S. Office of Technology Assessment. 1991. *Competing Economies: America, Europe, and the Pacific Rim.* OTA-ITE-498. Washington D.C.: Government Printing Office. Oct. 1991.

van Wolferen, Karel. 1989. *The Enigma of Japanese Power: People and Politics in a Stateless Nation.* New York: Vintage Books.

Vogel, Ezra. 1985. *Comeback, Case by Case: Building the Resurgence of American Business.* New York: Simon & Schuster.

Wakasugi, Ryūhei. 1986. *Gijutsu kakushin to kenkyū kaihatsu no keizai bunseki* (An Economic Analysis of Technological Innovation and R&D). Tokyo: Tōyō keizai shimpō-sha.

———. 1990. "A Consideration of Innovative Organization: Joint R&D of Japanese Firms." In Arnold Heertje and Mark Perlman, eds., *Evolving Technology and Market Structure,* pp. 209–26. Ann Arbor: University of Michigan Press.

White, Geoffrey M. 1981. "Comments." In Herbert Giersch, ed., *Emerging Technologies: Consequences for Economic Growth, Structural Change, and Employment,* pp. 375–79. Tübingen, Germany: J. C. B. Mohr (Paul Siebeck).

Yagi, Tsutomu. 1992. *Dō naru kompyūta gyōkai* (What Will Happen to the Computer Industry?). Tokyo: Nihon jitsugyō shuppan.

Yamaguchi, Jirō. 1987. *Ōkura kanryō shihai no shūen* (The End of Rule by MOF Bureaucrats). Tokyo: Iwanami Shoten.

Yamamura, Kozo. 1982. "Success That Soured: Administrative Guidance and Cartels in Japan." In Kozo Yamamura, ed., *Policy and Trade Issues of the Japanese Economy: American and Japanese Perspectives,* pp. 77–112. Seattle: University of Washington Press.

———. 1986. "Joint Research and Antitrust: Two Perspectives on Industrial Policy." In Hugh Patrick, ed., *Japan's High Technology Industries: Lessons and Limitations of Industrial Policy,* pp. 171–210. Seattle: University of Washington Press.

Index

In this index an "f" after a number indicates a separate reference on the next page, and an "ff" indicates separate references on the next two pages. A continuous discussion over two or more pages is indicated by a span of page numbers, e.g., "57–59." *Passim* is used for a cluster of references in close but not consecutive sequence.

Abegglen, James, 200
Advanced Research Projects Agency (ARPA-U.S.), 131, 193; response to Fifth Generation, 131; short funding cycles, 176; Sematech funding, 198
Advanced Technology Program (U.S. Department of Commerce), 194
Agency for Industrial Science and Technology (AIST-MITI), 61
Aiso, Hideo, 26, 68–72
Alvey program (U.K.), 16
Apple Computer, 54, 173
Anchordoguy, Marie, 7
Apollo Computer, 77
Applied Materials, 197
AT&T, 39, 77

BTRON (Business TRON). *See* TRON

Canon, 161, 197
Carter, Jimmy, 166
Center for Educational Computing (CEC-Japan), 9, 29, 84
Compaq Computer, 83
computer industry: liberalization of Japanese market, 37, 116–18; increasing Japanese domestic market share, 151; Japanese production, imports, and exports, 153
consortia, Japanese high tech: and book's methodology, 5–6; decreased corporate contributions to, 153–54; shrinking

size of MITI consortia, 154–55, 157–59; declining share of total Japanese R&D activity, 158f; expanded length of MITI consortia, 175–78; eroding effectiveness, 182–84; cooperation and conflict within, 182–83; and Japan's economic transition in the 1980s, 183; lack of intrusion of domestic politics, 185–86. *See also* industrial policy, MITI, Fifth Generation consortium, VLSI, Supercomputer consortium, TRON, Real World Computing consortium
consortia, U.S. high tech: analysis of, 194–97; Japanese views on, 195. *See also* Sematech, MCC
Convex Computer, 128
Cooperative Development Laboratories (CDL), 17, 91–97. *See also* VLSI consortium
Corrigan, Will, 166
Cray Computer, 128
Cray Research, 19, 169
Cray, Seymour, 19, 128, 147
CSF-Thompson, 44
Cypress Semiconductor, 112

Defense Advanced Research Projects Agency (DARPA), *see* Advanced Research Projects Agency (ARPA)
Dell Computer, 83
Digital Equipment Corporation (DEC), 112, 114

Library of Congress Cataloging-in-Publication Data

Callon, Scott, 1964–
    Divided Sun : MITI and the breakdown of Japanese high-tech industrial policy,
    1975–1993 / Scott Callon.
        p.   cm.
    Includes bibliographical references and index.
    ISBN 0-8047-2505-5 (cl.) : ISBN 0-8047-3154-3 (pbk.)
    1. High technology industries—Government policy—Japan.   2. Electronic
industries—Government policy—Japan.   3. Japan.
Tsūshō Sangyōshō.   I. Title.
HC465.H53C35   1995
338.4'762'000952—dc20
95-11675   CIP

Original printing 1995

Last figure below indicates year of this printing:

04 03 02 01 00 99 98 97